To Norma and Lew Gr[illegible]

through the [illegible] ras
and with the feelings of love
and respect they know I harbor
for them,

Herbert Weiss [illegible]

The Wild Goats of Ein Gedi

HERBERT WEINER

The Wild Goats
of Ein Gedi

A Journal of Religious Encounters

in the Holy Land

DOUBLEDAY & COMPANY, INC.,
GARDEN CITY, NEW YORK, 1961

BP145

Material from the author's article, "A Quest for Spiritual Life: The Yuvalites", is reprinted with the kind permission of the *Jewish Heritage*. Copyright 1961 by B'nai B'rith.

8/23/02

Dedicated to
JONATHAN, CARMI, *and* ALISA

Contents

Preface

Why do I feel the need to offer an apology rather than the customary word of acknowledgment at the beginning of this book? Some feeling of guilt, I suppose, at having used (the word betrays me) friendships, intimacies, certain moments of life. To be sure, I have an excuse. My hope was to engage the reader in a kind of journey to the Holy Land which was not only a trip abroad but, like the pilgrimage of old, a search for personal source-springs of spirit—and that involved, I thought, encounters with real people. These people did know that I wanted to write about them. Still, the ambivalent nature of such encounters—one eye on the meeting and mood of the moment, the other eye on the future reader—is a disservice, both to the person and the moment. In any case, it has left me with the need for what the ancients might have called a "sin offering."

My confession done, I feel more free to express the gratitude richly owed to a number of people. Every page in this book reflects the good judgment and help of my wife. I am sincerely grateful to Clement Alexandre of Doubleday and Company, to Marie Syrkin and to Nathan Glazer for their encouragement. The technical assistance of Coty Blank, Regina Levin, and Irma Pecsi was indispensable. As to the men, women, and children in South Orange with whom I have mingled my prayers for more than thirteen years, I hope they know how delightful has been their friendship and how precious their encouragement.

Parts of this book have appeared, in different form, in a number of magazines—*Commentary, American Judaism,* and *The Jewish Heritage.*

Herbert Weiner

Land, Light, and Soul

There is an almost merciless clarity in the sunlit air of the Holy
Land. It can reveal the crevices in hills miles away, or penetrate the make-up of a woman's face and reveal its true age
lines. And twilight moments, the pleasant intermingling of shadow
and light so familiar to European eyes, are more fleeting. The
bright red sun drops swiftly into the Mediterranean, and it is
sudden and complete night. The moment "between the suns" is
the Hebrew term for twilight. It is the moment which the Hebrew poet and mystic associates with the mysteries of life and
the deepest secrets of creation, "the tong that made the tongs."
Could it be that this moment of in-betweenness is so precious
because it is so fleeting? Like the praise of the Song of Songs
for spring when "the vines in blossom give forth their fragrance,"
for spring too is an all too brief interval between cold winter
rains pouring into a soggy earth and long, dry summer months
when a brazen sky beats down upon a hard-packed, thirsty
ground. Even the contours of the land are a pattern of extreme counterpoint. It is so small—one can stand on a mountain in Transjordan and like Moses see its whole breadth and
length, but it is packed with every kind of vegetation, climate,
and soil. From Mount Scopus in the center of the land one can
see Jerusalem on a lower hill below, then turn the head and
look back and below upon the frozen undulation of the Judean
desert, descending swiftly into the Dead Sea, and the deepest
cleft in the earth's surface. In the wintertime the snow may
fall here upon one's hands, while forty miles away within clear
sight, the green tropical vegetation of Jericho can be seen. There
is little rest for the traveler's eye as he moves in a few hours or
minutes from the stony-ridged hills and mountains in Judea to

the heat-baked sands of the Negev, through the green Sharon plains and up to the mountains and water-bogged valleys of the Galilee. Like the climate and the light, the topography in Israel has little patience with the in-between.

Might this either-or mood of the land have something to do with the harsh, polarized extremism of its prophets?

"Is it thou, O troubler of Israel? . . ." asks King Ahab of the wild-eyed, leather-girded zealot Elijah. Why so severe, he asks, why so little patience with human fallibility, with the natural weaknesses of man-made institutions? Why always bring this piti-less, penetrating human judgment upon man's human attempt to compromise, to cover up a bit? It is so hard to fulfill the com-mandment "with all one's heart, and all one's soul, and all one's might." "All" is so much to demand of fragile human beings. But it is an "allness" that has characterized the mood of the prophets and religious teachers here.

Can the contours of a land or the quality of its light affect the soul of its inhabitants? Would this be a way of explaining the peculiar association between the strip of Mediterranean soil called Israel and that dimension of life we call religion?

An American poet, David Morton, wrote sonnets which told how the shape of his New England hills formed his soul. A non-Jewish geographer-historian of the Holy Land, George Adam Smith, tried to describe the effect of its landscape and climate on the inner life of its inhabitants, on their very "categories of thought." The dependence of Israel's agriculture on the heavenly "gifts" of rain and dew, make them look toward their heavens with different eyes than the Egyptians, whose agriculture de-pended upon the man-made arrangements which brought them water from the Nile. The fact that the early Hebrews dwelt in the hills while their early enemies, the Philistines, occupied the plains, was reflected in their language. "My help cometh from the hills," sang the psalmist; "God walks in the high places"—ideas which the Jews later took with them to the steppes of Russia or the flat deserts of North Africa, calling their summons to the reading of the Torah in the synagogue an aliyah—an ascent. The extremes of temperature and climate also had their effect on the polarized temperament of the Hebrew, suggested Smith, who also referred to the uncommonly bright light in the land of Israel.

The idea that in the land of Israel things can be seen which elsewhere may be veiled, is an old Jewish and Christian theme. "The eyes of the Lord are upon this land," says the Bible, and an old rabbinic commentary explains that what in other lands may be less noticed, must in the land of Israel be sharply exposed and called to account. Here the coverings are stripped away, and the souls of men and institutions are more fully revealed. What may pass in other places—compromises, weaknesses, surface pretense —will here not be tolerated.

That the Holy Land can reveal to individuals and peoples an intensity of truth that may remain somewhat veiled in other places —this has been the faith that has brought so many pilgrims here. It is also the feeling which underlies this journal of encounters with religious life, problems, and personalities in modern Israel.

It would have been interesting, I have often thought during these visits to Israel, to bring together some of the people described in this book. They live, after all, only a few minutes' or hours' travel from each other, and they have so much in common. Most of them are strongly searching for a way of life which promises a maximum of truth and meaning. Many of them share a keen interest in religion—not only in problems like the relationship between church and state, but in the "interior" religious experience. Were subjects like this to be discussed by a number of people representing the great historic religious traditions, they might be provocatively illuminated. But it is a meeting which can hardly take place. Uri, the young Jewish farmer in the kibbutz of Ein Gedi, and Martin Buber, the distinguished professor in Jerusalem, may speak the same language or pass each other on the street, but they really inhabit different worlds of discourse. It would be even more difficult to arrange a meeting between the white-bearded rabbinical leader of the Orthodox Yeshiva at B'nai Brak and the pretty Protestant nuns from Darmstadt, Germany, and even more impossible to think of them talking with each other about the function of celibacy in religious life. Yet, through these dialogues in the Holy Land, these people did confront each other in a way.

Of course, every human dialogue has its lapses of understanding, and the lapses are even more inevitable when the confrontation involves not only individuals but complex historic religions. I hope my partners in these discussions that so often turned into relationships which I cherish, will forgive my own misunderstandings.

The Wild Goats of Ein Gedi

CHAPTER I

A Troubled Landscape

"It is called terra sancta being the name only for all holiness is banished therefrom . . ."
—from the diary of an 18th-century English pilgrim

A frequent sight in the Mid-East are hillocks so rounded as to be obviously man-made. They are called *tels* in Hebrew or Arabic —remains of civilizations piled strata on strata, waiting for the archaeologist's "dig."

Even children in Israel know the technique of the dig. One selects a promising site, perhaps on top of a *tel*. Then carefully, with pick, shovel, and brush, a hole is dug in the hope that material will be found revealing something interesting about the conditions and quality of life which once existed about this location.

In a sense our effort here is to make a series of digs. Journalistic excavations, so to speak, into the life of modern Israel's major religious communities. There would seem to be no lack of interesting sites to begin with. There is probably no more crowded spiritual landscape anywhere. Nowhere do such an abundance and variety of religious institutions and faiths confront each other in such close proximity. Christianity and Judaism in particular are represented here in all their historic fragmentations. That such a landscape should be continually sputtering with religious problems seems almost fitting. Government coalitions break up because of disagreement over the definition of the word *Jew*. A parliamentary censure motion is offered when a Prime Minister dares offer an unorthodox opinion about the number of Israelites leaving Egypt during the biblical Exodus. The Christian press in all parts of the world becomes far more agitated over alleged

1

restrictions of missionary work in Israel than over the complete ban on similar endeavors in surrounding Moslem lands. True, the religious faith which once brought pilgrims and crusaders to these shores burns low in our day. Yet in the consciousness of Western man still lurks the feeling that happenings in the land of Zion may have a significance that goes beyond the small territorial population actually involved. Nor are these happenings associated, as some Israelis think, with the efficiency of the land's chicken farms, the impressive draining of its swamps, or even the fighting ability of its little army. They should, many Christians and Jews still feel, have something to do with holiness, for they occur in the Holy Land, the cradle soil of three great faiths. Hence, there are international echoes to events and issues which in other lands go unnoticed. Church and state, for example, are not separated in many countries. In Israel the lack of such separation is a frequent cause for violent criticism by Christian and Jewish groups in America. In many lands the right of ecclesiastical authorities to control matters like divorce or burial arrangements, or to set the standards by which an individual is to be considered part of a specific religious community, is taken for granted. In Israel, when these questions arise, they become a matter of concern not only in that land, but abroad. They became so, for example, in a particularly poignant way some years ago, after an important American newsweekly reported an incident it captioned, "The Stolen Fence."

Shmuel Steinberg, the article reported, had come to Israel in 1955 with his wife Luba and two sons. Like many Jews in Poland, Steinberg had seen his family killed by the Nazis. He himself had been put to forced labor for many years in Siberia. Upon returning to Poland he had married a Christian girl, Luba, and she bore him two children. They found anti-Semitism in Poland still prevalent and accepted the invitation of the Jewish authorities to emigrate to Israel. Not long after arriving, Aaron, their five-year-old son, died of polio. For three days, reported the article, Shmuel Steinberg carried the small linen-wrapped body of his son about in a taxi, looking in vain for a burial place. The rabbis had refused to open their cemeteries, because according to rabbinic law only Jews could be buried in Jewish

2

cemeteries, and the child of a Christian mother was considered a Christian. The Catholic priest refused to allow the child burial in Christian hallowed ground because he was not baptized. Finally, said the report, a rabbi permitted the child to be buried on the outskirts of a Jewish cemetery, on condition that a fence be erected about the little grave, and that the father refrain from saying the traditional prayers of mourning for the dead. A few nights later the fence "mysteriously disappeared."

The incident had aroused vigorous protest in the Knesset, with some Jewish representatives accusing the rabbi of a "Nazi racist" kind of religiosity. Some kibbutzim and the municipality of Haifa offered their cemeteries to the Steinberg family. The nation, and the foreign press too, was moved by Luba Steinberg's remark: "In Poland they persecuted us for being Jews, and here for being Christians."

Years passed, but the image of the father trundling the body of his little son about in a taxi for three days remained in my mind. It seemed to bring together in an agonizing nexus the issues of religious freedom, church and state, intercommunity relationships and larger questions about the relevance of religion in modern Israel.

I decided to visit the Steinbergs. To find out where they lived and something more about them, I went to a Catholic priest in Jerusalem who was actively concerned with what he called "Israel's Christian problem." Some two thousand mixed-marriage families had immigrated to Israel in recent years from behind the Iron Curtain. Many of them were unhappy in their new environment, and part of their unhappiness, according to the priest, was caused by the Jewish religious authorities who were using "indirect methods" to convert their children or at least to make them reluctant to openly express their Christian faith. Since the Steinbergs were one of these mixed-marriage families, I was surprised that the priest did not recall their name. Finally, however, he remembered.

"We had nothing to do with them," he told me. "Luba Steinberg was a Greek Orthodox Christian. But he thought that the family still lived in the village of Pardess Chanah. "But they are very poor people." He wrinkled his nose as though smelling something unpleasant. "I don't mean just materially. You won't get much out of them."

An official in the Jewish agency, who usually delighted in incidents embarrassing to Israel's rabbinic leaders, displayed a similar lack of enthusiasm on hearing of my desire to meet the family. He had read recently that the child's body had been transferred to another place in the cemetery, in a ceremony which had been attended by important officials. Evidently they still lived in Pardess Chanah. He too thought there would not be much purpose to a visit there.

One pleasant summer day I visited Pardess Chanah, a pleasant country town with green gardens and white plastered homes, some of them still inhabited by the original builders of the village who came here fifty years ago. The pharmacist in the village drugstore told me that the Steinbergs still lived in town. He was polite, but curious as to my reasons for wanting to see them.

"You'll find them very simple people, really." His shrug reminded me of the Jerusalem priest. "Look," he added, as if to explain his attitude, "this is the kind of person Steinberg is. One day he came in here and gave me his name to charge some item. When I didn't say anything on hearing his name, he seemed disappointed. 'Don't you remember me?' he asked. 'I am the father of that child—you know—in the papers.' He seemed so proud of it all."

The druggist shrugged again. "Look, you're welcome to visit them, but if you want to know the facts of the case, you ought also to visit the rabbi who was involved in the whole affair. He is very fine, uncommonly intelligent man—a real Litvak— and he lives not far from here."

I accepted the suggestion and drove to the rabbi's house, a modest, somewhat dilapidated structure. A knock on the door brought the answer of a soft voice, then the slow shuffling of feet. A slightly stooping, gray-bearded gentleman with warm, shrewd blue eyes invited me into a room where a large talmudic folio open on a stand indicated that I had disturbed him in his studies. When I told him of my concern, he sighed, closed the folio, and sat down with me at a small table. Folding his hands, he very quietly repeated the story he had evidently told many

4

times. His first meeting with the Steinberg woman, he said, occurred about a year before the child died, when she appeared as a would-be witness for a marriage. Since witnesses in a Jewish marriage are supposed to be Jewish, he had ventured a few questions to the woman, who had not otherwise indicated her faith. By questions about her neighborhood of origin and other matters he had found out that she was not Jewish. That was the only contact he had with the family until he received a telephone call one afternoon from a social worker in a Haifa hospital. The social worker had told him that the Steinberg boy had died.

"The child was, perhaps you know," the rabbi looked up from his folded hands and sighed, "a sickly child, retarded, as is the other son. It's a tragic family history." The social worker, said the rabbi, was upset because the priest to whom the father had first brought the child did not want to bury him. "Could I help? What could I do? I said I would try. When the father and mother came I took them to the cemetery—it is on the outskirts of the town. I showed them a place near some trees where the child might be buried. I had to keep in mind that the cemetery would have to expand and therefore he could not be buried in just any place. She seemed a little discontented with the first location, so we looked for another place, where she seemed more satisfied."

"Was it outside the fence?" I asked, remembering the dramatic headline in the American magazine. The rabbi looked up surprised.

"We have no fence around the cemetery. There are only a few trees which set it off from the road. But you know, a Jewish cemetery, like a Christian cemetery, is consecrated by a specific ceremony as a burial ground. The woman didn't object to the boy not being buried in a Jewish cemetery. She just didn't like the first location I suggested. Well, I did my best, and tried to comfort her too. That was all that there was to it—except that the incident happened to occur before the elections."

Didn't the man carry the body of the child three days?

The blue eyes of the rabbi opened. *"Chas v'shalom*—heaven forbid. He didn't carry the child at all. The boy was taken here

5

by hospital car. Well," he continued, "a reporter from one of the nonreligious party papers who had not even been here wrote some story and suddenly the matter became a political issue. Steinberg, who till then had been friendly and even grateful, suddenly found that he had a good thing. Some people from the political parties spoke to him, and he co-operated with them. Now he has a good job in a factory and seems to be content. But the other boy is still very sick—I fear he will not get well— and the woman," the rabbi looked down, "I am afraid there are unpleasant stories about her."

The story was, of course, quite different from what I had expected, and so was the soft-spoken, kindly rabbi. Still, I told him, I wanted to meet the Steinbergs.

"You may be disappointed," he said quietly as he led me to the door and pointed out the directions.

The Steinberg house was a newly built concrete structure of three or four rooms, surrounded by a large, still uncultivated garden. A chunky, blond woman with Slavic features dressed in a black, formal dress let me into the house. Yes, she was Mrs. Steinberg, but she spoke no Hebrew or English. There were two buxom ladies, however, sitting on a couch in the room with her, and one of them offered to translate. They were neighbors, recent immigrants like the Steinbergs. The ladies passed a bowl of fruit back and forth smiling, and Mrs. Steinberg seemed rather amused by my questions. She confirmed the rabbi's story, only snapping, her smile for a moment gone, that she did not want "the child to be buried near the road where the dogs could get at the grave."

Was there any trouble now in the village between Christians and Jews? The three ladies laughed.

"We are all neighbors here, but none of us care about churches or synagogues." They giggled at the very thought.

"What we don't like here," the Jewish woman suggested, "is the dullness of life. It's boring. We should never have left Europe. I come from Russia; my neighbors are from Poland. We should have believed what they told us at home about capitalism." The others nodded genially. I heard what sounded like animal outcries in a nearby room.

6

"The other child is sick," explained the neighbor. "Maybe you can get them some money." She laughed.

A few minutes later Mr. Steinberg came home. He was a short, bald-headed man, and though tired went over the story with some feeling. He too agreed with the rabbi's version of the story, but vehemently denied asking a priest to bury the child.

"May I live to see my other child walk," he said excitedly, "but that is completely false. My children are Jewish. They couldn't be circumcised because they were ill, but they are Jewish, and I am a good Jew. You know that after the publicity I got letters from all over—from Rome, from priests, they wanted me to make propaganda against the state; but I am a good Jew, I wouldn't do it. Still, we need money for the other boy. He needs good food, perhaps you would like to see him, take his picture." He had noticed the camera I was carrying. I wasn't eager, but accompanied him into the room, where a child at least twelve years old was lying in a crib. I took the pictures hastily—the older Steinberg child was a living vegetable, completely degenerate, more animal than human.

I left Pardess Chanah and the Steinbergs with a feeling of almost physical nausea.

In terms of some insight into religious realities the Steinberg dig seemed to have offered little. If there were religious questions here, they were to a God who permitted human life to be mangled and cast aside by what seemed like cosmic malevolence or indifference, questions more difficult than the issues of church and state.

Church and State Complexities

Yet there are serious problems of church and state in Israel. Scarcely a day passes without charges in the local or international press that Israel is a theocracy, or converse claims by the Orthodox Party that the Jewish state is governed by atheists. An American Protestant journal suggests that "the right to freedom of worship and assembly is still to be gained in the young state of Israel." The writer of the article goes on to offer illustrations of religious suppression by the "will of Orthodox Jews." Some

7

examples listed are the alleged closing of Protestant churches, restrictions on Christian missionary endeavors, marriage laws which prevent one from exercising "freedom of conscience." Even the suppression of Reform Jewish groups, which according to the writer must meet underground in secluded places "under much the same circumstances as did the early Christians in the same city" of Jerusalem. Most observers from the West simply cannot understand why Israel in 1948 did not work out the kind of church and state separation which would avoid most of these problems and which seemed so attractive to Jewish communities in other lands.

When along with my impression of the Steinberg case, I brought some of these questions to a scholarly friend in Jerusalem, he lifted a caustic eyebrow.

"If it is religion you are looking for, you have come to the wrong land."

My friend had a reputation for seeing the underside of life, particularly religious life. And he did seem to enjoy hammering his point home.

"Oh, you may find a few spiritual athletes, as I call them, performing their spiritual gymnastics in some cell in a monastery. But if by religion you mean anything associated with theological thought, ideas, spiritual creativity in any civilized sense, you will not find it here."

No religion in the Holy Land—what a frustrating paradox for a would-be commentator on spiritual life here to encounter. But was it true? The cradle soil of Judaism and Christianity, the land where Mohammed is supposed to have said, "One village is more precious than all of Medina"—a soil so saturated with religious memories, the wrong land for religion?

The Israeli seemed to enjoy the silence effected by his remark, lighted his pipe, and proceeded to offer me a capsule description of Christian, Moslem, and Jewish life in his land.

"The Christians here—I don't mean the ignorant peasantry who are held in contempt by their own clergy—but the hierarchies, the various orders and sects, look upon themselves mainly as sentinels in a cold-war truce. Their main function is to act as guards over the ever-continuing war over the holy sites, and their

8

main task in this war is to see to it that they are not dislodged from positions that their particular religious army has acquired on these sites, by deceit, thievery, and murder. It's been a little more polite in recent years, but still, there have been incidents where holy hands have snatched candelabra from Christendom's holiest shrine, the Church of the Holy Sepulchre, and thrown them at the holy heads of Christian sects who lingered beyond the time allotted them for the Mass at some disputed niche. Of course, compared to past Christian history in this land, today's condition is almost heaven on earth. You know how Runciman, the authority on the Crusades, summed it up, '. . . a desecration of the Holy Spirit in the name of God.'"

"The Moslems?" My friend puffed furiously on his pipe and began the second part of his analysis. "They don't even pretend to be interested in religion. The peasant holds on to his superstitions, paints his house blue, and draws pictures of hands on his trucks and doors; but the only thing the educated, city Moslem worships is Nasser and Arab nationalism. They don't even pretend any more to abstain from the liquor which is forbidden every good Moslem by his Koran. Of course, the most repellent religious group of all here now—mainly because they suddenly have power—are the Jewish Orthodox spiritual authorities."

The scholar looked out through a window. For a moment his voice lost its strength, even choking slightly.

"I have been wondering lately—this will shock you—if the whole business hasn't been a bluff, if these Orthodox professional Jews ever believed in anything. Did you read about the Chief Rabbi of the Sephardic community who went around to kibbutzim and paid children an Israeli pound if they would sing a religious song? And, surely, you have heard about the swimming pool?"

The swimming-pool controversy, though apparently settled now, is remembered as a classic among the numerous cases of strife between the government, the "free-thinking" population, and Orthodox religious leadership. It started when a group of Israeli businessmen decided that they would build a swimming pool on the outskirts of the city. Jerusalem, situated in the center

9

of the country, was miles away from any beach or lake, and since Sabbath laws prevent the buses from running on the only day when most Israelis could go bathing, a swimming pool obviously would be very attractive. But Orthodox Jewish authorities in the city claimed that a swimming pool where both sexes could swim at the same time would lead to lewdness, juvenile delinquency, and be "an utter profanation of God's name and the Jewish religion."

The fact that there were some Orthodox religious kibbutzim which for economic reasons also had only one swimming pool and permitted both sexes to swim in it at the same time did not influence the Orthodox Jerusalem authorities. Jerusalem, they said, was "the holy city."

"Would you build a swimming pool and have mixed swimming in your synagogue or church?" asked the advertisements placed by Israeli religious authorities and their American friends in the New York papers. The threats of the Orthodox authorities and their spokesmen in the Israeli Knesset reached the point where the businessmen who had started the venture sold out their holdings to some Israeli kibbutzim. The latter not only sent a delegation of husky lifeguards to be present on the opening day of the swimming pool, but what was even more distasteful to the Orthodox who were threatening trouble, they stationed a number of angry-looking watchdogs around the pool. The Orthodox left the pool alone, but their frustrated feelings found outlet in a midnight rite of excommunication, complete with black candles, prayer shawls, and shofar trumpets, which solemnly declared everybody who had anything to do with the swimming pool as excommunicated from his faith and his people.

"You may not know," my Jerusalem friend told me, "that there was a postscript to the affair. We have in our Jerusalem zoo two small wading pools—one for male and one for female children, according to the Holy Writ as interpreted by our rabbis. Some of the children in the pools, however, are too young to read the Holy Writ, so in their play they jump from one pool to the other. This caused the Orthodox representative in Jerusalem's city council to break up a meeting one night by rising and accusing

10

the honorable mayor and his party of deliberately corrupting the morals of the young.

"Yes," my friend concluded his analysis, banging out his pipe against the ash tray on a desk littered with papers, books, and the remains of two cups of tea, "that is religion in the Holy Land—politics, organization, and power drives; spiritual warriors who specialize in being against—but if you're looking for something else, spiritual creativity or theology, you're in the wrong land."

"At any rate," I said, clinging to one aspect of religious life which was certainly of intense concern to Israelis, "you do have a problem, as you yourself have indicated, of religious freedom, a lack of separation between church and state."

"Separation of church and state—religious freedom—that is a subject you Americans don't begin to understand as it applies to this land, and most Israelis don't understand it either. There will be some lectures on this subject in Jerusalem soon. You might find it worthwhile to attend."

The actual subject of the lecture to which my informant referred was the history of the Christian community in the Holy Land. It did contain information with which any attempt to understand religious life in modern Israel must begin.

Unfortunately, it was a rather warm summer morning. The Christian educators and ministers who comprised the audience were weary after two weeks of touring the Middle East, the lecturer's voice was flat, and soon there were nodding heads. The speaker tried to ignore the disinterest of his audience and doggedly set about trying to simplify a complex subject. The history of religious communities in the Holy Land is a difficult subject, if for no other reason than that most of this history is so largely a reflection of events and ideas which originated in other lands. The creative centers of Moslem life have been Mecca, Cairo, Constantinople, Baghdad. The wellsprings of Christian power and creativity were in Europe; the centers of the Jewish Diaspora for the last two thousand years have been Babylonia, Spain, North Africa, and Europe. Even the forms of communal religious life in Palestine were mainly imported from models created abroad. An attempt to trace a line of history in the country now called Israel is further complicated because for centuries Pales-

11

tine was hardly recognizable as a political or even geographic entity. Population-wise, religiously and economically, as well as politically, it was a rather unimportant appendage to other territories and administrative structures. During the centuries of Moslem and Turkish rule, Palestine was but the tail-end of Syria.

Despite the difficulties which these historic facts place in the way of an attempt to trace an indigenous thread of religious and political development within the Holy Land, the lecturer managed to point out the historic origins, beginning in 425 c.e. with the decrees of Theodosius, of Israel's present-day religious structure. The name for this structure, rooted in hundreds, even thousands, of years of legal precedent and history, was the Millet system. Under this system each religious community had its own self-appointed hierarchy, which controlled not only church rites, but matters affecting the personal status of its members, their marriages, divorces, burial, personal inheritance, etc. Some of the churches and clergy of the minority communities received government support. Many of them owned their own substantial property. These arrangements, permitting a large measure of autonomy to minority religious communities in Palestine, were spelled out in further detail by a decree or Turkish firman issued in 1852 by Sultan Abdul Mejid, in which he ordered the maintenance of the status which each church had in 1757. This status quo ante confirmed by the Congress of Berlin in 1878 included agreements with respect to the holy places. The historic rivalry between the various Christian churches over the holy places is one of Christendom's most unpleasant chapters.

Even while the last crusaders were preparing to leave the Holy Land, representatives of the Roman Catholic church were already carrying on secret negotiations with Saladin which would give them further advantage over the Eastern Christian groups. When in 1870 the Church of the Holy Sepulchre was partly burned down, more money was spent in bribes to the Turkish authorities by the various Christian groups competing with each other for privileges within the church, than was spent on the actual construction. The key to the Church of the Holy Sepulchre is to this day in the hands of a Moslem, by mutual agreement of the Christian churches, who would rather see it there than in the

12

hands of a rival sect. This bickering and the bribes to the Moslem rulers which were its side effect were encouraged by the Turkish powers. But the quarrel between Eastern and Western churches threatened to become an excuse for war. Indeed, the Crimean War was, ostensibly, started by a quarrel over the disappearance of a silver star in the Church of the Nativity in Bethlehem. Trying to forestall this kind of difficulty, which could drag him into active conflict, the Sultan issued his *status quo* arrangement. A modus vivendi between the various churches was achieved. Among other details in its decrees the government appended a list of Greek Orthodox, Greek Catholic, and Roman Catholic communities, along with smaller Christian sects with national colorings like the Maronite, Armenian Catholic, Syrian Catholic, and Armenian (Gregorian). The Coptic and Abyssinian churches were also given "official" status. In following years this *status quo* arrangement was further validated by treaties between the Turkish sovereignty and other governments, and by agreement of the Congress of Berlin. There were also supplementary agreements with various church groups.

When the mandatory government of Great Britain assumed control of Palestine in 1919 after the First World War, it gave quick assurance that this religious *status quo* would be respected. So eager was the mandatory government to avoid upsetting the volatile religious arrangements that it even refused official recognition to the relatively new Anglican Protestant community, despite the Old School ties and the fact that the community had achieved a sizable following. The Protestants were late arrivals in the Holy Land, coming in the late nineteenth century, after the *status quo* arrangement had been set up. The British were not eager to upset the arrangement which after so many centuries of strife had achieved a relative peace between rival church claims. In 1922 an Order in Council was issued by the British, again reaffirming the *status quo* and listing the communities which enjoyed official recognition. In 1947 the United Nations' resolution bringing into existence the Jewish state had contained a specific clause again ensuring the *status quo* of existing religious arrangements. Among its first acts the Israeli government had not only affirmed the principle of religious

13

freedom in its constitution, but also had given assurance that it would maintain the *status quo* which had been bequeathed to it by previous governments and affirmed by so many international treaties. Hence, the lecturer concluded, even if the Israeli government were inclined to make changes in the present religious structure of the Holy Land, it would be confronted with long-established international commitments which could not easily be flaunted. For example, a law which would permit members of the official religious communities to be married outside the authority of their hierarchical authorities, could certainly be construed by these authorities as a change in the *status quo*.

Even an attempt to give official recognition to the numerous Protestant sects which had arrived in Palestine and Israel during the past few years might be interpreted by the official communities as an abrogation of the pledged *status quo*. Therefore, the government had to step slowly. Even though it did not at present grant official recognition to some of the smaller, newly arrived Protestant sects, it had given them "marriage books," which ensured them *de facto* rights. The defects of the present system were obvious, but complaints were easier to offer than cures.

The lecturer finished, mopped his brow, and seemed then to be waiting uneasily for an inevitable question. It was not long in coming, this time from a Protestant minister, whose undershirt shone brightly through a transparent nylon shirt. His stentorian pulpit tone shattered the torpid quiet which had reigned in the room during the lecture.

"Can you tell me, sir, why it is so difficult for a Protestant to get married in Israel by a minister of his own faith? Why does this state, which claims to assure religious freedom in its constitution, make itself an instrument of the ecclesiastical authorities? Ought there not to be a separation of church and state along the lines we have in America?"

The Israeli lecturer sighed. "But don't you understand, religious freedom has different connotations in the Mid-East than it does in the West. In your country one thinks of religious freedom in terms of the individual's rights, including the right to be free from all religious authority. In the Middle East religious freedom

14

has for centuries connoted the right of a minority community to ensure its existence. To take away from a religious community the right to supervise its church rites, or to control the personal status of the individuals who belong to it, would be considered by these communities as an infringement of their religious freedom. Don't you see?"

The minister shook his head to show that he did not see.

The lecturer went on feebly. Did not the people present in the room with him realize that the Millet system with all of its faults also had some advantages. A historian like Toynbee, for example, offers the Millet system as the ideal of a spiritual community that transcends geographic and national boundaries. In a way the Millet system, which has existed in the Mid-East for centuries, is not unlike the "cultural pluralism" which was once enthusiastically preached in America by men like Louis Adamic and Horace Kallen. Of course, what proponents of cultural pluralism do not often realize is that communal religious liberty and individual religious freedom are not too easily reconciled. From the point of view of the community, when the state allowed the individual to be married or divorced under auspices other than its own, it deprived that religious community of its inherited and sacred rights.

Again the minister shook his head. "But I thought that the Israeli Constitution promised everybody religious freedom."

"But this *is* the concept of religious freedom in the Middle East . . ." the lecturer began again. Then his voice trailed off and he wearily closed his brief case. The visitors shouldered their cameras and moved on to their next stop.

After the tourists left I thanked the disconsolate speaker for his presentation of a difficult subject. He was not reassured, and agitatedly kept on opening and closing his brief case.

"How in the world am I going to explain to you Americans that Thomas Paine and Thomas Jefferson, who have been a part of your way of thinking for centuries, are simply not known here?"

We walked out of the hotel together into the bright light of the street outside. Still shaking his head and gesticulating, the

15

lecturer continued his debate with the now absent American audience.

"You know, there isn't another state in the Middle East where Protestants carry on their religious activities with such freedom. There are probably more missionaries per square foot here than in any other part of the world."

We passed a large, imposing granite structure which houses Israel's Chief Rabbinate, and the professor looked at it.

"This is what we call in Israel the Datican—*dat,* you know, means 'religion' in Hebrew. You see its size—typical of all small states which pretend to power—large, heavy architecture, empty within. Humph—of course the position of Chief Rabbi is empty now too. The Jewish religious leaders can't agree among themselves or with the government. Why in the world we need a Chief Rabbi or a Minister of Religion in this land, I don't know. I don't know if there is any real basis for it in Jewish tradition and history. We've had our spiritual leaders—Maimonides, the Vilna Gaon, and others—but they were not Chief Rabbis. They achieved their eminence because of their scholarship and personality, and not by the vote of political parties, more interested in government subsidies and job allotments than in candidates' piety or scholarly attainments. The concept of a Chief Rabbi was invented by the English during the years of the Mandate. The Christian and Moslem groups had a chief ecclesiastical authority with whom they dealt, so we decided to have one too. Fortunately, the first Chief Rabbi, Kook, was a great man, but now——"

A loud explosion across the street interrupted. The Israeli saw me start.

"They are only excavating; that's dynamite, the only way to dig into the hard rock of Jerusalem. What you thought it was is also possible." He waved a hand in the direction of the Old City of Jerusalem, whose walls appeared to be little more than a stone's throw away, certainly within easy gunshot of the street in which we were walking.

"That's another thing people ought to remember when they speak about resolving religious problems here. Some time ago they had a debate on the radio in which representatives of the

16

different parties spoke on the theme of 'What unites us.'" The lecturer's thoughts ran on. "You know what they decided? The bullet on the other side of the wall, that's all. If not for that threatening bullet I think all these differences about religious issues and the tensions between the ethnic groups here, who hardly know and understand each other, would make us explode from within. In a way the Arab wall of hostility is our salvation, for at least this period of our history. This is not quite the time to begin setting off religious explosions here, while over there they are waiting for us to fall apart."

There was another loud dynamite explosion, then taps of hammers against chisels, a centuries-old sound in Jerusalem, where all the buildings are constructed of stone.

"Do you hear the sound of those chisels?" My companion had a facility for matching his thoughts to the sights and sounds about us. "That's the way you have to build, like they do, patiently, not with explosions. Dynamiting, blasting away everything, isn't enough. When you build you have to see what kind of rock, what kind of strata, you are building on. You can't judge by the surface alone, you have to know what's underneath, what hidden traps you might fall into by an incautious step, or by setting down a weight on an area that can't bear any weight. That's why we need some knowledge of historic facts, some appreciation of how heavily the hand of the past rests on religious life in the Holy Land. You know"—he stopped, intrigued with his own image—"what we ought to do with these groups is not give them a two-hour lecture in a stuffy room, but take them on a field trip, where they can meet some of these communities, and then see how they feel about offering us Western-style religious solutions."

At the corner we parted, the professor went on his way, still gesticulating and continuing his monologue.

The troubled lecturer is, I am sure, still having difficulties explaining Israel's religious problems to visitors from the West. There is no question but that there are such problems. But the hand of history does lie upon this land and is heavier than even some of those who live in it would like to admit. At times its pressure upon those who will not or cannot conform to its

17

mold is hard, even cruel, as in a case like the Steinbergs', who do not fit into one or another of the "established" communities. In the not too distant future, changes will have to be made, in the religious structure which the state has inherited. Despite past precedent or the opposition of the present established churches, official room will have to be made for new religious arrivals in Israel. For Protestant denominations and, what will be more difficult to achieve, for some of the non-Orthodox Jewish groups. Nor will the religious institutions, Christian, Jewish, or Moslem, be able to continue imposing laws which are at variance with the will and conscience of large numbers of people. The gap between official pretense and reality will require official adjustment in the direction of Western-style individual religious freedom—an adjustment already being asked even in some Orthodox Jewish quarters by those who think that an unsubsidized synagogue, which will have to attract people on its own merits, will be a healthier institution. But it is well for the Westerner to realize, before offering his solutions, that the issues involved are volatile, their historic roots legally complicated and connected with the areas of the mind and heart which are not always susceptible to reason and calm agreement. The history of religious strife in the Holy Land is proof that the line between the demoniac and the holy is thin indeed. And the Western critic would be wise to make his judgments not in terms of his own environment, but within the unique historic and religious complex of the Mid-East and the Holy Land.

Furthermore, those concerned with religious problems in Israel might ask themselves whether the legal structure of church and state arrangements in that land are really the most pressing of these problems. That there is a religious problem in Israel more serious than the Millet system, was the feeling that began to develop as I proceeded to make the kind of field trip among Israel's religious minorities which the lecturer had recommended.

18

CHAPTER II

Needle to the Faith

The Moslem Spiritual Predicament

The population centers of Israel's minorities are concentrated in the northern part of the land, around Haifa and the Galilee. Some of the groups here would make interesting studies for the religious connoisseur but are not particularly indigenous to the Israeli landscape. Near Haifa, for example, we can find a small community of Almoades, a branch of the Moslem faith, who were driven by religious persecution out of their native land of India in the nineteenth century and found their refuge here. In Haifa also is the world center of the Bahai religion, which was founded in Persia by a young man who came to be known as the Bab, the "gate" whose mission it was to prepare the way for Baha-ullah, main prophet of the new faith. The latter was driven out of his native land and incarcerated by the Turks in Acre, where he is buried. The Bahai faith is a mixture of Eastern spirituality and undogmatic nineteenth-century liberal ideas which conceive of God's will as manifesting itself about every five hundred years with new revelations and new prophets. It is one of the world's newest religions, and now numbers about six million followers, the bulk of them in India, but several hundred thousand enthusiastic supporters can also be found in the United States. The remains of the Bab rest now in the lovely golden-domed Bahai Temple, surrounded by beautiful gardens which can be seen miles out at sea as one approaches the port of Haifa. But there is no Bahai community to speak of in the Holy Land. The few officials who live here explain that their historic experience has taught them that it is wiser to forego missionary work in the land where their world center is located.

19

Also near Haifa, in the hills above, we can visit some Druse villages. There are some 15,000 Druse in Israel, all of them proclaiming their loyalty to the new state and proud of their unit in the Israeli army. Though speaking Arabic, the Druse are eager to deny any spiritual connection with the Moslem faith, claiming that their religion is a secret which is confided only to the initiated within the Druse community. Despite their loyalty to the new state, the geographic and spiritual center of the Druse faith remains in the hills of Syria and Lebanon, rather than Israel. There are other small religio-cultural groupings, like a few Moslem Circassian villages in northern Israel. But they too do not claim any deep-rooted historic connection with the Holy Land. The three main communities which do make this claim are in order of size the Jewish (1,800,000), the Moslem (200,000), and the Christian (50,000). The largest centers of the latter two groups are also in the North, where an artificial borderline set by the accident of war forms a triangle which has divided families and villages, and which poses a nightmarish security problem for the new state.

It takes very little time to discover that the problems of Israel's religious minorities are far more concerned with borders and security than with religion. Abdul Shukri, recommended to me by the government as Arab representative in Haifa, was in fact quite puzzled by my questions about his community's religious problems.

"Well, if you're interested," he had said, "we can visit the mosque in Acre—it's Friday, our Sabbath—and we'll find somebody there."

First, Shukri suggested that we go to the offices of the Moslem community in the port area of Haifa. As we drove down he told me a bit about himself. His late father was the Arab mayor of Haifa before the war. Shukri wanted me to know that he received no money from the government for entertaining visitors they sent him. He had his own prosperous insurance business. But he enjoyed speaking to visitors from abroad, he told me, and only a few days ago he had entertained a large delegation from the American Legion. Shukri was a tall man, heavily built, with large, dark, hard eyes, a gruff voice, and an easy manner.

20

Within a few moments after our meeting he was launched into what he called a frank discussion of Moslem-Arab problems in the new state.

"We are very happy about the Jewish state, though dissatisfied that the government doesn't see the difference between Moslem and Christian Arab here. Bishop Hakim, for example," Shukri pointed toward the hill where the leader of Israel's 20,000 Greek Catholics had recently built a lovely home overlooking the Mediterranean, "puts stuff into his magazine for which he would be hanged if he lived in an Arab country." He was only trying, Shukri suggested, to escape the "Crusader" label by being more nationalistic than the real Arabs—an old and fruitless attempt of Christians in the Middle East.

At the time of our conversation Shukri's cynicism about the possibility of Christians in the Middle East ever being accepted as "real Arabs" seemed to be realistically borne out by the news of the latest intercommunal strife in Syria and Lebanon. Ostensibly, the periodic fighting there seemed to be between pro- and anti-Nasser elements, or between pro-Communist and Western sympathizers, but there was also another source of conflict, less openly discussed by mutual agreement of both sides. For years Christian Arabs had been trying to prove to themselves and their Moslem neighbors that there could be a difference between Pan-Arabism and Pan-Islamism. Both the Catholic University of St. Mary and the Protestant-sponsored American University in Beirut take pride in having produced the most fervent theorists and leaders of modern Arab nationalism. As church leaders in Syria frequently and rather pathetically point out, no one has done better service for the anti-Zionist cause in the West than Christian Arabs. But there is irony in the situation which has developed for these Christian communities in the Middle East today. Despite the theoretical division, Pan-Arabism has become synonymous with Pan-Islamism, and Christian Arabs have not been able to escape either their historic association with the Crusader label or the suspicion of their Moslem neighbors that they are sympathetically connected through their church loyalties to the "imperialist" West. Christian Arabs continue to proclaim their fervent Arab nationalism while Moslems continue to hint that

21

beneath their public anti-Zionist statements is an unspoken relief that another non-Islamic island like Israel exists in the midst of the Moslem sea which threatens to engulf them. The attempt of the Christian Arabs to prove their Arabism by attacking Jews and Israel was not convincing to "true Arabs," suggested Shukri.

"Now, we Moslems here don't hate Jews. That is, we hate our Arab leaders who in 1948 could have accepted partition or earlier could have accepted the parliamentary idea. Then Jews would have been only thirty per cent and we wouldn't have been what they call a minority. That's what they call us here, you know," he said bitterly. "A minority. We're not a minority. We're the original inhabitants of the land."

The office for Moslem affairs is located in a section of Haifa near the port, an area where the rubble of houses and factories bombed during the war is still not completely cleaned up. A white-shirted gentleman with smoothly combed gray-black hair and a well-trimmed mustache was sitting behind a desk in a corner of the office. Shukri threw him a brusque greeting in Arabic, then switched to English for my benefit.

"Tell me, Muchmad, the gentleman wants to know if there are any fifth columns among the Arabs. Have you heard of any fifth columns?"

Muchmad hastened to respond to the question I had never asked. No, he had never heard of an Arab fifth column. Furthermore, said Muchmad, there was no need at all for security regulations, which the government still applied to Arab travel in the "triangle" area.

"Never mind . . . never mind . . . these regulations are still necessary." Shukri shook his head as if both he and Muchmad were aware of things which need not be discussed. The real complaint which Moslems had against the government, said Shukri, was not the security regulations but the "unfair" political representation in government.

"Why don't they give us our proper percentage? There are about 200,000 Arabs—Moslems—this means we ought to have about twelve or fourteen per cent in office." Furthermore, suggested Shukri, the United Nations representation should have Arab Moslems on it.

22

"Why, do you know that some of the people sitting in the other delegations are my relatives. I would know how to speak with them, and they would speak with me in a different way than they would speak with Jews."

Shukri went on to tell me how successful his speaking efforts had been in raising money for the United Jewish Appeal in New York. Muchmad listened to him politely, fingering a string of black beads. He saw me looking at the beads and smiled.

"Everybody thinks they are for prayer, but they are just for holding and for playing with the fingers. For Arabs they are an empty symbol—no religious meaning."

Muchmad's remarks gave me the opportunity to remind Shukri again that it was the Moslem religion rather than the political problems that interested me. Both men looked at each other and smiled.

"Of course, if you're interested," said Shukri, "but neither of us pray much. We don't need it. We want our children to know the Koran, of course, like the Jews know the Bible. They should know who Mohammed is—but religion is for older people. But we will go to the mosque."

The mosque in Acre is a half-hour drive from Haifa along a good highway which alternates between lovely palm trees, smelly oil refineries, and noisy iron works, and curves about the perfect semicircle of Haifa Bay till it enters the thick walls of the historic town.

Inside the old courtyard which enclosed Israel's tallest and loveliest minaret, an old man showed us into a room nearby. A few moments later the local cadi, dressed in baggy pants and a frayed vest, arrived scratching his short-cropped gray hair and several days' growth of beard. Islam makes no distinction between religious law and civil matters. The cadi, a Moslem judge, is qualified to officiate in matters of marriage, divorce, and burial, and also to adjudicate disputes of "personal status" which fall under Moslem law, Shukri explained. There was also a school for Moslem religious studies in Acre which the cadi headed. I asked about the school. The cadi shrugged and Shukri translated his brief reply.

"He says there are no students in the school now." The Israeli

23

government had provided a budget for a Moslem religious school, but there were no candidates. Further questions to the cadi about the interest of Israel's young Moslems in their faith elicited a similar series of indifferent shrugs and brief answers. Only once did the cadi's sleepy eyes and voice come to life. I had asked him how Moslems felt in earlier days, before the Jewish state.

"Ah, I remember even under the Turks, whom we didn't like— yet how proud we were on a festival day when the Pasha in his red uniform and with his soldiers would all come to the mosque. When we watched them we felt—well, we felt, even the small ones, that we were part of something big and strong." The cadi's voice warmed in memory. Shukri smiled tolerantly and asked if I wanted to hear the Moslem prayers which were being conducted now.

At a fountain in a courtyard outside, a few women with blue tattoo marks on their faces were dabbing water on their forehead, and on the soles of their feet and hands. This was the rite of *tuma*—the ablution rite prescribed for all Moslems before prayer. Women are not required to pray in the Moslem faith, but these ladies were evidently ready to participate, though from a distance.

Three or four elderly men were sitting cross-legged on the patio outside the mosque. Inside the cool darkness of the mosque six or seven more men squatted, their heads drooping, while the aged, white-bearded Imam—the local preacher—from a small balustrade connected with circular stairs to the ground, delivered his sermon in a high, monotonous voice. Near the door a young Moslem—he had arrived late—was going through the meticulously prescribed posturing which is part of the Moslem prayer ritual. Methodically and carefully he assumed standing, kneeling, and prostrate positions. His face was drawn together in rapt concentration as he performed the rites, which are graceful even when performed alone, but when carried out by large masses in perfect unison, are most impressive. Westerners, even if they see nothing else in the Moslem faith, might consider what is lost in Western religion, which inhibits or discourages the movement of the body in its prayer expression. The most natural expression of any human feeling, be it the love of a parent for a child or

24

the love of a human for his God, would seem to be in physical even more than in verbal movement. Physical movements, like the stretching out of hands or the full prostration of the body face downward, were part of all early religious expressions, and are still a part of the Moslem and most of the Eastern Christian religions. Is it possible to suppress them, as they are suppressed in the stiff formality of Western ritual, without suppressing the intensity of religious feeling?

Then again, I told myself, as I listened to the Imam's monotonous tone and watched the dull-eyed, unresponsive faces of the few people in the mosque, perhaps my little meditation was a forced attempt to stir up some sort of religious idea where even the thought of conversation about religion seemed silly. Shukri was impatient to leave. The undulating chant of the Imam followed us to the gate and Muchmad stopped.

"You know," he put his hand on his heart, "despite everything, it pulls back a memory, touches here."

Reflecting later on this dismal encounter with the Moslem faith in action, I tried to remember that it might not have been a typical expression of Moslem religiosity in the Holy Land—though I had been at Israel's most beautiful mosque, on the Moslem Sabbath. The Acre cadi, a Moslem in Jerusalem told me later, was not really qualified for his position because he had not studied in the famous Al Ahzar School in Cairo, which is the main spiritual center of Islam today. My informant bore the same name as this Acre cadi—Taburi—but hastened to disclaim any relationship. He was a lawyer from Nazareth, where his father had been "the only real cadi in Israel." Young Taburi was much more interested in religious matters than Shukri, but agreed with him that the religion as it was, was for "older people." There ought to be, he thought, in the Moslem religion, some attempt at the kind of reform and adaptation to modern thought which had taken place in Western religions. To his knowledge, there was nothing going on in that direction now. I asked the well-spoken young lawyer how his father felt about the situation. It was not the religious situation among the Moslems that mainly aggravated his father, said young Taburi, but rather

25

the acts of insult which perhaps unconsciously the government was guilty of in their relationships with their community.

"I will give you an example. My father hated to receive letters from the government because they would be addressed to the head of the local 'Arab minority.' Often when he saw a letter addressed in this way, he would tear it up without reading it. Technically I suppose we are a minority, but why does the government have to use the word? It is psychologically unpleasant for us."

"Yes, that is the primary problem of Moslems in Israel," a government official admitted, "and the only way to solve it is by giving up the Jewish state. Their problem is that they were licked in the war."

This may indeed be the basic problem of Moslems in Israel, but its implications for the spiritual life not only of the thoughtful Moslem but of Christian and Jew go deeper than the matter of a military victory. There is, of course, tragedy in the sudden change from majority to minority status for any human group. This tragedy can be sensed in a glimpse of Arab faces in Jaffa, once an almost all-Arab town, or in the streets of Haifa and Jerusalem. The old men and women who still walk there, dressed in Arab costume, are, one can see, strangers in their former homes. Official government policy may prohibit discrimination, the economic and even political conditions of their life may be superior to what is enjoyed by the Arabs over the border— but they still have what the Bible calls "the heart of the stranger."

On the level of official government policy there is often a genuine effort to fulfill the biblical commandments of remembering that the Jews too were once strangers in the land of Egypt, and a will to prove to the world that a people so long a minority knows how to treat its own minorities. In daily life, while the Arab radio stations across the border blast their daily threats of "another raid," the commandment is hard for most Israelis to keep in mind. The pathetic implications of the situation for the individual Moslem was highlighted for me by an incident related by a social worker. She had just returned from visiting a Jewish family whose young child had been sent into a condition almost of traumatic shock. The child had for years been going

26

to school with a young comrade who lived nearby. They had become friends, with all the eagerness and depth of childish hearts. One day another boy in the class had come and told him that his friend was an Arab. The Jewish child didn't believe it, but when he had asked his best friend, the latter had burst into tears and admitted that he was an Arab. Both children had returned to their homes that day, heartbroken and literally sick, the Arab boy because he had been "revealed," the Jewish lad because his best friend had turned out to be a member of the "enemy camp." The mothers of the two children had met and tried to reconcile them, but it was no use. The stereotypes of "enemy" and "friend" were stronger than the real life situation. The social worker had recommended psychological counseling for both children. In time the Jewish child will recover from his "betrayal." He is in the majority camp. But what of the Arab lad? His problem is deeper than the fate of a minority rejected by the majority. He has to fall back on a spiritual tradition which offers him no way of understanding his minority situation in a positive way. Christianity and Judaism do offer such a way—but there is no tradition in Islam which says Blessed are the meek and the weak and the disinherited. There is no teaching that power and glory may be associated with the humble person who rides on a donkey, or with one who is crucified, or with a people that is scattered in exile and a minority everywhere. To Moslems, the crucifixion of Jesus makes all claims of the Christian Church to victory and power ridiculous. In this sense the minority status of Moslems places them in a spiritual predicament more difficult than that sensed by a Christian or Jewish minority.

This is further deepened by the changes in the spiritual quality of Moslem life which have taken place in the last century. Unlike early Christianity or later Judaism, Islam never attempted to distinguish between earthly and heavenly principalities, between what belongs to Caesar and what belongs to God. The glories of the true faith were always identified with the power of the state. The religious element of Mohammedanism is still strong in many sections of the Arab world, in Saudi Arabia, Yemen, or among the uneducated Arab masses. But for the more so-

27

phisticated leadership of most Arab communities today, Pan-Islamism is seen as only superficially connected with religion. The Arab nationalist leader may speak about the genius of his people and the glories of their past civilization. In fact, the purely religious element of his culture has been almost completely swallowed up by a secular nationalism. His sense of belonging to a historic group expresses itself very weakly in terms of a positive God faith, ritual observance, or study of the Koran. The vacuum which ensues from the elimination of the religious core of Pan-Islamism is filled instead by a group nationalism which in turn must find its unifying bonds more in terms of what the Moslem is against—"imperialism," Zionism—rather than what it is for.

The above observations are, of course, by no means original and have been offered by better-qualified observers of the Moslem scene. They are not repeated here in order to cast aspersions on the spiritual potential of a religious faith which even today in Africa is apparently more successful in its work with the colored masses than white Christian missionaries. The success of Moslem missionary work in Africa is attributed in part to the preaching of dervish missionaries, whose primitive emotionalism is more satisfying to uneducated Negroes than the sophisticated religious images offered them by Westerners. The fact that Islam permits more than one wife also makes it preferable often to the monogamic demands of Christianity. Even more important is the fact that Moslems have been far more successful than Christians or Jews in establishing a brotherhood of faith which rises above color or racial grouping. There is no doubt that on the continent of Africa and in various parts of the Moslem world, the faith of Islam is very much alive. It is far less meaningful, however, for the sophisticated Moslem intellectual, because, as Taburi pointed out, it has not yet gone through a real "conflict" and "response" of the type which Christianity encountered and survived during the Renaissance. At any rate, if there is a renaissance along spiritual levels taking place in the Moslem world, most educated Moslems in Israel are yet unaware of it. In this land, where Mohammed thought one village was better than the whole of his native Medina, Islam seems to be a matter for old people and

28

of little help to the spiritual predicament of Moslems who do not wish to be called a minority even though they are no longer the majority.

"Leave Things as They Are"

Theoretically, Israel's Christian Arab community of 50,000 should be better prepared for its spiritual predicament.

"We are, you know, as Christians, accustomed to being a minority," pointed out Bishop George Hakim, leader of 20,000 Greek Catholics. The impressive-looking bearded Patriarch, with bald head and alert though peaceful brown eyes, received me in his spacious new Haifa residence overlooking the Mediterranean. Fingering a large, red-jeweled crucifix resting on his saffron robe, and seated comfortably in his tastefully upholstered chair, the Greek Catholic leader needed little prompting to launch into his analysis of what he considered the major problem of Israel's Christian community.

"At the beginning we were very well disposed toward the state. After all, we are taught to believe in Paul's words, that 'all principalities and powers are from heaven.'" But, said the archbishop, the continuous suspicion shown by the government toward its Christians, and the needless security regulations and travel restrictions which are enforced in the triangle area and other sections of Northern Galilee, had dissipated the original good feeling among Arab Christians toward the Israeli government and made them feel like second-class citizens.

"The government made a bad mistake in failing to differentiate between the potential loyalty of Arab Moslems and Arab Christians—the latter could have been very loyal citizens of the state. By now the government knows who is a good and who is a bad Arab," said Hakim sarcastically. "It doesn't need these regulations. There is only one reason, in my opinion, for maintaining them, and for transplanting Christian Arabs from their native villages to other areas. That reason is," the priest's quiet voice took on an acid edge, "economic greed—that's the basic motivation of the state here."

George Hakim has for years in his church publications, pulpit, and interviews with foreign visitors, given vent to his bitter feelings about these matters. The government officials who arrange the meetings between the archbishop and anybody who wants to see him often try to anticipate the effect of his views.

"You'll find him very polite, a gentleman," said the Israeli who made the appointment for me, "and incidentally a shrewd business operator and real-estate owner himself. Why, do you know," the Israeli official said, "he has more travel privileges than anybody else in Israel? Not even a United Nations official can freely cross the border as he does—despite his outspoken anti-Israeli sentiments."

Though denying that he was anti-Israeli, the archbishop did devote himself at first to examples of what he felt were government discriminations against the Christian minority. He seemed surprised, then pleased, when I told him that I was interested in his opinion on specifically religious rather than political problems.

"Why, I can't remember when somebody has come here to talk to me about religious matters." It took him a moment to adjust himself to the new topic.

"Well, you ought to know that I am the only native Christian leader in this region. All the others are from abroad. We are the largest Christian group in Israel." The archbishop had no complaints about church and state arrangements, nor about his community's situation. In fact there was less danger of intermarriage now between Jews and Christians than before. "Then again, the fact that we are a minority brings us closer in feeling to the original Christian community in the Holy Land."

This was exactly what I wanted to ask him. What did it feel like to be a Christian living on the holy soil where Jesus lived, walked, and suffered?

The archbishop's eyes looked out of the balcony window toward the blue Mediterranean. "You know that if you live close to something, you don't continually notice it. We are so close to the holy places. But yes, I think there is a difference in Christian life here. We are less mechanical, we are closer to nature—there is more peace. . . ." His voice trailed off, as if searching for more examples of the specifically different quality of religious life in Israel.

30

"On the other hand," the archbishop said more strongly, "the time has not yet come for the kind of Christian-Jewish religious dialogue which Monsignor Vergani and others speak about."

The line of authority which flowed from the Vatican to the Greek Catholic archbishop, and to the late Apostolic delegate to the Holy Land, a Roman Catholic, was, I had heard, a delicate matter.

Vergani had made a number of statements praising the government for its respect of Christian rights and holy sites, while Archbishop Hakim had been critical. Vergani had also, on occasion, expressed a desire for meetings between Christians and Jews on a friendly, religious plane. Archbishop Hakim didn't agree.

"We have lost our spiritual elite here. Our intellectual leaders are across the border now, exiled. We must first build up our strength here before engaging in any dialogues." He interrupted his thought again to say wonderingly that he had many conversations with visitors, but this was the first one on theological matters. It apparently didn't occur to the archbishop that a visitor might be as surprised as he was at the lack of "theological" discussions which come the way of a Catholic archbishop in the Holy Land.

In Nazareth I met the head of Israel's 17,000 Greek Orthodox Catholics, Archbishop Isidoros. The Greek-born Patriarch, who once fought with the partisan forces in his native land, received me graciously in his spacious but simple quarters at the courtyard of his church in Nazareth. He was tall, with gentle, regular features, dark eyes, long, flowing black hair and beard, and a somewhat bashful smile. He answered all my questions, with careful words that he had obviously used many times before. There was, he admitted, a large Communist vote in the Arab sections of the country—but they were undoubtedly Moslems. Yes, he knew the Russian Archimandrite in Jerusalem, and there was both a historic and a present-day relationship between them, but it was a church matter which had nothing to do with politics. The relationship of his church with the Israeli government was fine, said the archbishop.

"We have our own wealth and do not need the subsidy which

31

they give to other churches. You know," he pointed out softly, "that the Greek Orthodox church was descended directly from the Christian church founded in the Holy Land by Peter." He himself was Greek. In past centuries the fact that the head of the Holy Land's Arab Greek-Orthodox population was always a Greek was frequently a source of some internal dissension. The Holy places under Greek Orthodox control were also in the hands of Greeks rather than the indigenous population.

Archbishop Isidoros denied knowledge, however, of any resentment today over the situation.

I mentioned the church and state issue.

"No, we are satisfied with present arrangements." The archbishop shook his head. "If we have problems between us, among the Christian communities, we know how to settle them. We have been living together for a long time and know how to make arrangements."

What about the Christian groups in Israel, like the Protestants, who were very unhappy about the present system?

Isidoros shook his head gently. "It would be better to leave things as they are."

"But aren't things as they are often disappointing to Christian pilgrims?" I asked the Greek Orthodox archbishop. How does a Christian feel when he comes here to Nazareth and sees several churches, each of which claims to be built on the exact site of the Annunciation, or in Jerusalem finds two Gardens of Gethsemane.

The handsome black-bearded archbishop looked out through the window. "Yes, living here can be—what shall we call it—a needle to the faith. Maybe it's better for the faith to visit the Holy Land than to live here." The pleasant smile on his face had disappeared as he said these words, and his dark eyes were serious. Then he smiled again and waved a hand in the direction of the town below. "But it can be very pleasant here on a Sunday morning when all the bells of the churches are ringing."

Outside in the bright sunlight of the church courtyard, the archbishop willingly posed for a picture, though first hurrying back to his chambers to get the black elongated round hat of his office. In front of the rosebush in the courtyard, he posed, lifting up the crucifix hanging about his neck, his eyes rolled slightly heavenward, as he waited for me to snap the photograph.

After leaving the Greek Orthodox spiritual leader I walked toward the center of the town through the narrow streets filled with the wares of artisans, with vegetables, and with gunnysacks of pleasant-smelling spices. Nazareth's history is reflected in the faces and costumes one passes on its streets. The dark-visaged Mediterranean type bargains in Arabic with the villager who has the blue eyes and flaxen hair left here by the Frankish Crusader. Tattooed Arab girls bearing tin water cans on their heads pass by sandal-footed Benedictine monks and small-bodied Coptic priests with round, black conical hats. Occasionally everyone in the street presses against the building walls as some large black car flying a church banner ascends to the upper levels of the city where some of Israel's Christian groups have their monasteries and administrative offices. I passed a dozen tourists following their guide wearily up the street, cameras on their shoulders and tired heads turning in weary response to the rapid-fire description of their leader.

"Over there, to the right, where the Franciscans are building a new church," called out the guide, "is the location of Joseph's workshop. We are going now to the school where Jesus studied. You will be able to see the stone table upon which he wrote."

The tourists' dull-eyed glance followed the guide's pointing finger obediently. They seemed unimpressed. The buildings to which he was pointing are remarkably drab, in architecture and inner decoration. The official guide's rapid patter was carefully coached so as to cover over the discrepancies in the historic claims made here by the various church groups. There is considerable scholarly question with respect to the traditional Christian claims in Nazareth. There is even a question as to whether present-day Nazareth, built on the slope of the Galilean hills of northern Israel, is the city referred to by the New Testament as the childhood home of Jesus. As late as the sixth century, Nazareth is reported in Christian chronicles as being simply a small Jewish village renowned only "for the beauty of its women." Even Jerome, living during the fourth century in

33

Bethlehem and reporting the visit of two Christian nuns to Nazareth, makes no mention of Holy sites within it.

Most of the Christian holy sites in the Holy Land were determined during a visit of Queen Helena, famous mother of Christianity's first emperor, Constantine. A chronicler of the day describes how "she was led by divine intimation . . . to the place of the sepulchre and beneath a former Temple of Venus, and contrary to all expectations, the veritable and hallowed monument of our Savior's resurrection appeared." In this Jerusalem cave Helena discovered, according to the chronicler, nothing less than the true Cross and two other crosses along with scrolls written by Pontius Pilate. (She promptly sent some nails from the true Cross to her son, who used them in the bridle of his personal war horse, an event in which his Christian confessors saw a fulfillment of the prophecy, "In that day shall be written on the bells of the horses Holiness unto the Lord.") Queen Helena conveyed news of her discovery to Constantine, who immediately gave orders that the Church of the Holy Sepulchre be built on the spot. In this way Queen Helena traveled through the land, turning vague conjecture and myth into confirmed sacred sites.

We can only guess at the mood and circumstances in which these discoveries were made. The Queen came on her pilgrimage to the Holy Land bearing dark and heavy memories. There were rumors that her son had been responsible for the murder of his sons and wife, a jealous and mistaken shedding of blood which even the pagan faiths refused to condone. Was it this burden of guilt that the Queen Mother bore to the land of her new faith? In any case, she came from a world where religion insisted on "seeing" as well as hearing evidence of the Divine. And the Queen Mother's desire corresponded perfectly with the ambitions of the then Bishop of Jerusalem, Macarius. He saw in her visit the opportunity to give his bishopric, which till then had been an unimportant adjunct to Antioch, something of the status he felt it deserved. Both the number and the fame of Christian holy places grew with the passage of time. In the fourth century a pilgrim lady from London was able to see the tablets which Moses had broken after descending from Mount Sinai.

At Cana until recently tourists could see the wine jugs allegedly used at the wedding mentioned in the New Testament, and the splinters of the true Cross which have been exported from the Holy Land are easily equivalent to the wood of a small forest. As sects multiplied within Christendom, so did the holy sites, each group protesting the inauthenticity of the holy sites held by the others. Was it this knowledge that had made the Greek Orthodox archbishop feel that living here could be "a needle to the faith?"

There are other problems in the Holy Land which can be a needle to the faith of a man like Isidoros. He knows that the bells of Nazareth's twenty-four churches, pleasant as they may sound on a Sunday morning, do not bear witness to the greater harmony of the church. Rather do they remind anyone who knows something about past history here that the "body of Christ" is split into many fragments. And these fissures in Christendom have released more violence and hate than love. Furthermore, there is another problem even more difficult to discuss openly.

The Byzantine church which the archbishop represents has deep historical ties with the chief Patriarchate in Moscow. In Tzarist days Moscow never hesitated to use the church as an instrument of the state power. In the latter part of the nineteenth century Russia used the Greek Orthodox church to acquire land and influence in the Middle East. Then, as today, the Holy Land became a focus for the struggle of power between East and West. Russia set itself up as a "protector" of Greek Orthodox interests. The Latin church was backed by the European powers. Ostensibly, the quarrels were about the repairs of the Holy Sepulchre, or about the stolen ceremonial object in the Church of the Nativity. The religious pretexts were used to touch off active conflict, as in the Crimean War. The parallels of the situation are all too evident. The Greek Orthodox church today is very much involved in a nonpublicized struggle for power between East and West for influence in the Middle East. Archbishop Isidoros himself is now almost isolated from his ecclesiastical confreres who reside in nearby Arab lands. His personal relationship with the Israeli government is good, which means that his standing in his own church is not so good because the influence

35

of the Russian-centered Chief Patriarch in the Arab lands is increasing. Archbishop Isidoros will not speak publicly of the political power struggle within his own church. But it is more than vested interests that move him and other Christian religious leaders in Israel to suggest that "things ought to be left alone—as they are."

"Needed—A Shaking Up"

The only religious leader in Nazareth who is eager not to leave things as they are is the minister of the Baptist church. It was not difficult to find Nazareth's Baptist church. Several teen-age youngsters dressed in Western sports shirts and neatly pressed trousers were sitting on the wall surrounding the Well of the Annunciation. They pointed toward a huge sign with the words "Southern Baptist Alliance of the United States," a few yards away. Behind the sign was a substantial concrete building used by the Baptists as a school. Nearby was the church, a structure whose sloped wooden roof and simple beamed interior are more reminiscent in architecture and feeling of a Midwestern town than of the Galilee hills which supply the white blocks of granite that most buildings use here. Typically American and Midwestern in appearance also was the church's minister, Dwight Baker, in his American-style eyeglasses and gray-blue suit, shaking the hands of his parishioners as they entered the church for vesper services. Mr. Baker's little blond boy brought me a hymnal and prayer book, and I sat down with the twenty or thirty people who had come for the service. The interior of the church was a welcome relief from the cluttered statuary, altar cloths, icons, and mediocre art of the other churches in Nazareth. There was only one attempt at color and visionary inspiration—a large painting hung in back of the pulpit, lighted by a neon light.

It was a portrayal of a gently flowing river, turning and winding downstream from a distant, blue-green mountain, flowing through verdant banks whose trees trailed green boughs in the soft flowing stream. It was evidently a representation of the

36

river Jordan, and it had been painted, Mr. Baker told me later after services, by his mother, who used "a bit of her imagination." The minister knew that this Jordan of Western imagination bore little resemblance to the shallow, sinuously curving stream which descends quickly from the hills of Galilee into the barren, steaming crevice of the Dead Sea 1286 feet below sea level. The few hymns weakly sung by the congregation were obviously European melodies. Mr. Baker's sermon was delivered in English, though he could speak Arabic. It was pleasant, but had no more indigenous relationship to the land than the Midwestern twang of Mr. Baker's Arabic. Only at one point in the service did the atmosphere change, and the sounds of the service became native to the throats that were uttering them. That was when the minister asked the congregation to read a chapter of the New Testament in unison. Then the strong, melodious chant of the Arabic flowed forth naturally from the throats of the congregation, and for a few moments the "translation" atmosphere was gone.

After the service the American minister offered to show me a Coptic church. He suggested we go there since he was curious to see it himself. We walked over a field filled with stone rubble to a small, newly built red brick building. We found the Coptic priest resting on a couch in a little room off the courtyard of the church. He was very old, with small wizened features and yellow complexion. Near him sat a large, black-mustached Arab wearing a gray-and-white striped robe and a large black leather belt. The priest, who spoke Arabic to Mr. Baker, told us that his friend was an Orthodox Christian, "but a good friend."

Hearing the conversation, a bulky, dark-haired woman looked in and disappeared to come back with a tray holding some small cups of coffee and thimblefuls of banana liqueur. The woman was a Copt who lived in Jaffa, and had come to spend a week in Nazareth, "for the climate." She was not particularly religious, she told Baker. "All people are the same, and it's a different age now." The little Coptic priest heard her and smiled.

I asked the priest what the attitude of the Coptic church was at present toward Israel. Only that week the Israeli government had accused a Coptic priest who had been traveling to and from

37

the old city of Jerusalem of transmitting military secrets to the Jordanian government. The priest listened with a little smile, and Baker translated his answer.

"He has just quoted from the Bible—'And Jacob blessed Pharaoh'—which he takes to mean that there can and should be peace between Egypt and Israel. He has only feelings of gratitude to the Israeli government," Baker translated. "The government recently made possible the construction of his church."

But did people come to the Coptic church? I asked.

"It doesn't matter," the priest replied, "what church a person goes to, so long as he goes to church. Nobody need try to change the religious opinion of another." The Greek Orthodox Arab nodded his head in agreement. Things had indeed changed since the time when the Coptic church, because of its doctrinal differences with the rest of Christendom, had decided to break off from the Byzantine Empire and surrender to the Saracens.

The priest donned a robe and a low, black, conical turban, and took us into his newly painted building. As in most Eastern Christian churches, there were no pews in the center but long benches running around the sides. Most Christian prayer services in the East are carried on in the manner of the Orient—in standing or kneeling positions. The priest took us to the small altar where a large book was resting on a wooden stand. This was the Bible written in the ancient Amharic language. He read some sentences from one of the pages. Baker asked if he would read a passage familiar to us, in the Amharic language. The little priest seemed puzzled and after thumbing through a few pages in the Bible, shrugged.

"I don't think he understands what he is reading," Baker whispered. Outside in the courtyard the priest agreed readily to pose for a picture, but first, like Isidoros, ran back to his room and brought out a large crucifix which he held before his chest for the picture.

Later that evening Baker joined me for supper at the Galilee Hotel. The Baptist minister thoughtfully talked about Israel's religious problems. He didn't agree at all with Isidoros and Hakmi about keeping the *status quo*.

"The religious sterility here is the result of the Millet system —it is a relic of the feudal system of the Middle Ages. Like the dukes and barons in their day, the church hierarchy has inherited its property and its populations. It wants to keep things as they are." The Protestant minister shook his head with a touch of wistfulness.

"If spiritual leaders had to attract their people here on a religious basis rather than inheriting them as organized communities, it might shake things up. What we need here is a real change of heart and spirit. A real dying and resurrection of life as we Baptists conceive it." He had often dreamed of what might happen if a person like Billy Graham were to visit Israel and to preach not in Jewish areas but in Christian communities like Nazareth. A gleam of anticipation came into the thoughtful and rather sad eyes of the Baptist when he thought of what might happen. Of course, he reminded himself, Graham's pro-Zionist attitude might make for more problems with the Arab Christians whose faith had not been able to transcend the bitterness of the nationalist struggle in Israel. Eighty-five per cent of the Arabs were probably pro-Nasser in their hearts, he said. The minister did not approve of the security regulations with which the Israeli government restricted the movement of Arabs in this area. On the other hand, he realized that even if these regulations were to be lifted, the Arabs in Nazareth and other communities would simply go on to the next set of complaints. The basic problem was psychological rather than political or economic—the deep hurt of a majority suddenly become a minority. If only there were some way, said the Protestant, to get the Arab youth out of the communities which have become like ghettos and breed a ghetto-like mentality, a "closed miserable brooding which can get them no place." The minister shook his head as if dreaming again of the impossible.

"Christians in the Holy Land could have the opportunity to bear witness to their faith in a way which would make a bridge between Arab and Jew in the Middle East. But," he sighed, "what we need is a real shaking up, a complete change of heart and spirit, the sort of thing the prophets here asked for."

Meditation in Nazareth

After Baker left I walked out on the small balcony of the hotel, which looked over the main street of Nazareth. A wicker chair there had a broken leg, but by leaning it back against the wall I could achieve a comfortable position, my back touching the cool granite of the building, my face upward toward the sky. The moon and stars hung low, and the cubical houses gleamed white against the black hill upon which they were built. The night quietness muffled the occasional voices which rose out of some distant quarter of the town, and blunted the click of footsteps on the cobblestones below. Two couples walked along the street. The women trailed a few yards behind the men and were dressed in black, with black scarves on their heads, the usual garb of Christians in the Holy Land. The men were dressed in more typical Arabic style. Their long robes gleamed in the moonlight, under their Western-style jackets. The white robes pulled away from their legs, revealing sockless feet in heavy high shoes. Both men wore Arab kaffiyehs, white scarves pressed around their heads with a circular black cord. The fringes of their Arab headdress flowed gracefully over their sport jackets.

"You Westerners think it's strange to see us wear Oriental robes with European jackets," an Armenian storekeeper in the old city of Jerusalem once told me. "With you everything has to match, be part of a set. We in the Levant don't see why we can't combine any styles we like. That's the secret of our survival here—clothes, furniture, ideas, we don't insist that they all fit together."

Why indeed does everything have to match? Let him who hungers for "system" beware lest he disturb that tolerance of incongruity which permits Moslem tarbooshes to live together with Western jackets; bare-sandaled, ascetic monks to kneel before glittering, gem-studded altars; and people of assorted languages, skin colors, and religions to assume sufficient indifference to each other so that there is the possibility of survival. Wasn't this what the Patriarch of the old Eastern church was trying to tell those who wanted to "shake things up," here and bring Western order and system into the East. It is a lesson the world too must learn if it would survive.

From some distant quarter of the town a flute and accompanying drum had been playing for more than an hour—perhaps the continuation of the wedding celebration which I saw that afternoon. It had been a typical, brief Moslem ceremony—the young bride was led from her house by a procession of adults and little children to the courtyard of the groom's house. There a few people crowded into the room where the Moslem cadi perfunctorily sealed the marriage while somebody beat a drum outside and everyone chanted a few songs and clapped hands. Now the flute and drum wove a melody like an interminably winding river. So too does Eastern song go on without apparent climax or goal, only the pulse beat of the drum marking the passage of time. This is the message of the East—the reminder of the never stopping river of time which makes all plans and hopes flicker for a few moments like lights upon the water, then vanishes into the flowing stream. The Western ear likes music with a beginning and end, with a goal and clash, climax and resolution. It is more than a difference in musical style. In it is an affirmation that all in the future need not be as it was in the past. Time for the Westerner is not like the unwinding of a film which has already been made—seemingly new for its viewer, but not really. Time can bring into existence that which has never been before and which a man may see—an utterly new world. Strange that this message of time being more than an illusion, time as something real and creative, should have come out of the East and been brought to the West by way of Nazareth. For certainly this was what Jesus preached—newness, differentness, it need not be as it was—a new heart, a new world, a new birth. It was the message of Christianity but also of Judaism, of the prophets, who dreamed of "That Day."

Perhaps there is an affinity between the Jewish soul and this idea of time's reality. In the last century Henri Bergson, a French-Jewish philosopher who almost became a Catholic, presented this theme in a metaphor startlingly relevant to our day —the image of a climbing rocket which in its flight drops behind dead layers of burned-out matter. Wasn't it this sense of dead, burned-out matter everywhere that is the real "needle to the faith" in the Holy Land, not only in Nazareth, but in the mosque of Acre and in the synagogues of Meah Shearim?

"Up above on the hills," says a Christian resident of the town, "away from the cluttered altars, the competing claims of the churches, I feel something—up there where I can see the valleys and sky that Jesus saw, or down below in the grottoes."

The original town of Nazareth was built more below than above ground, and some of the original caves have been revealed beneath the excavations. It is quiet and cool in these grottoes. The stone steps leading into them are worn smooth. Some of the stone walls have thin projections from which baskets of supplies were lowered by rope into storage holes dug into the ground. In one corner the walls of the grotto may appear more smooth, as if it were the place where the family gathered or where a child's crib would be placed. Here, the visitor may remain a moment after the guide's voice fades away and the other tourists have followed after him. Here, near the bare stone, he may feel "something"—something which will disappear as he walks back past the layers that have been deposited by man, past the faded Byzantine mosaics, the Crusader columns, the nineteenth-century carpentry, statuary, and colored windows, and into the streets where the radio blares forth American jazz and the cafés advertise shish kebab and soda pop. The radios and the cafés are at least alive, but the cluttered layers of stone are dead. Dead too is the potpourri of robes, hats, and priestly uniforms that set apart Copt, Greek Orthodox, American, Maronite, Abyssinian, and the other two dozen sects of Christendom that pass each other on the streets of Nazareth without looking at or knowing each other. It is all dead—like the ashes of a burned-out rocket that at one time were formed by fiery life thrusts. These differentiations of uniform and church were once symbols of fiery controversies. But there is no more life in them now than in the dead hand of the ancient Patriarch Isidore which the Armenian Christians still use to consecrate their new Patriarchs. This is what disappoints the pilgrim who comes to Nazareth—and what Christian who comes there is not somewhere in his soul a pilgrim? More than the doubtful authenticity of the historic sites or the petty bickering over who can whitewash which stairway, more even than the quarrels about *status quo* and religious freedom, is this sense of spiritual lifelessness in a land which the religious heart has always associated with the power of rebirth, the dream of the utterly new in life and in society. This is the real problem of religious life in the Holy Land today.

"But they don't want this land to be alive," an old rabbi once told me when I asked him to analyze the difference between Jewish and Christian feelings about the Holy Land. He was a white-bearded Patriarch with twinkling blue eyes who was called the Posiviezher Rabbi. In Europe he had been head of a famous talmudic academy which was destroyed by the Nazis. The old man's warm voice had broken in a laugh as he told of the fund-raising gimmicks with which he had built his new talmudic academy in Tel Aviv. He had broken the cost of maintaining the school into hours and minutes, then traveled through the cities of the United States offering Jews a chance to support his Yeshiva for one full day or even a part of an hour. The rabbi's voice had become more serious when I asked him about the meaning of Israel for Christians.

"For us this land is a house of life. For them it is a house of graves. They don't want this land and its people to be alive. It might remind them that Jews are alive, and Judaism is alive. They might even have to think of Him [the rabbi, of course, wouldn't pronounce the name Jesus] as part of our history, just another Jew, and this they don't want."

The Posiviezher Rabbi doesn't realize that to many Jews as well as to Christians, he and his students would appear to be more fossilized than alive. Those who visit his Yeshiva in B'nai Brak see a scene that reminds them of a frozen tableau lifted out of long ago. Hundreds of young men and boys, wearing North European garb, their long side curls reaching down to their shoulders, lean over large folios chanting in the Aramaic tongue, which has not been spoken for a thousand years, and study laws which were relevant to life in fourth- and fifth-century Babylonia. To non-Orthodox eyes, the scene of the Posiviezher Yeshiva in B'nai Brak would seem as artificial and imported

43

and as essentially irrelevant to life as the Gothic churches and European hymns in Nazareth.

Still, is there truth in the old man's analysis of Christian interest in the Holy Land? Is there a kind of Christianity which prefers graves to life, the sureness and peace of death to life with its uncertain and unknown possibilities? Surely there have been and still are Christians who insist that Israel—both the land and the people—ought to be dead or at least fossilized. Their faith assumes that Jewish history has long been finished and supplanted by a new Israel. The actual land of Israel need no longer play any role in the life of the new Israel, the Christian church. Angrily they reject what is occurring today in the Holy Land as a "historical anachronism," the wrong and useless attempt to revive a fossil.

But there are also Christians today who think that this revived Israel may not so easily be labeled a historic anachronism. They see here not only graves but a re-quickening of life, which has implications for Christians as well as Jews. To them the phenomenon of the new Israel calls for a reopening of a theme which Christian theology includes under a category of discussion called "the mystery of Israel."

CHAPTER III

The Mystery of Israel

Oh, night that guided me, Oh, night more lovely than the
dawn,
Oh, night that joined Beloved with lover, Lover transformed in the Beloved . . .
—*Ascent of Mount Carmel by St. John of the Cross*

Beneath the sterile surface of present-day Christian life in Israel
there is at least one point of ferment. It has to do with a topic
which flared into brief but violent open debate during the World
Ecumenical Conference of 1954, held in Evanston, Illinois.

"Our destiny as a Church," said a group of prominent Protestant theologians, most of them from Europe, with searing memories of Dachau and nazism, "is in a mysterious way bound up
with the destiny of God's old Covenant people. Before the full
number of Jewish musicians have joined in, the Eternal Kingdom
orchestra cannot start performing the jubilant symphony of the
love of God in Christ, the Redeemer of all. It can only do some
rehearsing."

The conclusion of those who circulated this memorandum was
that "the Church cannot rest until the title of Christ to the
Kingdom is recognized by his own people according to the flesh."
A group of students under the influence of Karl Barth, famous
Swiss theologian, circulated another memorandum referring to
the state of Israel as a "sign" of the vitality of the Messianic
hope which still persists in the Israel of the flesh.

These special references to Israel were vehemently opposed
by other speakers and memoranda. Christians from Arab countries feverishly urged the Conference to avoid any special mention of Israel. Some American liberal Protestants joined them,

45

not because of anti-Zionist feeling, but because they did not agree with the call to missionize the Jews. Charles P. Taft, mayor of Cincinnati, argued that such a proclamation would "jeopardize my friendships and my relationships with my Jewish friends." Thus liberal Christians friendly to Jews worked with fervent anti-Zionists to deny that there "is no final hope for the Church without the Jews, without Israel."

It was not without significance, a Catholic observer commented after the Evanston conference, that "it was over the people of Israel that the Protestant Assembly expressed its division," although the Catholic admitted a similar division on the same subject could be expected in any large conclave of Catholic theologians. By a small majority, those who wanted to say something about the "mystery of Israel" in the final statement of the convention were outvoted. But everyone at Evanston knew that the discussion of this "mystery" had entered into a new and lively plane with the birth of the new state.

Just how lively and how fascinating in its possibilities I began to realize only after my meetings with a group of Catholic priests in Israel.

It was the late Apostolic delegate to the Holy Land, Monsignor Vergani, who introduced me to them. Monsignor Vergani was already ill with a cancer which was to take his life in 1959. A white hospital-style bed could be seen behind a screen in the small room of the Italian consulate where he received me. The white-robed priest was very Italian-looking, with a dark complexion and a small black mustache above a receding chin. He kept looking at the green pad on his desk as he spoke.

"The question you raise," he said softly, "is included under a subject which the church calls 'Mysterium Israelis, the mystery of Israel.' There is a monk who lives not far from here, on Mount Carmel. He has thought a great deal about this question, and I recommend that you speak to him. He was born Jewish himself."

The priest had written the name of the Carmelite monk on a small card, and along with it some other names of individuals in Israel whom he thought I ought to meet. The humid heat of the Haifa port had penetrated into the room, despite the drawn shades, and Vergani continually wiped his brow with a handker-chief.

"Yes, there is a difference in Christian life here." Vergani had returned to my question. "For example, we cannot demand as much of our monastic orders in a climate like this. Here religious life lends itself less to activity and more to mystic contemplation."

Monsignor Vergani spoke fluent Hebrew—one of the reasons for his popularity in Israel. When I mentioned the respect in which Israelis held him, he smiled.

"Perhaps it is because I have tried to be a spiritual and not a political leader that I have also had some political influence. But there is no reason why there should not be the friendliest relationship between Israel and the Vatican. There is nothing in Catholic doctrine which makes it necessary for the church to either support or oppose the Jewish state. As a matter of fact, the possibility of official recognition by the Vatican is excellent. Even the question of Jerusalem's internationalization can be re-discussed if the holy sites can be protected through another plan. Of course, there are serious problems. A great tragedy has taken place here with respect to the Arab refugees. There is fault on both sides. Who is to blame only history can show, only God knows."

A black-robed nun had served us with cups of Turkish coffee while the papal delegate continued to speak softly, his face look-ing downward on the small desk.

"Yes, we would be very interested in a Christian-Jewish dia-logue, though it seems impossible with the Orthodox Rabbinate. Such meetings on a religious plane could be mutually stimulating." He paused and looked up for a moment.

"It's interesting, but I think this is the first time that somebody has wanted to speak with me about matters other than political."

I still have Monsignor Vergani's card of introduction with "Father Elias, Our Lady of Mt. Carmel" written on one side, and on the other side, "Father Bruno, Father Roget, Father Jochanan and Father Stiassny." Today these names are associated with warm human beings and with discussions that range far beyond an abstract theological theme into areas of intimate per-sonal self-revelation. But I remember that summer day, sitting

for a while in a café near Monsignor Vergani's office and thinking about the subject which he called Mysterium Israelis.

Across the street crowds were plodding through a public arms
exhibition that had been set up by the Israeli government. It
was a few months after the victorious Sinai campaign, and the
prize exhibit being displayed was the Egyptian destroyer *Ibrahim,*
which had been captured off the shore of Haifa. Young boys
and girls in army khaki walked among the exhibits, casting
knowledgeable eyes at the guns, which most of them could easily
handle. Newly arrived immigrants from Europe and dark-faced
families from North Africa, speaking Arabic and munching the
peppery *pitta* of the street vendors, looked about with less comprehension. All was movement—the crowd at the exhibit, the
lines waiting to board the buses, the traffic. There was an almost
angry restlessness on the faces and in the voices of this Israel of
the flesh.

"They cannot seem to be quiet, or remain alone," a young
American Quaker working in nearby Acre had observed the
other day. "On the beach, if there's a space, they'll avoid it,
and only go where the crowd is. In a group, if there happens
to be a moment of quiet, somebody will immediately start clapping his hands, and the people begin banging, as if they cannot
stand it."

Jacques Maritain, another Catholic interested in the "mystery
of Israel," has made a similar observation.

"Israel which is not of the world—[and still] at the deepest
core of the world, [is there] to irritate it, exasperate it, move it.
Like some foreign substance, like a living yeast mixed into the
main body, it gives the world no quiet"; and has no quiet itself.

Of course, implies Maritain, Israel of the flesh would lose its
restlessness if it rejected the world and chose the Christian God.

I wondered that day if the Father Elias I was about to meet
would bear out this particular thesis.

When later that afternoon I went to the monastery of "Our
Lady of Mount Carmel," a massive red-brick structure surrounded
by a high wall, on a promontory overlooking the Mediterranean,
I found the huge wooden doors of the church barred. A note,
handwritten in English, French, and Hebrew, explained:

48

"This church is closed to the public because of repeated acts of vandalism on the part of the Israeli armed forces."

I rang the bell several times and was walking away when the face of a young man appeared in a window on the second floor. I waved the little card Monsignor Vergani had given me, and shouted my desire to meet Father Elias.

"He is sleeping," was the reply in heavily accented English. "Come back at three thirty." He closed the window. I walked across the street. A church which had been borrowed by the British for a military base was now occupied by the Israeli navy for the same reason. A young sailor slouching in front of the gate knew nothing about the sign on the monastery.

"I think some ground in the garden was damaged a few weeks ago by maneuvers, but they always get compensation. We don't bother them." He shrugged.

I walked to the edge of the cliff. Below, trains and buses moved like toys on the heavily traveled strips of rail and concrete connecting Tel Aviv to the bustling Haifa port. The noise of the traffic in the port below hardly reached up to the high cliff. It was quiet and hot, and the thought of the monks taking a midday nap make me look speculatively at a pine tree, but it was small and offered too little shade. Still, one should nap, I thought to myself. The semitropical heat of Israel's summer demands such naps rather than the bustling dynamism that was going on below. Perhaps Monsignor Vergani was right in suggesting that religious expression here should be less active and more contemplative. He was thinking then of this Carmelite order on Mount Carmel, whose monks claim kinship with the disciples of Elijah who once lived on this hill. But then, how close in mood were these Carmelite monks to the zealous, angry Elijah, who had walked on these slopes? The mystical "Carmel" which they tried to ascend in their dark cells had been outlined for them by one who had never been to Israel. The "crags of the mountains and the paths of ascent, and the pine trees and flowers" described by St. John of the Cross were different from those known by the disciples of Elijah who once lived in these caves. The monks behind the stone walls of their monastery might have a problem trying to combine the Carmel of St. John with the real Mount Carmel.

When I returned to the monastery an hour later and rang the bell, there was again no answer. Then I heard an irritated voice from the side.

"Yes, yes, come this way. You want to see me?"

Father Elias, whom I presumed it was, stood a few yards away near a small side entrance. He appeared to be in his middle thirties, of average height, stocky, with gray eyes and a slightly aquiline nose set in a full face. His russet robe was worn, and the center of his circular tonsure was in need of a fresh shave. Without a word the priest strode ahead through a dark stone corridor and into a large room which contained a table and some chairs. I waited while he carefully inspected my letters of introduction, making notes on a slip of paper. Then we sat down and the priest indicated his readiness for questions. I referred to the sign on the front door of the church.

"Yes, yes, it is a terrible situation." Father Elias spoke with a clipped South African accent. "They are surrounded here on three sides and now they want to take on the Catholic church as well. Well, they have made a mistake." He put his hand to his mouth to cover an outburst of stomach gas. "Mind you, it is not a matter of damages. All the brothers here want is an apology, a bit of courtesy."

When I told him that other priests in Israel had praised the Israeli government for their efforts to respect church property and even help in the rebuilding of churches damaged by war, the priest shook his head.

"Yes, yes, they have done that." He continued speaking without raising his eyes from the table. "But there has been a change in their attitude lately. I can even give you the exact date for it . . . for the revelation of their true attitude. June 9, 1957, that was our Pearl Harbor Day. That was when they torpedoed us." He tapped his finger on the table loudly.

"You see, we have recently had some mixed-marriage immigration from Poland and other countries behind the Iron Curtain. About two or three thousand Christians, including baptized children, who have come this way . . . and they are loyal to the church . . . loyal. There have been some Christians coming to Israel before this time, but very few, and they have been afraid to show their heads. But the new Christian immigration is different. And I have proof of what I suspected all along. . . . You wait here, I will get it."

The priest stalked out, his robes swishing. I remembered the Steinberg case and wondered how many of the Christians upon whom Father Elias placed such hopes were like Mrs. Steinberg in her "loyalty" to the church.

A moment later Father Elias reappeared waving a large paper. "There Is a Christian Problem in Israel!" was the headline in capital letters on the mimeographed sheet. There followed a paragraph explaining that ". . . twenty to thirty per cent of Jews marry non-Jews in Europe. . . . Between two and three thousand Christians married to Jews have recently come to Israel from behind the Iron Curtain. . . . Today we have proof that there is a deliberate campaign on the part of the Orthodox Rabbinate and the Government to convert them." The paragraph was signed "A Catholic Priest."

"That's me," said Father Elias, compressing his lips. "If they want to deport me, I would just like to see them try. If you want me to sign this sheet, I will. Give me a pen." He reached out his hand as if to receive a pen.

The mimeographed sheet reprinted an article from an Orthodox Jewish newspaper, *Hatsopheh,* dated June 7, which suggested that if the children of mixed marriages who lived as Jews were converted, there would be less danger of religiously illegal marriages, and the children's adjustment to Israel would be helped.

"There it is, collusion between the state and rabbinic authorities. Well, let me tell you, the matter has gone up to the highest authorities, the very highest."

When I told the priest that I had not come here to find out about the newly arrived Christian families from Europe, but to hear his ideas on the "mystery of Israel," he looked up from the table and his voice softened. "Well, it's an involved subject. I have put my ideas down in a book. But we can make a beginning."

Vigorously the priest presented his theory. Jewish history could be divided into periods of "sinning" followed by exiles—to Egypt, to Babylonia. But the latest exile, after the destruction of the second Temple, was different from all the others. The Temple and the altar were no longer available to make amends for their sins. This time the exile was a "complete scattering . . . because the crime and the sin was vastly different . . . namely," the priest tapped his head, "the rejection of the Messiah. From that point on the Jews have been cursed, uncreative."

I interrupted the monk's fluent stream of words to ask whether Hasidism or the Golden Age of Spain, which produced poets like ha-Levi and philosophers like Maimonides, might be considered creative spiritual periods? The monk shook his head vigorously.

"The spiritual creativity in the exile amounted to a flea bite. Things like Hasidism were purely local events. All you have to do is compare it with the church. Just think of the architecture, music, art, of the Christian world." Father Elias kept tapping the table. "However, something has happened now, an event comparable to the Exodus from Egypt, only this time it is a spiritual exodus. . . . You can see it every place here. The young people have left Orthodoxy—the dry rabbinic law—never to come back to it." The priest interrupted his thought. "Of course, the youth here are different. They have fewer complexes. On the other hand, they have a lot of impudence, and no respect for chastity. You can see it on their faces. But there is some sign of hope—some hope. All Israelis are mad about archeology. It is—a looking for spiritual roots, an effort to define themselves as Jews. But this they will never do. This is the basic problem of Jewish history today—no authority. They will never be able to define who is a Jew."

Father Elias presented me with a personal example of the difficulty of defining "who is a Jew."

"When I came here I applied for citizenship. According to Jewish law, anybody born a Jew remains a Jew. You know that the Israeli law differentiates between Jew and non-Jew, and makes it easier for the Jew to become a citizen here. Well, there was a long correspondence in which they tried to evade the question. I have the correspondence in Vergani's office for use some day. But to come back." With an effort the priest brought himself back to his theory.

"We have to examine something about Christian history in order to understand the meaning of all this. For four hundred years now, since Luther, the Christian world has been degenerating, falling away." This fact, said Father Elias, had to be seen alongside the change which took place in Jewish life in the eighteenth century. Then, the Jews were beginning their "spiritual exodus" from Orthodoxy. These two events, the falling away of Christian life and the beginning of a Jewish spiritual exodus, were part of a providential pattern. This was the heart of his theory, based on the prophecy of St. Paul, ". . . that a branch of the original tree would be grafted back and give life to the olive tree."

Two Jewish brothers named Ratisbon, Father Elias told me, converts to Catholicism, had thought along similar lines. They had come to Palestine in the nineteenth century and built a monastery in Jerusalem which still bears their name.

"But they were ahead of their time. Now there are signs all about." In about twenty-five or fifty years there was to be a mass conversion of the Jews into the church, predicted the priest. Within the church they were to form a specific Jewish group, making their own "life-giving contribution" to the church. To be sure, this thesis was not yet the official thinking of the church. Even his Catholic confreres in Israel were not altogether convinced, but they were very interested.

"Have you met Fathers Bruno, Roget, Stiassny?" He mentioned the names given to me by Monsignor Vergani. "Or Father Jochanan? You should—he works as a potter in Tel Aviv. You see," Father Elias said, "the Catholic church does not yet have any consistent thesis on the subject of the 'mystery of Israel.'" But Father Elias hoped to present the church with a firm dialectic of Jewish history. "After all, if the church is willing to deduce certain theological facts from the dispersion of the Jews," the priest raised his thumb like a talmudic student deducing the logic of an argument, "then it should also have an open mind as to the significance of the return, of what's happening now."

Before leaving the priest that day I commented on his articu-

53

lateness, a talent which evidently had not been lost through the strict Carmelite rules of silence.

"It's a gift," Father Elias said. If I could come again, he would try to tell me more about his order and the circumstances of personal life which had brought him here. I suggested that we see each other in a few days, when they would be celebrating the Feast of St. Elias. It seemed to me that the priest hesitated a moment before agreeing.

The Greek Catholic archbishop in Haifa, Hakim, had urged me to see the Feast of St. Elias as it was celebrated on Mount Carmel. It would be a typical Christian folk festival, and he was going to conduct a Mass. There was indeed a folk atmosphere around the red brick monastery. Several dozen families were camped around heaps of blankets, mattresses, and cooking pots. The older men wore traditional Arab garb—long robes and head-scarf with black-ringed *agula*. The younger people were dressed in Western clothes, and thronged the courtyard before the church. Some vendors were selling refreshments, and a sharply dressed young man was taking bets on a gambling wheel. Some young men started a traditional snake-line *debka* dance, chanting and clapping hands as a husky youth in army uniform waved his bayonet knife in the air and led the dancing line. Father Elias suddenly appeared at my side. He greeted me warmly, almost smiling.

"I have talked with our Superior since your last visit here. He gave me permission to tell you everything, to take out the whole dossier. I'm going to open everything to you—an act of faith."

We left the crowd outside to enter the church, where a few dozen men and women stood listening to the weak singing of the choir. People walked in and out freely while the bell announced the transubstantiation of the Host. Underneath the altar was a grotto containing a statue of St. Elias on a small platform. Some mothers were lifting small children onto the dais of the statue, where they reached up and wiped the face of the prophet with handkerchiefs or pieces of cloth. The young man whose face I had first seen peering at me from the second floor of the monastery was in the grotto, selling postal cards and candles. Father Elias genuflected and seemed eager to take me away from the

54

service, which he said was for the Maronites. They were to be followed by the Roman Catholics and the Greek Catholics.

"The truth is," he led me up the stairs toward the roof, "that the church here has become Moslemized . . . Orientalized. The Arab Christians here are degenerate. That is, not in a sexual sense. A Christian boy here would not dream of having intercourse with a married woman, they are very chaste. But they are degenerate spiritually. You cannot impose spirituality on them. They are poor material."

The wind on the flat roof of the monastery was strong and Father Elias had to shout to make himself heard, but he was bubbling with all kinds of information.

"They have uncovered part of a statue of the god Carmel near here. Undoubtedly this was a place which was always dedicated to religious idol worship. It may be, of course, that Elias also had his cave here, but we do not know. We are not compelled to believe all the legends we are told."

The priest kept apologizing for the festival atmosphere around us. It was really "something like the Druids, a matter of group survival and memories, rather than a living religion. To tell you the truth, we have not gotten even one priest here from the native population in all these years."

From one corner of the roof we could look into the naval encampment alongside the monastery. "There are girls there." Anger started creeping back into the priest's voice. "They run around here almost naked. We have no proof, of course, but they are probably turning this place into a brothel. On the other hand," the priest tried to pull himself back from his irritation, "there is something healthy about the new Israeli type. He has dignity and he knows the Bible. There is material here for a new type of Jew," Father Elias again made an effort to smile, "even if it does not seem so."

The wind on the roof got too strong for conversation, and we went downstairs toward the room we had used during the last discussion. It was occupied by another priest talking with a family.

"He is a Lebanese priest, very pro-Israeli," Father Elias said. "You know, some of the help here is also Maronite. When they heard about the Israeli victory in the Sinai, they threw their

55

hats up in the air in exultation. For them the Israeli army is a guarantee against persecution."

I reminded him of his promise to tell me something of his own personal religious experience. Without hesitation the priest fulfilled his promise. He had been born to a prominent Jewish family in South Africa, and received a traditional Jewish training. During his youth in South Africa he had felt a great restlessness, been attracted for a while to the Communists, and gone through college and medical school. While in the army, serving as a medical orderly, he talked to the chaplain. The Padre had said to him, "You Jews have always been too nationalistic about religion." He was still not satisfied, and hesitant. But one day, while walking alone along the sea, he was suddenly "overwhelmed . . . it was almost frightening and not pleasant, but it was as if a strong presence said, 'You will be a priest.'" He was "flooded with certainty," but waited six months, until he was discharged from the army, before going to the Irish brothers in London. There in the library he felt another "overwhelming compulsion," as if his elbow were being seized and pushed toward the writings of St. John of the Cross. Not long after that he decided to join the Order. His coming to Israel was "purely providential."

"I will tell you—my family life was very unhappy, very unhappy. I was not hard to satisfy . . . they could have made me happy. But they did not."

"Do you think this had any effect on your conversion?"

"Only that I did not have much to lose. I have family here in Israel, you know, but they have never seen me."

Father Elias appeared disappointed when I told him that I had to leave. I promised to return again.

"Any time, any time," he said warmly. "I'll be waiting for you."

The Mystery of Christianity

More than a year passed before I saw Father Elias again. But the name of the angry priest on Mount Carmel came up often in conversations with Christians and Jews in Israel. Some of the

56

Catholic priests whom I met were gently critical of their colleague.

"His theories have no *nuance,* as we say in French," a priest in Jaffa suggested. "He is a brilliant thinker, but much too definite in his ideas about the conversion of Jews, too specific about time and manner. Besides, a servant of God should make himself anonymous and not try to force his theories upon the church."

Another Catholic priest in Jerusalem tried to explain. "Father Elias is overreacting. It may have something to do with his family—they treated him very poorly when he became a Catholic, and here in Israel he has relatives who have never been to see him. I am afraid Father Elias has been going through a crisis lately."

With respect to Father Elias' "Christian problem"—the two thousand mixed-marriage families—both priests agreed that the Ministry of Religion had acted foolishly. "But the government has apologized for that foolish editorial in *Hatsopheh.* No, we have to give them a chance to catch their breath here."

A Jewish official in the Ministry of Religion quickly dismissed the charges of the Carmelite monk. Dr. Warhaftig, who was then Deputy-Minister of Religion, wore a large-brimmed fedora as he sat behind his desk, sipping his glass of tea. He let me know quickly that there were more important matters on his mind than Father Elias.

"He has cut himself off from his people," said the Jewish official angrily. When I asked Dr. Warhaftig, who has a reputation for Jewish scholarship, whether according to religious law Father Elias was not indeed a Jew, since he was born of a Jewish mother, he dismissed my question with a wave of the hand. The Deputy-Minister of Religion was equally curt with regard to the "Christian problem" outlined by the Carmelite monk.

"First of all, there are not two thousand, but probably less than one thousand mixed marriages that have recently come to Israel from Poland. Most of them don't have the slightest intention of settling here. They are using the country as a stepping stone to America or Canada. Secondly, what the priests don't tell you is that all these immigrants said they were Jewish when they applied for immigration to Israel. What bothers the priests is that they want permission to visit the camps and find out who is Jewish and not Jewish. But do we have the moral right to let the priests "spy out" these people? After all, anybody who wants to profess his Christianity and go to church is free to do so."

The Israeli official was equally emphatic in denying any plot on the part of the government or Orthodox Jewry to convert Christian children.

"In fact, our main concern is keeping Jews and Christians apart, so that we know who is a Jew and who isn't. As to the question of definition, you'll have to leave that to the rabbinic authorities, and not to priests, or even to Ben Gurion."

Dr. Warhaftig, with a sweep of his hands, figuratively swept all the criticisms and complaints I had brought to him off his desk.

As a matter of fact, one of the questions which was occupying the mind of the Jewish official was the definition of "who was a Jew." It was a question which was to be vigorously debated in the Israeli Knesset during the ensuing months. It was even to result in the breakup of Ben Gurion's coalition government and the exit of the religious parties from this government. Among those who lost their desks was Dr. Warhaftig. The problem was raised by Ben Gurion's insistence that an Israeli citizen could define himself as a Jew on his identification card by a simple affirmation. This definition was violently opposed by the religious authorities who held that the definition of a Jew ought to be based on Jewish religious law. The vitriolic debate which ensued in the public press and in the Knesset for months finally caused the resignation of Dr. Warhaftig's party from the government. This gave Prime Minister Ben Gurion an opportunity to appoint a rabbi upon whom he could count as antagonistic to the larger religious parties. The political and religious battles which followed carried over into irreconcilable disagreements about a proper candidate for the Chief Rabbinate, a post that was later left open by the death of Rabbi Herzog. In the excitement over this still unresolved question the debate about "who is a Jew" was tabled without resolution. In this respect at least, the prophecies of the angry priest on Mount Carmel seemed to have been correct. There is little prospect of the Jewish community, as it is now constituted, agreeing on the definition of a Jew.

Many months passed before I visited Father Elias again. Despite the passage of time the priest readily plunged into the discussion of his favorite subject and brought me up to date.

"The church wasn't ready to go to war and back me up in the matter. They are interested in peace." From the priest's tone I gathered that he had not reconciled himself fully to the church's view. Father Elias looked pale. He was still bothered, he said, with attacks of colitis, which he described in proper medical terminology.

"Once a doctor, always a doctor," said Father Elias, smiling at his own medical diagnosis. "Like a Jew—once a Jew, always a Jew."

He looked at his watch. "We do not have much time, but I can show you some things this afternoon." I followed him through the high-ceilinged empty stone corridors and the huge rooms of the monastery. At a large closet he slid open a paneled door, behind which several dozen stiff silken robes with elaborate brocading hung on hangers.

"These are the gowns which are reserved for use by visiting church officials from other lands. Of course," the priest smiled ironically, "we are a little out of the way for most of the church activities, so we do not use these much now."

We entered a chapel where a monk was standing at a lectern and chanting from an open book, while three Carmelite brothers sitting on a side bench joined at certain intervals, standing up occasionally to genuflect.

"Most of their readings are from the Psalms, you know," Father Elias whispered. In another room, where long tables arranged in an open square were being set for dinner, we passed a monk with a white apron tied around his russet robe.

"We have only about twenty-four brothers here now." Father Elias did not try to hide his disappointment. "We once had many more and we had hoped that this monastery would be a school, a sort of academic center for the Order . . . but the money has been diverted to other places."

59

I remarked on how strange it was that of all the Carmelite monasteries the one on Mount Carmel should be weakest in number and spiritual quality. The priest nodded without replying, and hurried me along to another room. He showed me some booklets and papers.

"I had these prepared for you. But you asked me the last time about the mystic tradition of the Carmelite order. You might say we are the keepers of the mystic tradition in the church. You might call it a psychological approach to the needs and hunger of the soul in its yearning for salvation and faith.

"Perhaps you noticed the reference to Elijah over the altar in the Chapel, which is the insignia of the order? *'Zelo zelatus sum pro Domino Deo exercituum'*—I have been very jealous for the Lord God of hosts.

"You see," continued the monk, "we trace our monastic tradition back to Elijah and to his school of disciples. They lived here among the hills and in the caves. Of course, there is no proof, but it is very possible that they might have practiced silent meditation not dissimilar to ours. Here too, each monk lives in his own cell, where he practices silent contemplation. *'Hit'bod'-dut'* you call it in Hebrew. It is not impossible that the monastic traditions of the church go back to Elijah rather than to Egypt, as is usually thought. Now you take the Dead Sea Scrolls. They are finally getting around to the possibility that there can be monks in Judaism. In respect to this kind of research and thinking, we watch eagerly the work of a man like Yigael Yadin, who recently published a paper showing the relationship between Paul and the Dead Sea sects. A person like Yadin is for me like the moving finger of Jewish History." The priest moved his finger across the paper toward himself, indicating that the Jews were moving toward the church. "Incidentally," the monk reminded himself, "you remarked last time how quickly and vigorously the brothers here walked about. You were right—we do emphasize vigor here. There is a dynamic element in our mystic tradition—we call it the 'Eliasian spirit.'"

The monk looked at his watch. "Well—I'm sorry we have so little time left." It was almost time for vespers. Soon the monk would begin his period of absolute silence, and after prayers retire to his cell for his spiritual exercises.

He walked with me out of the monastery and through the courtyard to the road. We shook hands.

"Well—good-by." He hesitated, and I thought I heard him say "bless you." As I turned the bend of the road, he was still standing outside the gate, outlined against the large orb of the sun, which was beginning to descend into the Mediterranean.

Among the pamphlets Father Elias gave me was a magazine, *Scapulaire*, containing an article he had written, *"Israel, ou vas tu?"* While waiting for the bus, I opened to it and read a paragraph:

"In the Epistle to the Romans St. Paul predicts the conversion en masse of the Jews. 'All Israel will believe.' This national conversion is envisaged as being for the Gentiles 'a resurrection from the dead . . .' We interpret this to mean that national conversion of the Jews will occur in an epoch when the gentiles are also in large part, lost. The conversion of the Jews will be the principal cause of a spiritual renaissance of these very gentiles. . . ." It occurred to me that Father Elias was as antagonistic toward the Christian world as toward the Jewish, was in a way as disappointed in his Christianity as in Judaism. Could that have been the reason for his "overreaction," as one of the other priests called it, to the adjustment problems of the new Christian-Jewish families to the Holy Land. For it was more than the spiritual influx of a few hundred souls that concerned Father Elias. These new Christian families were a key link in a theory upon which he had staked his life. For there was a weak spot in his "dialectic." Granted that the Jewish Israelis, as Father Elias called them, had made a "spiritual exodus" from Orthodoxy. What was to attract them to the church in the Holy Land? Certainly not Christians who were "effete" and "degenerate." Nor, despite the priest's dreams about "loyal" Christians from behind the Iron Curtain, did families like the Steinbergs offer much hope for a revived Christian church in the Holy Land.

It was the same problem that troubled a Protestant missionary in Nazareth, who felt that there was a great opportunity here for those who wanted to bear witness to their Christianity, but who could find nobody whose Christianity was strong enough to rise above the passions of nationalism. It was the problem of Archbishop Isidoros, who knew that Christian life in the Holy Land was a "needle to the faith." It was this barrenness of Christian life in the Holy Land that accounted for the explosive interest of the Carmelite priest in the newly arrived Christian-Jewish families who, he felt, were loyal to the church. These were Christians from a European church who he thought knew Christianity on its higher levels. They could be the "catalysts," the missing link in the process of conversion for which Father Elias hungered with all his soul, his solution to the "mystery of Israel." That was why he so needed them, and resented the pressures he thought were holding back their emergence as a "converting" agent in the historic climax and proof of the thesis to which he was committed. But to one not committed to this thesis, a different question reveals itself through the stiff network of the Carmelite priest's theories.

Why after almost two thousand years of Christian pilgrimages, missions, and crusades should Father Elias have to depend upon a few hundred or a few thousand recently arrived Christians to reveal the church's glory to Jews in the Holy Land? Why has the land which was the fountain source of Christian faith apparently produced no living waters for the followers of the Nazarene? Economic and political conditions, population figures, wars, etc., cannot be sufficient answer for religionists like Father Elias. The religious spirit has obviously been able to flourish under the most unencouraging of environments—the condition of the Holy Land at the very time when Christianity was born is an example.

In this amazing sterility of Christianity on its cradle soil, might not those who think about Israel in terms of a mystery see also a mystery of Christianity?

CHAPTER IV

Missionaries—Converting or Converted

Is There a Missionary Problem?

Even if not a mystery in the theological sense, it is still strange that the cradle soil of Christianity should after all these years require intensive missionary effort. One might think that a land so crowded with sacred sites, with representatives of every sect and church in Christendom, would hardly require additional missionary efforts sponsored from abroad. Actually, the missionary population of Israel is probably, on a per capita basis, the highest in the world. At least, this is the claim of an Israeli antimissionary society which holds that there are three hundred monks and nuns and seventeen Catholic orders in the country, and "of these a large number have missionary tasks." There are also more than seventeen Protestant organizations represented in this little country, whose Protestant community numbers only about two thousand. Most of their leaders, claims the antimissionary group, are avowedly interested in a missionary effort.

Some literature published by the society says that several thousand Jewish children have been attracted into the "missionary net." It offers pictures of the "attractive missionary automobile which takes children for a ride to return them in the evening as better Christians to their Jewish parents. . . ." "Help us," concludes one of their appeals, "to counteract these false joys and prevent the alienation of Jewish children from their people and their heritage by establishing club programs in the slum areas where the missionaries set their nets for Jewish souls."

The missionaries have a different view of affairs. Some Protestant organizations in America accuse the Israeli government of harassing Christian missionary efforts, closing their churches, refusing them passports, persecuting converts—charges denied by government officials in the Ministry of Religion.

"Can you show me any place in the Middle East where Christian missionaries have more freedom?" replies one official. "Do you know what would happen to these missionaries if they tried to carry on in Amman or Saudi Arabia as they do here?"

The missionaries appreciate his point. They know that missionary work in all Moslem lands is flatly forbidden by law. Still, they would like to find a more permissive atmosphere for their work in Israel. Israel proclaims itself to be a state which offers to its inhabitants freedom of religion, and this offer should include the opportunity to change religions.

My look into the realities of missionary endeavor in Israel revealed a situation quite different from that printed by both missionary and antimissionary statements. It also evoked some reflections which, I am sure, will surprise the missionaries if they should read them. But it might be well to point out first that the fervor of Christian missionary endeavor is of little concern to most Christians and Christian leaders in Israel. The major Christian communities in the land do not share their concern. In fact, the leaders of the land's major Christian communities are inclined to be as resentful of missionary efforts as the Jewish authorities. The reasons for their attitude are both historic and practical. The majority of Christians in Israel are Arabs belonging to the Greek Catholic and Greek Orthodox denominations. That delightful delineator of Eastern church history, Dean Stanley, points out that "in the Mohammedan East, the Greek (Christian) population remains like islands in the barren sea, and the Bedouin tribes wandered for 12 centuries around the Greek convent on Mount Sinai, probably without one instance of conversion." The psychology of the Eastern church, affirms Stanley, is ". . . in my Father's house there are many mansions." It does not have the compulsion which seems to have driven the Western church to stamp all other groups in their specific spiritual image.

As a matter of fact, until recently, Western Protestant groups like the Anglican have also appeared uninterested in missionary endeavor, setting themselves the modest goal of servicing the Protestant community, mostly tourists and diplomats, or trying simply to be "represented" in the Holy Land. It is the newly arrived Protestant groups without indigenous roots in the Holy Land who are today openly out to win new souls. Since most of the souls they win seem to come neither from the Moslem nor Jewish communities, but from the established Christian groups, the hierarchy of these groups naturally look upon the newcomers as poachers.

As for the Jewish community, rumor had it that the missionaries were meeting with most success among the new immigrants to Israel, especially those living in the poorer neighborhoods of towns like Jaffa. It was to Jaffa then that I went one Sunday morning to seek some evidence of missionary work.

My first conversation with a Catholic nun in a school drew a blank.

"We have very few Jewish children here, and we are not interested in missionary work," snapped a nun in her Irish brogue. My attempt to relax the tone of our conversation by reference to religious life in the Holy Land was equally unsuccessful.

"This isn't the Holy Land, this is Jaffa. There are only holy places in this land, that's all."

A few minutes later, though, at a nearby Presbyterian church, I accidentally stumbled upon a conversion case in the making. The elderly minister of the church received me graciously in his home and invited me to attend services with him. Despite his friendliness, he avoided any discussion of his church's missionary interests. The congregation at his church that morning was small, a few dozen people, some of whom were tourists. The pleasant Scottish bur of the minister and the quietly sung hymns of the congregation had begun to produce a pleasantly soporific mood when I noticed a short, middle-aged man alongside me holding his prayer book upside down. His face was set in an angry mold, and he moved his lips in a way that had no relation to the words of the service. He may have been conscious of my glance, for he placed the English hymnal back in the rack of the seat in front of him, and took out a Hebrew Bible which he opened to the first page. He read it silently, with the same angry look of determination, while the minister gave his sermon. When the congregation rose to leave at the conclusion of the service, he stood looking about awkwardly. I asked him if he was a member of the congregation. He didn't understand my English, so I asked the question in Hebrew.

"No," he answered in Hebrew, his lips pressed together in determination, "but I want to be." I introduced him to the minister, who did not seem happy about my services as an intermediary. But since he spoke no Hebrew he reluctantly accepted my offer to translate. We went into a small room.

"What kind of a Christian does he want to be?" the minister asked irritably, while changing his robe. The question confused the would-be convert, who pressed his lips tighter.

"Any kind."

"Tell him to be here Tuesday at two o'clock," said the minister, terminating the conversation. I accompanied the prospective convert outside.

"I hate it here." My companion motioned to the stalls of food and the little stores which we were passing. He had come to Israel several years ago from Poland, where his first wife had been killed, brought with him his little boy, and married an Israeli girl. He didn't like his second wife, and she didn't like him. He would be perfectly willing to have his little boy convert along with him if they could get a visa to enter some other country and leave Israel.

"Tuesday, two o'clock," he muttered with angry determination as we parted.

A few days later I related my experience to a Dominican priest, Father Bruno, who then lived in Jaffa. He laughed and admitted that this kind of candidate for conversion in Israel was not unusual.

"Sometimes they knock at the door and tell me that they want to become Christians," the priest related. "I ask them if they are willing to study for two years, for that is what the Catholic church in Israel has set up as its policy. They say yes, they will study but can't they study in some other country. That's when I tell them to go to Hayarkon Street, because that's where the travel agencies are. They don't really want me—they want a ticket abroad."

Father Bruno denied any personal missionary goals—"That is in God's hands"—he himself had other ambitions in Israel. He apologized for his English but was actually an exceedingly fluent speaker. Within a few minutes he had presented me with a capsule biography of his life and a revelation of his secret ambitions.

"Perhaps I should tell you, I am really of Jewish descent, but I don't like to tell people that at first because of—well, I don't like them to look at externals and prejudge."

Father Bruno, a tall, good-looking man with intelligent, dark eyes, had come from Egypt to France with his mother, sister, and father. The priest grimaced, I thought, when he mentioned his father. In France he had lived a "normal life, going out with girls, and thinking about marriage." While studying in Lyons he met a girl whom he liked. But she was Catholic and this presented him with problems which he had not considered before. About the same time, by coincidence, he heard a provocative lecture on the problem of evil by a Catholic professor. He began reading and posing questions to his Catholic girl friend which "she herself could not answer." He had at that time no thought of becoming a priest, but he began reading the New Testament. One evening in his room alone at night he felt himself powerfully moved. It was no vision, but he felt strongly that Jesus was speaking to him. In his mind the Catholic church and Jesus were identified. From that evening, one by one his intellectual doubts fell away and shortly afterward he spoke with his girl friend.

"I would like to ask you if you would marry with me," Father Bruno remembered his words. "She seemed troubled and told me she would give me her answer in a week. I never prayed so hard. I knew I wanted to be a Catholic regardless of her answer, but I decided that if she said 'no' that it would be a sign that I was destined for a vocation in the church. I did not know what branch of the church at that time attracted me. For a while I thought it was the Cistercians—the deep, deep prayer when they meet at midnight, it's a wonderful experience. But later I was drawn to the Dominicans. I liked their intellectual and preaching

67

tradition." A week later he received his answer. His girl friend had decided to marry his best friend. Then Father Bruno knew that he was to be a priest. "Incidentally, two years ago I had the pleasure of returning to France and officiating at the christening of my former girl friend's child."

"Now my dream really is," the priest went on, "to form an institute for Jewish studies here in Israel, where priests could study Hebrew and the Bible in the original. You know that through the church I have finally become a Jew." As a Jewish Catholic, the priest explained, he was fulfilling his ancestral faith. And he had other secret ambitions. He wanted to offer the Mass on Saturday as well as on Sunday morning. Sunday was a difficult day for people to come to church since most people worked in Israel, even though Christians were officially excused.

"But didn't the church deliberately move the Sabbath to Sunday in order to differentiate itself from the synagogue?" I asked. After all, the Dominicans in Spain during the Inquisition might have considered Father Bruno's ideas as the kind of Judaizing influence it wanted to eradicate.

The priest's ebullient flow of language hesitated. "But no, I am a believing Catholic. I don't see anything wrong with trying to have permission for a Mass on *Shabbat.*" He used the Hebrew word for Sabbath. "I've written for permission to offer my personal Mass in Hebrew. After all, most of the Breviary consists of Hebrew psalms. Why should we say them in Latin?"

Father Jochanan, another priest in Israel, who belonged to the Order of the Little Brothers of Jesus, had received such permission, Father Bruno said.

"Do you know them, the Little Brothers? They're remarkable. They are not here for the purpose of saving souls or for any kind of activity about which you can make statistics. It's wonderful. In a world which asks for accomplishments and for efficiency they want to accomplish nothing—only to sow love where there is none, and be 'truly little.' Wait here a moment." Father Bruno's white robes swirled gracefully as he swept into the next room and returned with a book about the Order of the Little Brothers and Sisters, called *Seeds in the Desert*.

I agreed to return the book to Father Bruno a few weeks

later, when we would both be in Jerusalem to attend a World Congress in Jewish Studies at the University.

"I hope I'll be able to follow the Hebrew," said the priest. "How I want to master that tongue!"

Some weeks later, I met a Baptist missionary in Israel who spoke Hebrew like a sabra—a native-born Israeli. With his open-collared shirt and broad shoulders, Robert Lindsay looks as well as speaks like a sabra. I visited him in his "church" in Tel Aviv —an apartment which he had converted into a meeting room and library. Lindsay introduced me to a tall, good-looking young-ster of about twenty who said he was the librarian of the Baptist center in Tel Aviv. A bit nervously the Israeli said he was not a Baptist, but that he was interested in the group and appreciated Lindsay's making it possible for him to carry out his literary work. At present he was translating Pascal's *Pensées* into He-brew.

Driving out to the Baptist farm in Petach Tikvah, Lindsay showed me a book about the Dead Sea Scrolls. "The Dead Sea communities were important, because they revealed a type of Judaism other than the Pharisaic which has indigenous roots in this land." It was important for Israelis to know this, he pointed out, because the religious orthodoxy which they encountered was simply a closed world to them. Not that there weren't religious personalities to be found among the Orthodox Jews, but they were embalmed in a legal formalism which Israeli Jews could not appreciate. On the other hand, books like the Dead Sea Scrolls emphasized the "covenant" relationship between Jews and their God. This, thought Lindsay, was the essence of the biblical experience—an inner affirmation of the covenant relationship which had to be renewed in every generation.

The Baptist farm in Petach Tikvah is a spacious and pleasant establishment, with fruitful fields and a large swimming pool. The several dozen young boys and girls splashing in the pool were Christian children on vacation from Nazareth, Lindsay informed me. In his comfortable apartment, with its air-conditioner and large stone fireplace, the minister told me about the latest devel-opments in his running battle with the Israeli government on the issue of marriage regulations. The Baptist point of view is that

69

there ought to be complete separation of church and state along American lines in the Holy Land, but if this could not come about, then Lindsay wanted his group to enjoy the official privileges which were accorded by the government to the established Christian denominations, including the right to officiate at marriages. The government had already given the Baptist ministers a "marriage book," which was *de facto* recognition, but Lindsay wanted it to be completely official. As regards conversions, the minister shrugged. "You would be able to count the actual number of converts on the fingers of both hands."

But missionary work in terms of numbers was not his main concern at present. He wanted to establish the Baptist religion as part of the Israeli scene. "Also, I'd like to have Baptists coming from all parts of the world to study Hebrew and the Bible here. We ought to have a school here for Baptists," said the Protestant missionary enthusiastically. His wife served us some lemonade and smiled at her husband. "He is like a sabra."

I told the Lindsays about my meetings with Father Bruno and his ambitions about Hebrew and schools in Israel. "You both strike me as Judaizers," I told Lindsay. It was a thought more facetious than serious at the time. But the idea clung, and took on new dimensions after a meeting with a fervent female Protestant missionary in Haifa.

Why Converts Convert

A provocative writer, Eric Hoffer, who likes to state what he admits is only one side of the truth, but the side usually avoided, has an unkindly analysis of the "true believer" and his missionary impulse. This impulse is not, as missionaries like to believe, "an expresion of an overabundance of power," but rather the result of "some deep misgiving, some pressing feeling of insufficiency at the center. . . . The proselytizing fanatic strengthens his own faith by converting others."

But that "true believers" could have very opposing feelings about the need for missionizing became very clear in the course of a discussion that took place one evening at the home of a Presbyterian lady missionary, Lily Wrechsler, who lived in Haifa not far from the monastery of Father Elias. Like the Carmelite monk, Lily Wrechsler was born Jewish and like him was bitter about the Jewish State and its attitude toward converts. She had not made many converts in her years of missionary endeavor, Miss Wrechsler admitted, all she could do was "to sow the seeds and leave the results to God." There had been a few people who had come to Christ through her efforts; for example, a young woman who since becoming a Christian had suffered a great deal from official Jewish institutional disapproval. The missionary's voice took on a bitter edge as she related the difficulties of her convert, who was a nurse.

"It is not that she deliberately tried to convert people, as the hospital authorities claimed when they discharged her. She doesn't talk about her faith unless asked, but patients seeing her so alive and happy will sometimes ask why. Then she has to tell them. She cannot bear false witness to her faith."

Miss Wrechsler was tall, with a rather long, high-bridged nose, dark complexion, and frizzly gray hair arranged in a careful knot on the back of her head. Quietly, somewhat bashfully, she related the circumstances of her own conversion. She had been raised in a strictly Orthodox Jewish home in Switzerland. Her father was a prominent professor of medicine and she herself had studied psychology. She did not like to analyze her own conversion in psychological terms. "That was like using a dirty knife." But it was not, she thought, frustration or unhappiness that had brought her to her religious faith. As far as she could remember, she was always "searching for the truth and for God." As a child she was always so happy that the family called her *"sonnenschein."* She also had a boy friend who wanted to marry her if she would accept Orthodoxy. They had studied together at the University in Berlin—he was about twenty then —and she had been trying to learn more about Judaism. But "I simply couldn't feel the presence of the living God." One Friday, after trying to study from some Orthodox Jewish literature with her boy friend, she left him with a feeling that something was about to happen. The next day she broke the Orthodox religious law by riding on the Sabbath. She became an atheist for three years.

"I was very unhappy then and thinking often about suicide." At school she sat next to a student girl friend. "One day this girl told me that she had been praying for me." Lily was very much affected by this, and about the same time she was helped by a professor to whom she spoke of her problem. She wanted to speak to this man about religion and Christianity, but he always avoided the subject, because he knew her father and did not want to hurt him.

Finally, at the urging of the girl who was praying for her, she had gone to a pastor.

"You are not right with yourself," the pastor had said, and Lily had poured out her heart to him. Suddenly, for the first time in years, she had felt "peace, and warmth, and wholeness."

"One day, as the pastor was praying with me, my eyes were closed and I didn't even know that he had left the room. Until then I hadn't associated my feelings with Christ. But when the pastor returned, he said, 'Do you think I could have helped you without Christ?' I felt slapped in the face." Lily was at first horrified at the thought of conversion, which "would make my father turn in his grave." But she started going to church and reading the New Testament. Suddenly certain verses, especially in the book of John, appeared to her with new force, verses like "I am the door, and the truth, and the life," and "If you will pray in my name, I will answer." She had tried to pray in the name of Jesus, and it worked. She suddenly felt changed. "The second birth," Lily explained.

A knock on the door broke into the quiet recital of the missionary's religious case history. Lily opened the door and two young girls burst in, bubbling with enthusiastic chatter in German. They stopped when they saw me, and said *Shalom,* excusing themselves to Miss Wrechsler for interrupting. The missionary introduced them as nuns who had recently come from Germany. The nuns came over and shook hands. The younger one was fair, with blond hair and blue eyes, and evidently accustomed to letting her older, dark-eyed friend talk for her. The latter was strikingly pretty, with regular fair features, full lips, brown hair, and large, dark-brown eyes. She had a very sweet voice, the kind

72

that can suddenly become strong even in its sweetness. Both girls were dressed in long, light-blue garments reaching almost down to their bare, sandaled feet, and on their heads were white bandannas, tastefully arranged off their brows. Bubbling with excitement, they told Lily Wrechsler about an experience they had had in their Hebrew class that afternoon. Later, when I asked them why they were in Israel, Sister Veronica, the older, dark-haired sister, explained quickly:

"We are here because we have sinned against the Jewish people. We cannot return the life which has been lost, cannot make it up, but we want to show that we are sorry."

They were Protestant nuns from Darmstadt. Their order had been formed after the Second World War. Israel was to them a "symbol of our repentance." They fasted on Yom Kippur and had an eternal light in their chapel in memory of the Jews who were killed by the Nazis. "On Yom Kippur we also read selections from the Jewish prayer book. Ach! Where can we find such prayers now."

My next question, I realized by the nun's surprised blush, was a *non sequitur*. I asked her how old she was.

"That is a woman's privilege to keep secret." She laughed, lowering her head, but her eyes sparkled. "But I can tell you," she said flirtatiously, "that when our order was founded about ten years ago, I was among the founders."

"They do everything in this order themselves," Lily interrupted in English. "Build, clean, do all the heavy work. They have had a great deal of influence in Germany, where they put on a repentance play which has been seen by many thousands of people."

"Is the object of your order to missionize?" I asked.

"No———" Sister Veronica looked hesitatingly at Lily Wrechsler. "We believe that in time the Jews and Christians will repent and the personal Messiah will come—but that is not our purpose here. We have made of Christ a repulsive symbol—a force of might. We must show him otherwise." There was something incongruous about the light, almost gay tone of the nun and the meaning of her words, but she was utterly sincere.

73

We spoke about Lily Wrechsler's "second-birth" experience. Miss Wrechsler again affirmed that "a second birth is a necessary part of the Christian experience."

"Nein, Ich glaube das nicht, Schwester Lily," the nun said quietly, a troubled look coming into her eyes. "I didn't have such an experience. One must have the light of repentance, but it needn't be a sudden breakthrough."

Lily shook her head. "Perhaps it is not necessary for Christians, but for Jews who are so hardened it is necessary. The Bible says that in that time there will be 'gnashing and wailing' among the Jews." Lily's soft voice had a sharp edge.

"Do you agree?" I asked Sister Veronica.

The nun seemed troubled. "Perhaps, but we need not talk about such things now. May I ask you a question?" the nun asked, obviously trying to change the subject. "Why don't more Jews come here from other countries? It's so wonderful and lovely, why don't they come in larger numbers?"

I promised to answer her question if she would first answer why a pretty girl, so eligible for marriage and family, found it necessary to give up these treasures. The two girls looked at each other and giggled.

"We are not forever committed," Sister Veronica said gaily. "But now we feel that we have a calling; as it is written in Paul, 'Virgins are called to serve.' That is the meaning of our gold wedding rings. If you are still wondering how old I am," Sister Veronica interrupted her thought, as if her previous evasion of my question had been troubling her, "I will tell you—thirty-five." She blushed again.

"But why should a good God ask such a sacrifice?" I asked.

Sister Veronica nodded and her face turned serious, as if recognizing the validity of the point. "But that is the meaning of the Cross? Suffering."

Lily Wrechsler again interrupted. "History has shown the only path to the personal Saviour through Jesus. All creativity and life come from suffering."

Sister Veronica looked at Lily as if wondering whether she agreed with what the missionary meant.

74

"It does say in the Bible that God is a 'consuming fire.' We offer ourselves up to him," she said slowly.

"Isn't that the meaning of the story of the sacrifice of Isaac in the Bible?" Lily again supplemented the nun's words.

"But why does a faith which preaches mercy and compassion give us a picture of a God making his beloved suffer in agony on a cross? The fascination with blood and suffering—is it not an image which has encouraged man's letch for violence,' as Rebecca West called it?" I quoted the author's criticism of the "hateful lie"—the theory that there is a mysterious causal process at work in the universe which relates suffering to blessing. Wasn't it all a rationalization of man's fascination with blood, death, and pain, rather than with life, mercy, and peace?

Sister Veronica nodded, as if she understood what I was saying. "But that is not the meaning of the Cross, or Jesus," the nun said worriedly. "Though I know that history has shown it that way to Jews and others."

Lily Wrechsler interjected, "We must be buried before we can be reborn."

"But there is some truth to what he says." The young nun turned to the missionary. "Life and not death should be the goal, and we should serve not only by good deeds, but by happiness."

As she spoke of happiness, the cloud passed from her eyes and she changed the subject.

"The country is filled with flowers and growth. We so enjoy traveling around with our Hebrew teacher. He is so enthusiastic, but we are so slow in our learning of the Hebrew." The nuns laughed at each other and tried out a few of the Hebrew words they had learned this week.

"But soon," the quiet nun chimed in, "we hope to know enough to go to work on a kibbutz in the Negev. We hope to be nurses there."

"Do you miss your homeland?"

Sister Veronica turned serious. "Well . . . there in Darmstadt we were in a warm nest, and here we are a bit alone, but everybody is friendly, more than we deserve."

"Have you met the Little Brothers and Sisters of Jesus," I asked. "From all that I have heard about them, you would seem to have much in common." They hoped to meet some day, said Sister Veronica.

More than a year after our meeting in Miss Wrechsler's home, I met the Darmstadt nuns again. They were working then as nurses in a hospital, near Tel Aviv. In their white uniforms and chattering in Hebrew, they were quite undistinguishable in appearance from the other Israeli nurses. They took me to their room on the hospital grounds and we continued the conversation we had started in Haifa. Sister Veronica was still the spokesman and told me more about the Protestant order to which she and her friends belonged. It had been started during the war in Germany by a woman whom she called Sister Basilea. Under the influence of Sister Basilea the order had decided to set aside a special place in its prayers and way of life for the people of Israel and the new Jewish state. An eternal light in their chapel commemorated the six million Jews who had been killed by the Nazis. On the Jewish holy day of Yom Kippur, the nuns recited passages from the Jewish Orthodox prayer book. The date when the Jewish state had been proclaimed is marked by special attention and prayers in their monastery. All of this, stressed Sister Veronica again, was without thought of conversion. "That is in the hands of God." They simply felt a special bond with Jews both because of the Nazi crisis, and because of the kinship which they felt existed between Christianity and Judaism through Jesus. "You know the passage in the Bible describing Joshua's spies carrying clusters of grapes out of the land, the grapes hanging from a staff between the bearers? That is how I think of our relationship with the Jews—we are on either side of the vine, of Jesus, united by Him."

Again the Protestant nun told me how much at home she felt in Israel. "We are like sabras," said her friend in Hebrew.

I didn't this time ask the question I had put on previous occasions to Father Bruno and Robert Lindsay—whether they were not being Judaized. It was still in the category of a semifacetious thought. But a few months later the thought came to me again in a context which struck even my missionary friends with its strangeness.

Some Strange Things that Can Happen
to Christian Missionaries in Israel

One evening I stopped at the seaside town of Natanya, to visit the Reverend Dwight Baker, the Baptist minister from Nazareth, who was studying at an Ulpan—a full-time, intensive Hebrew School. We drank coffee in the room Baker was sharing with a Jewish refugee from Hungary, and he brought me up to date on Baptist activities in Israel. There were now six Baptist ministers in the country, all of them speaking Hebrew, carrying on services, schools, farms—the largest contingent of Protestants in the country, and probably the most determined in their effort to become an indigenous part of the scene, rather than an imported church for foreign visitors. On the other hand, said the Nazareth minister, spiritual conditions of Christians in general were "rather moribund. Though," he brightened, "we finally have our first indigenous minister—a young man who has had a couple of years' training in the States, and will soon go back for more."

The Catholics, I told Baker, had also acquired an indigenous convert recently, an army major named Joshua Blum. I had walked, or rather run, through the Jerusalem streets one afternoon with this convert, for Blum had a vigorous military stride. People in the streets had gaped at the husky young monk in the brown robe and sandals of the Benedictine Order, striding by them speaking sabra Hebrew. The priest had not minded these looks, stopping only to ask a staring child, "You see something strange, lad?" Blum felt himself to be very much an Israeli, retained his reserve rank in the army, and went to yearly maneuvers. One of the reasons he had chosen the Benedictine Order stationed in the Dormition monastery on Mount Zion was because he could be assured of remaining in Israel. During our walk he had spoken briefly of his conversion. He was "almost" a native-born Israeli, and in his home he had seen something of the Jewish religion.

"I tell you this," he said, "so that you shouldn't think I became a Christian because I didn't know of the Jewish religion."

He had been married, and there were children, but he was unwilling to talk about this. All he would say was that in his opinion there was a conflict between "family attachments and the full love of God." He explained his conversion "logically."

"Stop me," he had said, "if any of the steps I offer you don't click." Rapidly then, he had offered an outline of history from the resurrection of Jesus through nineteen hundred years of world and Jewish history, all of which added to "irrefutable proof" of the truth of the church. I had asked him why, if the facts were so clear, so many remained unconvinced.

"Two reasons. Either they have not heard the facts or they are afraid to 'know' the facts because they might have to change their habits of life."

On a hill opposite the old city of Jerusalem, near the Dormition Abbey, Blum asked me to take some pictures which he could send to his father in Haifa. He had posed sideways, his bearded face lifted upward toward the heavens, his glasses glinting in the golden light of the sun.

Baker had read about Blum in the papers, and told me that the abbot of the Dormition monastery was also studying at the Ulpan. We went downstairs and knocked at the door of the little room where the abbot lived alone. A gray-haired, slightly stooped man with dark eyes and very thick glasses opened the door.

"*Shalom,* Daveed," he greeted the minister in Hebrew.

"*Shalom,* Arye," replied Dwight Baker, calling the priest, Father Leo, by his Hebrew name. "Arye," the Benedictine abbot, told us he was working on a Hebrew composition for tomorrow's class.

"Daveed" nodded in sympathy, and said that he also was preparing a talk in Hebrew, about the Arab problem.

We went down to dinner in the small dining room. A radio was blaring out American jazz and several dozen people were sitting around the tables, eating the ever-present green *salade* and olives which are a staple of most Israeli meals. Near us were some elderly white-haired women from America, and a teen-age girl from South Africa. A few chairs away a dark-mustached man smoking a cigarette nodded at Arye and Daveed as we entered. "He is a Christian Arab," said Baker. "Works in the Post Office and wants to learn Hebrew."

78

A short man with heavy spectacles and a long tie whose edge stuck out far below his vest came over to us.

"*Shalom,* Arye," he said to the abbot, smiling.

"*Shalom, shalom,*" said the monk, smiling back. "*Ma shalom ish-techa?*" (How is your wife?)

"*Tov* [good]," the man with the spectacles said, nodding. The two of them continued to speak together in Hebrew, nodding and smiling. They looked like a couple of Jewish scholars at the Yeshiva, I whispered to Baker. "He is a teacher here," the minister informed me, "and just got married last week. Arye offered a special blessing after the ceremony."

As we ate, the priest and the minister spoke about their work. Baker told us about a group of Baptists in Haifa who were pious and intelligent, but had presented him with peculiar problems. They didn't want to call themselves Christians, but preferred the name Messianists. They insisted that they were still Jews, though they believed in Jesus as the Messiah, and some of them still wanted to keep Jewish laws like circumcision and the observance of kosher food. The result of such a development, Baker pointed out worriedly, would be the formation of a Jewish church within the church. It paralleled the rift which had developed in the first century of Christian history between the Jewish followers of James and the group led by Paul. The Baptist minister didn't know whether such a development should be encouraged.

"Do you have anything in the Catholic church, Arye, like this?"

Father Leo nodded and mentioned the names of some priests who wanted to form a Jewish grouping within the Catholic church.

"Will you pass the bread, please, Arye?" The Baptist minister interrupted for a moment in perfect Hebrew.

"Certainly," Arye replied, also in Hebrew.

Father Leo discussed some of his problems. He too found it difficult to recruit indigenous Christian leadership in Israel. He had set up a school in the United States, in Vermont, with the hope of attracting some monks to his monastery on Mount Zion. The Baptist minister sympathized. He had difficulty in explaining the situation to visiting Baptists from his own country. They would come to Tel Aviv, point to some central corner and say,

"Now, here we ought to build a church. We'll rake them in by the thousands."

"They just don't understand," Baker sighed, and Father Leo nodded his head understandingly.

The incongruity of the scene and conversation in the Ulpan suddenly struck me, and I stopped eating. Baker looked at me, and guessed my thought.

"I suppose people just wouldn't believe it if we told them," he said in his Missouri drawl.

The scene was hard to believe—a Benedictine abbot chatting with a Baptist minister in Hebrew about the difficulties of missionary work, while a Christian Arab from Nazareth smoked a cigarette nearby and youngsters from South Africa ate food served by a Yemenite waitress while a radio blared American jazz. It was the kind of scene which set one to thinking again about the mystery of Israel—the mystery of a Providence which had so suddenly thrown together such a concatenation of people and faiths.

Who would predict what would happen to any of these people and faiths in the land which Israelis call their "pressure cooker," not only to these Jewish immigrants from seventy lands, but to the Moslems, even to Christian missionaries? It did seem to me that strange things could happen in the modern land of Israel to missionaries. Of course, we must not make too much out of what may be the atypical whims and dreams of a few people. Yet it is startling to meet priests who petition the Pope for permission to read some of their prayers in Hebrew, who want to return to the Jewish Sabbath, and who speak of rediscovering their Jewish origins in modern Israel. It is strange to hear Protestant missionaries discussing a problem which was argued nearly two thousand years ago in Jerusalem—the advantages and disadvantages of a Jewish-Christian church. It is hard to resist a feeling that some Christians in Israel feel that life here reveals an aspect and quality of Christianity quite different from the religion they knew outside this land.

Probably it would be going too far to say that Christian missionaries in the land of Israel are as much in the process of being converted as they are of converting. Yet is it possible for the Christian faith to be dipped profoundly in the life and reality of modern Israel without undergoing some profound changes? After all, a Christian encounter with Jewish life in Israel does evoke memories, sounds, and sights that have grown dim over the centuries. It is an encounter with the land, people, and language of the Jewish Jesus and, in a way, with the pristine Christian church, that is, the church before it had been severed from its Jewish matrix. The possibilities of such an encounter are at least thought-provoking.

But even more intriguing to me was the way Christians like the Darmstadt nuns fitted into the environment of modern Israel. It was a "fit" which raised the question we have touched on before. Even as there seems to be a kind of Christianity which was alien to this land and which, when imported, lay lifelessly on its surface, might there not also be a kind of Christianity, a religious seed, which was acceptable to this soil?

It was a question which became more insistent after my meeting with a group of young men and women who dreamed about planting "Seeds in the Desert."

CHAPTER V

Seeds in the Desert

The Little Brothers

In vain one looks over the centuries of Christian history in the Holy Land for some creative outburst of indigenous piety. If not an Augustine or a St. Francis, then at least some books or prayers worthy of notice by the rest of the world. But the Christian life was so sterile in Palestine, says James Parkes, that it could not even produce an historian of the Church. The Christian faith was born here, but shortly after its birth the cradle soil became a passive display case for ideas and rituals imported from abroad. This, of course, is a huge generalization, to which there must be some unnoticed exceptions. We might even today point out a small Catholic order of recent origin and wonder if it might be such an exception, though its founder also came from abroad. Charles de Foucauld was a Frenchman who lived in Nazareth for a number of years and there conceived a pattern of life which the Order of the Little Brothers and Sisters of Jesus tries to follow, calling it "The Way of Nazareth." There are some eight or nine members of this order who now live in Israel, and one of them is the Father Jean or Jochanan who had been mentioned to me so frequently by other Catholics.

I met Father Jochanan in a small ceramics factory near Tel Aviv, where he works. The factory is a small concrete building which serves both as workshop and office. A gray-haired man, evidently the proprietor, was sitting behind a desk talking excitedly on the phone about a business order. Two soldiers were standing by him and a short, slender young man in khaki pants and khaki shirt open at the neck, revealing his black, tangled chest hair, was working at a nearby table. I asked for

83

Father Jochanan. The young man at the worktable put down the ceramic block he was holding.

"*Ani hu*—I am he," he said a bit bashfully. He had large brown-hazel eyes, red-lidded as if from lack of sleep, and fine features with a full Gaelic underlip. While I asked for a chance to speak to him alone, he glanced uneasily at his employer on the phone. Then, looking at his watch, he said he might take a little time from his lunch hour, since it was close to noon. We walked outside and sat on the steps of a small tool building a few yards away. As with most conversations in Israel, the first matter to be cleared up was the language of discourse. Father Jochanan spoke English, but preferred Hebrew. I told him of my meetings with other priests in Israel, including Father Elias. Did he share the ideas of Father Elias with regard to the ultimate Jewish conversion to the church? The young priest hesitated and smiled. It was hard to be as definite as Father Elias. His own reasons for coming to Israel had really nothing to do with the thought of making Jewish conversions. His family had been rather lukewarm Catholics till he joined the church, and his own decision to become a priest had not come about through any startling event. He had gone to church schools for about fifteen years and during the war had become aware of anti-Semitism in France. He had felt himself drawn to the Jews since then. As to the purpose of his work here, Father Jean shrugged and turned up his hands.

"To work and to pray." He smiled as if knowing that this type of answer was not very convincing and added, "Also, if the opportunity comes, to bring human beings closer together." The Order of the Little Brothers and Sisters of Jesus was not like the working priests in France, Father Jochanan told me, though they were often confused in people's minds. The worker priests in France, whose program of labor among the people had recently been restricted by the Vatican, had a definite mission with respect to other souls. The Order of the Little Brothers and Sisters meant simply "to imitate the life of Jesus while being sanctified and set apart, while yet living with the people." Their rule was also more contemplative in character than the French working priests. Three hours each day were set aside for prayer

84

and solitary meditation. The whole of Sunday was given over to fasting and prayer. The young priest looked at his watch again. It was not easy to get a job under these conditions, since they could not work on Sunday and on Saturday business establishments in Israel were closed. He would have to go back to work now, but I could visit him at his home in Jaffa. I asked if I might take a snapshot of him. He preferred that I didn't, for the order did not approve of publicity. As he was walking back to the factory, I did snap a picture of the building in which he worked. He suddenly began sprinting. I wondered if he had heard the click of the camera and taken offense.

A few days later I tried to find the address which Father Jochanan had given me. It was not easy, and the taxi driver muttered angrily under his breath. The Jaffa city authorities had, since the Arab-Israeli War, renamed the tangle of streets in the ancient town and schematized them by a number system. Somehow, Street 150 insisted on ending up near Street 79. When the planners tried to straighten up the confusion by adding names to the street numbers, their troubles were compounded.

Few cities have had as many masters as Jaffa. It was an old town when the prophet Jonah walked through it to board a ship for his eventful journey. Greek legends associate the craggy rocks extending from the cruel shore into the Mediterranean with the myth of Perseus. The Canaanites used it as their chief port, before the Hebrews, and later King Solomon landed his cedars from Lebanon and dragged them from this town up through the hills to Jerusalem. When Simon the tanner had his shop in its streets, the language and population of the town was more Greek than Hebrew. After the seventh century the Arabs used the rocks which had been cut by Canaanites and Hebrews for building their mosques. In the eleventh and twelfth centuries the Crusaders used the same stones to construct their Gothic fortifications. From the end of the Crusades till the establishment of the Jewish state in 1948, Jaffa had been a populous Arabic city. Now most of the Arabs were gone and their houses were occupied by refugees from seventy different lands. A city which has seen so many changes and has managed through most of them to keep old names and designations for special quarters might be expected to take some sort of revenge at the haste of its new owners to cast off the old. In Middle Eastern tongues cities are feminine in gender, and regarded somewhat as personalities. They may be taken by different masters, willingly or reluctantly, but the wise conqueror has treated their historic personalities with respect. This attempt by city authorities to denude the old town of its ancient personalities was, I thought, as we blundered about the streets only to find the policeman of whom we asked directions equally confused, an appropriate reaction of a lady whose dignity had been outraged. My taxi driver was, however, not inclined to any philosophical approach to the situation and finally let me down in the approximate neighborhood.

"Everybody here should know where a priest lives," he advised. As it happened, I passed a man walking with a little girl who wore a gold cross on her neck, and he did know. He pointed to a stone house set in back of an empty lot. I knocked at the large wooden door. Father Jochanan opened the door. He held a spoon in his hand with a small slab of margarine on it. He was in the midst of cooking supper for himself and his roommate, who was out shopping. Politely he invited me to join them, but I sensed some restraint in his manner. Some feeling of guilt told me it might have something to do with the picture I had snapped a few days ago. I assured him it was not a picture for publication, and that I was not a newspaperman. My intuition was right. Father Jochanan seemed immensely relieved by my explanation. He had not wanted to say anything, he told me, but he knew that I had taken the picture and had been very disturbed.

"We do not want publicity here; articles which tell about the Brothers going to the natives as in Africa give the impression of a superior ministering to an inferior. That is not our feeling. We are all equal brothers."

Now that the barrier of misunderstanding had been removed, Jochanan began speaking gaily and freely about his order. He brought me some snapshots of priests in an Indian village in Peru and of a Little Brother who worked alone on a fishing vessel. Some of the Little Sisters, Jochanan told me, rode camels and lived in tents among the Tuareg tribesmen in North Africa, where Charles de Foucauld had been killed. De Foucauld, the founder of the order, had died a martyr's death, Jochanan told me, and the church was now considering his canonization. Five years after his death the Order of the Little Brothers and Sisters had been founded by René Voillaume. Now there were more than six hundred in the order who lived in various countries among the most poverty-stricken elements of the populations, dressed like them, and spoke their language. If possible, the members of the order tried to live in pairs. There were three pairs of Little Sisters living in Israel but until recently Jochanan had been the only brother. A few months ago, however, another young man had joined him.

A few minutes later Jochanan's roommate, a tall, slender young lad with rimless glasses and a college-style crewcut, entered carrying a bag of groceries. He also was French, but spoke fluent English with a British accent. Immediately Jochanan informed his colleague that the picture I had taken the other day was not to be used for publicity.

After their meal of olives, vegetables, and an egg Jochanan related his experiences as a priest in Israel. He had gone to a religious kibbutz, where he thought the atmosphere might be more congenial. He had liked it there, but ". . . I felt as if my presence with them made them feel closed up. Even when I removed the cross—we can do that if circumstances warrant— I still felt some embarrassment on their part. Perhaps they were not open because of their association with the meaning of the Cross in Europe. Anyway, after three weeks I left and found this job in town." Perhaps they thought he was a missionary, but ". . . we have no missionary goals. Of course, if it happens, it happens. But we are not here to convert people. We leave that to God."

"But doesn't the church's claim that it is the only road to salvation make it important for believers to bring nonbelievers into the church," I asked.

"Oh no," Jochanan said eagerly, reaching for a heavy book which lay on the table. "Look, I have just been reading a book on official theology." He leafed through some pages from theologians and popes to illustrate the point that "not only sincere

87

Catholics, but others who are sincere in their own way" can be saved.

"A person may not know what forces of salvation are working in him and whether there may not be a special grace in his life, even if he is not officially a Catholic. There are many things that are misunderstood about Catholic teachings by Catholics themselves."

"Still," his friend, who had sat down on a couch and drawn up his legs as if partaking in a college bull session, entered our conversation, "there are some things which it is hard for Jews to understand. I don't know, for example, if they can understand the Christian vow of poverty. Does that idea exist in Jewish religious writings?"

I told the young priest that there was in Jewish tradition an understanding of the virtues of abstinence and poverty, and mentioned a Rabbi Chen in Jerusalem. This rabbi had written a series of articles in which he demonstrated that the theme of poverty is an essential part of Jewish thought and of all the Jewish holidays. The booth on the festival of Sukkoth, the "bread of affliction" on Passover, the white prayer shawls worn by traditional Jews on Yom Kippur, etc., were examples of this theme. Jochanan wrote down Rabbi Chen's name and asked if there were other Jewish writings I could recommend, especially works dealing with personal piety.

"I have read Ibn Bachia's *Duties of the Heart*." The priest's soft brown eyes lit up with enthusiasm. "And I read him often. I also have some books by Rabbi Kook, the former Chief Rabbi of Israel, although I must confess I don't understand him as well."

Jochanan's roommate had been thinking about Rabbi Chen's thesis, and interrupted again. "Of course, come to think of it, you may be right. Jewish monastic communities existed we know, because we now have found the Dead Sea Scrolls."

"Still," now it was Jochanan who dissented, "it is difficult to explain to Jews the idea of celibacy. I have tried many times. For example, in the kibbutz we used to speak about the commandments, and they would ask how I could believe in the Torah yet not fulfill the first commandment "to be fruitful and multiply." I used to say that this commandment is of course necessary for the perpetuation of life and if there was any danger that most people would not fulfill it, then I would break my vow of celibacy. But I do not think that there is any danger. What people do not understand about our vows is that they are not negative commandments, but the result of positive feelings which result in some prohibitions."

"Yes, it is hard for Jews to understand the motivations of priesthood." Jochanan's young friend nodded. "But when they ask me, I try to explain by offering two reasons. First it is to bring a sacrifice as a symbol of dedication; second, it is necessary to sacrifice oneself and separate oneself from the world in order to feel a full love for God."

"But do you not think that there are married Jews and Christians who feel this full love?" I asked.

The young priest was quiet for a moment, his head bent downward toward the table. "No, I really do not think so," he said softly, lifting his eyes, still red-rimmed from the vigil he had kept last night before the Host. "I know that there are religious Jews, but I wonder to myself if these religious Jews can feel God as a dear friend, that is, someone always present and always with you. Perhaps, I don't know."

Before I left that evening, he had drawn a map for me of the street in Nazareth where I could find some of the Little Sisters of his order.

The thought that family relations or physical love is in some way incompatible with full dedication to God is indeed a thought alien to most Jews. The priest was right—there are few aspects of Christianity more difficult for Jews to understand than the principle of celibacy. "He who can and does not have children," says the Talmud, "it is as if he diminishes the image of God." The commandment to be fruitful and multiply is accounted by Orthodox Jews as the very first of the 613 holy commandments they see in the Bible. Rabbi Abraham Isaac Kook, former Chief Rabbi of Israel and profound Cabalist, makes note in his commentary on the Song of Songs that love is "one flame" which should express itself simultaneously on many levels—physical, communal, and spiritual. It is Rabbi Akiva, points out the

89

Chief Rabbi, who interprets the Song of Songs as a parable of love between God and his people. But Akiva, Kook says, was able to understand the Song of Songs this way precisely because he was a great lover—of his beloved wife Rachel; of his people, and of his God. This is the attitude of normative Judaism—that spiritual and physical love not only do not conflict with each other, but to diminish one is to diminish the other. The required celibacy of monk and nun is then an aspect of Christian life which does puzzle most Jews. It was this aspect of Christian life which became the central question of my discussion with the Little Sisters in Nazareth.

Chastity and Faith

André, a young Jewish scholar from France, and Ruth, an Israeli schoolteacher, went with me to Nazareth and began arguing about celibacy on the way.

"Most priests are cases of mother fixation," said the Israeli definitely. She was herself once divorced and had married again, with her second marriage going in the same direction as her first.

"I think you will find that most nuns and priests have some peculiar relations with their parents . . . the men with their mother, the women with their father."

André disagreed with her. "The idea of fleshly love getting in the way of spiritual love is neither as foolish or un-Jewish as most Jews think. Elijah as far as we know was not married; and Elisha, when he was called to follow him, had to say good-by to his family. Jesus too was unmarried, and even in Eastern Europe didn't Jews often leave their families for long periods of time, dedicating themselves to their studies?"

The argument continued as we ascended the hill and passed the police station on the outskirts of Nazareth. There we picked up two young men dressed in clean white shirts and khaki pants.

"Are you Christians?" Ruth asked them.

"One of us is Christian and one is Moslem," a dark-eyed youngster with a black mustache answered in perfect Hebrew, smiling. "Can you tell which is which?"

90

"I will guess that the Moslem is the one with the mustache," Ruth answered laughing. "Right?"

"Right," answered the young man, and they jumped out of the car with a *Shalom,* pointing in the direction of a store where Jochanan had told me the Little Sisters worked. The store was closed and a passer-by told us that the people who kept it were living now in the nearby convent of the Poor Clares. The wall gate to the convent was open, and within we saw a small cottage, its door marked with a large blue cross. A tall, sturdily-built girl of about thirty answered our knock. She wore a long blue-gray dress and a blue-gray kerchief neatly arranged on the back of her auburn hair. Her Hebrew was hesitant and disappeared completely into French when she found out that André was from France. We were fortunate, she told us, to have come this morning, for the Mother Superior of the group, Sister Jeanne, was visiting from Haifa. We were taken into a small room with whitewashed stone walls, completely bare except for a crucifix, a small couch, and a half-filled bookshelf. On the top of the bookshelf was a large framed picture of a man with dark, wild-looking eyes turned upward in a glazed, pietistic look.

The Mother Superior entered and introduced herself with a smile. She seemed to be no older than the other Little Sister and was pretty, with sparkling dark eyes and a lovely smile. We sat down on the small stools that stood in the corner of the room and chatted while another sister brought in small cups of Turkish coffee and a bowl of Israeli candies. After a few minutes of polite amenities Ruth, who had been looking curiously at the young Mother Superior, interrupted abruptly.

"What really is your work here?"

Sister Jeanne laughed. "Oh . . . it is embarrassing. Our shop where we sell ceramics is not yet fixed up . . . we are working on it now."

"No . . . I mean," Ruth said, narrowing her eyes, "what do you want to accomplish as a nun?"

"Oh . . ." The nun laughed again and lifted her hands, fluttering her fingers gracefully. "Only to work and to pray."

Since Ruth continued to stare as if waiting for more, Sister

Jeanne, still smiling, turned to André and added a few sentences in French.

"She says," André interpreted, "that they go to places where there is hatred and poverty and try to live lovingly . . . work with the population, adopting their language and culture, being in the community yet set apart."

"Would you mind telling us a little bit about your life before you became a nun." Ruth spoke in a rather patronizing manner.

The nun obliged in a mixture of Hebrew and French. She had come from a town in Southern France and had joined the Order of the Little Sisters ten years ago. Her house had not been particularly religious, though since her decision they had become more interested and her home was now a meeting place for North Africans and Frenchmen, a place where they tried to bridge some of the antagonisms which were troubling that land. Before joining the order, she had lived a normal life, going to church and thinking of marriage like other girls. Then had come the decision and she had been sent to Israel. Three years ago she had taken her permanent vows of poverty, chastity, and obedience and was now the Mother Superior of three other Little Sisters in Israel. The nun's dark eyes sparkled as she spoke, and she laughingly apologized for her awkward Hebrew. "Jochanan in Tel Aviv speaks much better."

"Do you mind if I ask you a direct question?" The Israeli said. "I have been looking at you and hearing you speak of love and it is puzzling to me. I look at your face and it is happy and content."

Sister Jeanne's eyes again sparkled and she nodded.

"But how can you really speak about love?" Ruth asked. "How can you know what love is when you do not have a husband and children?"

"But I do have a family." Sister Jeanne smilingly turned her head in the direction of the two sisters in the next room. "And we have our family problems. Of course," her face became a bit more serious, "It is not always easy. It is like making a sacrifice each day for a greater love."

The schoolteacher asked no more questions, but she was

92

clearly dissatisfied. Sister Jeanne had put on her sunglasses, and taking a large brief case in her hand, walked out with us. We left her standing near the wall of the convent discussing a construction problem with an Arab workman. Ruth turned to André.

"Did you notice her eyes and smile? She seems completely blessed. How do you explain it. Do you think they really know love? I do not think that a woman in love, even one whose love is requited, can have that kind of peaceful happiness."

The Frenchman grinned. "They think they have the most passionate and deepest of love affairs, and with a party who is very reliable."

"No——" The schoolteacher seemed aggravated. "There is something immoral about trying to possess great love and passion without paying for it with tears." She shook her head and went on as if speaking to herself. "Sure, she is happy. People can hypnotize themselves into happiness, and you do not have to be a nun. Any method of shutting out the contradictions of life, of forcing everything into one simplifying formula can bring some kind of peace. But . . . it is not right. Yes, you achieve some peace by cutting yourself off from that part of life which takes away your peace—the baby, the duty of raising children—but this is a cutting off from life."

"From the Catholic point of view," said André, "such cutting off opens the way to a better life. There was once a nun in Italy who had lost her husband and children, and afterward was able to thank God for each of the losses, which she said were an obstacle in the way of her love for God."

"That is what I think is immoral," Ruth replied angrily. "If one really loved . . . not in some hypnotized fashion . . . but really felt with the pain of human beings, he would not thank God so easily for taking away a good husband and lovely children. I think I prefer the Jewish love of God which lets them quarrel with Him and call Him to account for the defects in this world. But still," she mused as we started to drive down the winding road into the valley of Jezreel, "she seemed so blessed and content. Whose was the picture of that crazy-looking man on the bookshelf?" the schoolteacher asked abruptly.

It was a picture of Charles de Foucauld, André explained, the spiritual founder of the order to which the Little Brothers and Sisters belonged.

"If it's psychological dissections of spiritual personalities that you want," André said, grinning, "he would make quite a case, though the church is now thinking about making him a saint."

De Foucauld, André told us, was graduated last in a class of 860 at St. Cyr Military Academy. His classmates there remembered how his room at night would "tinkle with the clink of silver spoons scraping cans of *pâté de foie gras.*"

"Actually, though he resigned from the army because of his attachment to a courtesan named Mimi," said André, "his major lust even as a young man seemed to be food. His sexual attachments were rather weak and perhaps peculiar—at any rate by the time he was twenty-five he said that he no longer found chastity to be a great problem."

The real love of De Foucauld's life, according to André, was a cousin whom he thanked for having saved him from marriage. Their relationship was purely platonic, and it was this cousin, Marie de Bondi, who introduced De Foucauld to Abbé Huvalin. It was in a sermon delivered by the abbé that De Foucauld heard the words which would decide his way of life.

"Our Lord has taken the lowest place so absolutely that no one has ever been able to wrest it from him." To also take this lowest place soon became the goal of De Foucauld.

André's information about the soldier turned priest came from a biography by Anne Freemantle. It is a book which paints an unusually frank portrait of the man now being considered for canonization. Soon after his meeting with Abbé Huvalin, De Foucauld joined a Trappist monastery but found its severe regimen too easy. Freemantle tells of his complaints that the monks were using oil, a needless luxury, on their food. At one point Abbé Huvalin found it necessary to write him a note: "If you have and hold a hatred for yourself, let it be a tranquil hatred, like deep water."

The Abbé discouraged De Foucauld from dreams about forming a new church order out of his own desire for self-mortification.

De Foucauld had been thinking about a different kind of order, based on "absolute poverty, manual labor, abjection, and silence," where there would be no hierarchy and no relationship but the fraternal one based on equality. He put away his plans for a while, and in 1897 came to Jaffa dressed in a "long blouse, striped blue and white, a pair of blue cotton pants and a thick white woollen cap around which a piece of stuff was wound in turban fashion"—evidently his concept of an outfit that would make him anonymous. He traveled by foot from Jaffa to Nazareth and sought employment at the convent of the Poor Clares, one of the church's most severe and withdrawn orders of nuns. He told them nothing about his background, and they agreed to give him work as a gardener. They offered him a comfortable room, but he asked permission to sleep in the tool house on a bench, with a stone for a pillow. When one of the nuns protested that he would not even be able to stretch out in the hut, he replied that "Christ could not stretch out upon the Cross." In Nazareth he sought to "live exactly as possible the life of our Lord, living only from the work of one's hands, accepting no gifts, either spontaneous or solicited, and following literally all the counsels, possessing nothing, giving to everyone who asks, requiring nothing, depriving oneself of the most that is possible." It was the life of Jesus that De Foucauld wanted to imitate, but specifically that part of Jesus' life which was passed in Nazareth.

"What did he do during these thirty years?" asked De Foucauld. "He submitted to Mary and Joseph. The secret of this conduct was to suppress the desire to shine which is so natural to us. . . . This example takes away from me all the pretexts I have which self-love so subtly suggests persuading us that God's work is involved, that a neighbor's salvation is at stake. . . ."

This is the "Way of Nazareth"—the goal of some six hundred Little Sisters and Brothers, who in the most poverty-stricken areas of the world try like him "to be truly little."

The lives of individuals who are proposed for sainthood have the tendency to be fitted by their canonizers into patterns which omit or minimize matters that do not fit into the pattern. A classic pattern for sainthood is the Augustinian line of development from dissolute sinner to holy man. Another desirable conclusion to a saint's life is a martyr's death. De Foucauld's life also can be told in such fashion as to fit into this pattern, but it is strained. The last years of the priest's life were spent in North Africa. Here he engaged in unsuccessful efforts to make converts and later joined with French soldiers who were engaged in cutting out a new colony for France. De Foucauld's goal there was to "win souls for God and land for France." From the French point of view he is a patriot who helped the French to understand the Arab territory they were trying to conquer. Others, however, call him by a more nasty name, *mouchard* —stool pigeon or informer. There are other questionable aspects of his life in North Africa. He made a special study of the love poems of the Tuareg tribesmen and in the company of French soldiers he visited the famous love courts of the Arabs and eagerly watched the rites which Freemantle describes as similar to "an American teen-age get-together, with much petting to climax." He finally does die a martyr's death, killed by the Tuareg tribesmen among whom he lived, who evidently linked him, correctly, with the French against whom they were revolting.

One uncommitted to the proposition of De Foucauld's sainthood would find it hard to fit the latter years of his life into the classic saint-sinner pattern. But then perhaps it is wrong to demand a consistent and steadily growing process of perfection in proposed saints. Obviously there was enough inspiration and holiness in De Foucauld's life to inspire the order which now lives by his Rule. And it does seem that this inspiration reached its highest spiritual level in Nazareth. Whatever the judgment of history or the church will be about De Foucauld, it will be hard to feel anything but admiration and respect for the pattern of life pursued by those who try to follow the Way of Nazareth these days in Israel.

The Way of Nazareth

One day I met the Little Sisters who live in Jerusalem. I recognized them by their long gray dresses. They were standing at the side of the road amid a crowd of a dozen young boys and girls, trying to hitch rides. Reuven, my driver, snorted impatiently when I asked him to stop and back up. I beckoned to the girls, who began running. When they saw that my car was empty, they stopped. One of them called out, "We are looking for a hitch, not a taxi." I assured them that mine was a noncommercial offer, and they got in the car. One of the Little Sisters was about thirty, with lovely white skin and large, slightly protruding blue eyes. Her name was Aliza, she said. She did the talking for a younger friend who spoke little Hebrew and had been in Israel only a year. They were on their way to Nazareth, said the nuns, where one of their order was going to "receive the Cross," that is, take her permanent vows as a nun.

When I asked Aliza why she had become a nun, she laughed. "Father Jochanan in Tel Aviv is better able to explain these things—I am not good at expressing ideas and I can't speak Hebrew well yet." But, she said, it had really been a simple matter. "It was like what happened to Daniel. You remember how God seized him and brought him. . . ." She laughed again. No, it had not been the result of any single event. "It was only that at a certain time in my life I looked around and said 'This cannot be all there is, these passing things . . . there must be something more lasting, a greater love.'" She shrugged and opened the palms of her hands as if that explained everything.

I told the nuns that I could take them to the crossroad near Tel Aviv, but first wanted to stop and visit a Karaite village. The Karaites belonged to a branch of Judaism which in the eighth century had refused to accept the authority of the rabbis and claimed to be guided in their religious life only by the written word of Scripture and not the Talmud. The rabbis had considered them heretics and even refused to intermarry with them. For centuries there were Karaite communities in the Crimea and in the Near East who lived in tense and unhappy relationship with the "rabbinic Jews." But now some of the Karaites had come back to Israel. I invited the nuns to visit them with me. Aliza looked at her watch and consented.

A few minutes later we left the main road and drove up a dusty path past bare fields and several dozen cottage-like houses, shimmering in the summer heat.

97

We hailed a black-mustached young man with a khaki hat pulled down over his eyes and asked for someone who could tell us about the Karaites. We had found the right person, he replied. He was the son-in-law of the village chazan—the person who served as prayer leader here. But first, the young man insisted, we had to meet his wife, the daughter of the chazan. We stepped out of the car while the young farmer brought a cow into his barn, ran to his house, and returned with a light-complexioned girl of about eighteen who was carrying a tray with some cool water and strawberry-preserve syrup. The young girl shook hands with the Little Sisters, and did not seem at all curious about the blue crosses which were sewn on their dresses. After our drinks we walked up a few houses to a yard where a bald man dressed in white underclothes was digging around a newly planted tree. He was light-complexioned with blue eyes like his daughter. After rubbing his dirty hands on his clothes and shaking our hands, he finished spreading some fertilizer around the tree and invited us to his house.

Inside his small cottage we sat on couches against the walls. Our host disappeared for a few minutes into another room. His wife, a heavy dark-haired woman, came out of the same room carrying a large plate of fly-covered red watermelon slices in one hand, and a naked baby boy in the other. Soon our host reappeared dressed in a striped, pajama-like outfit which was evidently his formal attire. He told us that he was from the ancient Egyptian Karaite community. Nasser had not distinguished between Karaites and Jews, so the unity which they could not achieve themselves had been imposed upon them by outside forces, and now they were all together in Israel. Of course, the chazan said, "the rabbis still call us *mamzerim*—illegitimate bastards. Well, if they call us *mamzerim*, we say they are *mamzerim*."

It was a rather neat way of summing up a thousand years of cleavage and recrimination.

The chazan showed us a book which, he said, had just been examined by the scholars at the Hebrew University. Around the margins of the prayer book I saw little stories and comments

98

similar in style to those which could be read in the Talmud. Despite their opposition to the rabbinic oral tradition and their claim to the Scriptures as the basis of their tradition, the Karaites had developed their own oral tradition in the course of the centuries.

I told the chazan that the nuns sitting in his room were Christians. He nodded at them with friendly eyes.

"To us it makes no difference—all people are human beings."

Aliza was looking worriedly at her watch, and after a few minutes we returned to the car. Reuven started impatiently and in his haste drove over a large irrigation pipe. "Puncture," groaned Reuven as he heard the loud crack. "Puncture" in Hebrew has come to stand for any kind of mishap, ranging from a traffic jam to a sudden headache of the driver. But this was a real puncture in the gas line. An hour passed before we were able to find a telephone in the village and call up a nearby station for gas. The nuns sat in the back of the car quietly, but obviously worried that darkness might come before they caught a *tremp* to Nazareth. I suggested they take a bus to Haifa, and offered to pay their expenses. Aliza smiled and shook her head. "If we accept help from you, why should God help?"

Reuven finally closed the puncture in the gas line with a wad of soap, and we returned to the main road. Behind us the Judean hills gleamed bare and hard in the bright sun. "The land has been stripped," writes George Adam Smith. "It's bones protrude, and in parts it is very bald—a carcass of a land." The stony barrenness of Israel's hills, like everything else in the Holy Land, has been interpreted by visitors' eyes as being symbolic of more than natural devastation. Herman Melville in 1857 thought that "the abominable landscape in a great part of Judea must have suggested to the Jewish prophets their ghastly theology." For Melville, this landscape evoked something of his own theology. "Is the desolation of the land the result of the fatal embrace of the Deity? Hapless are the favorites of heaven." The Jewish writer Sholem Asch had a more optimistic interpretation of the empty hills surrounding Jerusalem. Each of them is waiting, says Asch, recalling an ancient Jewish legend, for the time

99

when "all peoples shall come to the mountain of the Lord." Then each people would take over one of these barren hills. Their present barrenness was therefore a reminder of the ultimate redemption that was to come.

I asked Aliza the same question I had once put to Jochanan—why this Holy Land was seemingly so barren and unreceptive to Christian teaching. Her reaction was the same as the Little Brother's—a puzzled shrug and agreement that it was strange.

"Still," Aliza brightened a bit, "there is something different here—though people sense it more after having left. I have received letters from friends who write that they know now that they have left behind something they cannot find elsewhere. . . . I am not expressing it well in my Hebrew—but always, after they've been here, it seems less real elsewhere. This land," she pointed to the rocky hills, "the Bible says that it 'devours its inhabitants,' but if you work hard, it can also be a land of milk and honey. I do not think I can explain, but it is both. Both descriptions in the Bible are true. It's *kashe*—hard—but real." Her large blue eyes widened in the attempt to express her feelings.

At the junction of the Tel Aviv-Haifa road Aliza and her friend left us with a gay *Shalom* and walked on to the crowd of "trempists" who were trying to hitchhike to Haifa. It was a typical Israeli grouping—an elderly Kurdish couple, the man in baggy pants with a turban on his head, his wife with heavily tattooed forehead; several slightly built Yemenite girls with white kerchiefs setting off their dark, finely chiseled features; some young men whose mustaches and European jackets indicated North Africa as their probable origin, and a large number of boys and girls in a variety of Israeli military uniforms. Nobody in the crowd seemed to notice the gray-clad figures with blue crosses on their dresses who had just joined them. Despite their costume, or perhaps because of it, the Little Sisters of Jesus seemed a very natural part of the variegated mélange of clothes, cultures, and faiths which make up the population of modern Israel. A tall bronzed Israeli soldier hardly glanced at the two nuns who took their place in line beside him. He looked like a sabra, and

100

sabras are accustomed to their land's heterogenous inhabitants. But what if this sabra were somewhat curious about his new neighbors in line and asked them what they were doing in Israel. He would probably get an answer similar to the one I had received. "We are here to work" or "to pray," all the rest being expressed by a smiling shrug. Strangely enough he might find such an answer satisfactory, I thought, as we drove away from the crossroad.

There is something similar, despite the obvious differences, in the way the sabras and Little Sisters explain their life decisions—a few bare words, a gesture, as if long speeches were so unnecessary. What is important to both is not the spoken word, but "realization" in life, as the sabra calls it.

It seems absurd, at first thought anyhow, to suggest similarities between the Little Brothers and Sisters of Jesus and the sabra, who proudly claims to be like the fruit of that name, with its tough, prickly skin and seeds which must be spat out before getting a taste of soft sweetness. But the comparison, I found out, could be made favorably by the sabras themselves.

Several years later I visited Aliza again in the little Jerusalem store where she and another Little Sister worked at their ceramics business. To supplement their income Aliza also did housework, but she was working at the potter's wheel in the store the day I came. She continued to work as we chatted.

"One has thoughts in work like this." She nodded at the vase which was taking shape under her hands, then hesitated as if embarrassed.

"For example?"

"Well, you can understand better when you do work like this what Isaiah meant when he said 'go to the house of the potter' in order to learn about the proper relationship to God. I have my own thoughts about this." She laughed and hesitated again.

"Well, you see how we make a vase. The center appears to be nothing, yet it is the real constructing factor in the work. If it is not straight, then the structure about cannot be properly built. That is how I think of God—the center, invisible, but everything depends upon it."

Aliza told me that Jochanan was studying in France for a

101

while, but would soon be back. Before he left, the Little Brother had been interviewed by a magazine which was read by young sabras.

"We don't want publicity," Aliza said. "Jochanan did not permit our picture to be printed, but could not forbid the writer to write."

The writer of the article had not paid much attention to details of the Catholic order's religious faith and rites. What attracted the sabra was the eagerness of the Little Brothers and Sisters "not to shine," their willingness to preach love not by words but by simply working, and their effort to be "seeds in the desert."

It was a kind of life, a sabra would think, which is indigenous to his land. After all, the sabra's ancestors came from the desert, and their descendants never forgot that Israel's most important life experiences were "in a land that was not sown." It was to the desert that the prophets retired when they sought to renew their knowledge of life's deepest realities. And it was through the efforts of a few who came to a desert and dreamed of a kind of life similar in many ways to the Way of Nazareth that modern Israel's first kibbutzim were formed. Only if the few will continue to be attracted to the desert, says Ben Gurion today, will Israel be able to fulfill its historic mission.

It was a twelfth-century Jewish philosopher, Yehudah Halevi, who suggested that even as certain crops grow best on certain kinds of soil, so there is a type of religious seed which will "take" only in a certain land. The land of Israel, he implied, would only permit a special kind of "divine matter" to root itself in its soil—all other "seeds" will be spewed out or lie lifelessly on its surface. Was this what Aliza implied when she said that the land was kashe—"hard." The land of Israel seems to have been hard and not receptive to the in-between, the sensible adjustment and compromise that in other lands has been the secret of a church's growth. Something there is about this land which does not prompt halfhearted movements of the mind and soul to take root. What has grown here and produced fruits which have become a spiritual diet of half the world has been produced by the few who pursue their goals with the quality of "allness."

Might this line of thought offer an answer to those who

102

complain of the land's spiritual aridity, especially Christians who call the holy soil "ungrateful" for not giving life to the seeds of Christian sowing. Perhaps it is the seed rather than the soil that has been at fault.

CHAPTER VI

The Real Dialogue

Theory of the Archetype

It was a Jesuit priest in Jerusalem who offered me an image which gave a final form to a thought that had been crystallizing throughout my encounters with Christians in the Holy Land. I met Father Stiassny and his colleague, Father Roget, also a Jesuit, for lunch in a Jerusalem restaurant. The priests were quite different, not only in their attitude toward the mystery-of-Israel question, but in their personalities. Father Stiassny was thin, with pinched nose, small spectacles, and a soft, careful manner of speech. Father Roget, black-bearded, stocky, and ebullient, roared up to the restaurant on his motorcycle, strode in removing a black beret from his balding head, and called out loud greetings in Hebrew.

"He is like a sabra," Father Stiassny said as his colleague sat down, took the menu which was written in several languages, and examined the Hebrew section.

"Yes, I do feel like a fish in water here," said Father Roget, who was of Jewish origin, and whose English still retained the flavor of the Chicago streets in which he was brought up.

"But you don't feel so happy about things here." Father Roget smiled at his fellow priest, obviously continuing a long debate.

"Yes." Father Stiassny nodded seriously. "I do think the government has done some unnecessary and foolish things here, especially with regard to the recent Christian immigration."

"Of course," Roget agreed, "but you are too hard, not to give them a chance to catch their breath. You can't expect spiritual miracles overnight. Just think, as we are talking, children are studying the Bible in the land of Israel. Do you think that you can put Jews and Torah together in Israel without having a spiritual explosion sooner or later?"

Actually it was summer, and most children were not studying the Torah or anything else at lunchtime, but Father Stiassny smiled and said nothing.

"Do you think all this is happening for no reason?" Roget continued. "The state and the return of the Jews?"

"Yes, it might be so," Father Stiassny said quietly. "It might be of great meaning, or it might be the prelude to another disaster, another Galut—exile."

Father Roget appealed to me. "Do you see any signs of a spiritual quickening among the sabras? Unfortunately, we don't have much contact with the native population. But we have the feeling that if something were to begin here, it would spread quickly, because they are all the same. I mean that sabras are so similar that if something started, it would spread like wildfire."

"But how do you feel about Israel?" I asked Father Stiassny. The soft-spoken priest lowered his head for a moment, then glanced at some Hungarian refugees sitting nearby and gaping at the Hebrew-speaking priest.

"If you want to know what I think, I'll tell you the truth." He hesitated. "What amazes me is that others are not more amazed at what is happening here."

Father Roget looked at his colleague in surprise.

"As for myself, personally," the priest spoke quietly, but with feeling, "I couldn't visualize my own life without Hebrew. By that I mean that I couldn't personally conceive of understanding the New Testament and Christianity in a way it should be understood without the knowledge of Hebrew."

"Well!" Father Roget was both surprised and delighted at his colleague's reply. "Of course," Father Roget said, turning to me, "you mustn't think that there are many of us in the church so interested in this question—the mystery of Israel, as we call it. But when we tell others about it, they lap it up like milk."

After lunch Father Roget roared off on his motorcycle, and I accompanied Father Stiassny up the street toward the Sisters of Zion Convent, where he lived.

"I don't find it possible to be both socially gregarious and also to accomplish anything real in studies." Father Stiassny sighed as his friend's motorcycle disappeared down the street. "I know that some others are gifted that way, but I can't."

At the stone gate of the monastery a freckle-faced blonde girl ran up to the priest.

"Shalom," Father Stiassny said, in Hebrew, chucking her chin in his hand. "Is your father well?"

We walked up the stone stairway of the monastery and Father Stiassny led me into the library on the second floor.

"We have a fine collection of rabbinical literature here, as you can see." Across the hallway the priest's study offered a magnificent view of the Old City walls. The heavy granite buildings of the New and Old Jerusalem were beginning to take on their familiar golden hue in the afternoon sunlight.

"This is where I spend most of my time and do my work." Father Stiassny seemed to be in a confessional mood. "My field is the Jewish Hellenistic period—what I would like to show is that the influence of Greek thought in Christianity is overexaggerated. Much of what some scholars think had its origin in paganism, is really rooted in Judaism. This, of course, is what discoveries like the Dead Sea Scrolls tend to prove." The priest rose and took down some manuscripts from the shelf in back of his chair.

"I am also trying to retranslate some of the New Testament back into the original Hebrew and Aramaic. Here is something I am doing on the Beatitudes. It illustrates what I mean about not being able to understand Christianity and the New Testament without a knowledge of living Hebrew. You take the word *blessed,* which is so often used in the Sermon on the Mount. How can one really understand it unless one knows the Hebrew word *ashrei*—meaning something like finding favor in the eyes of God. It is not the same in Greek or English. But it isn't often that I have a chance to talk about these things," the priest said, as if amazed at his own loquaciousness. "With the present rabbinic leadership, frankly, we have no contact—there can be no dialogue at all."

The priest told me about his own decision to enter the church. "It didn't really come about in a sudden fashion." His father, a Hungarian, had not been very religious. His mother was born Jewish, but had converted to Catholicism at an early age and was a very pious Catholic. He took after his mother in both appearance and feelings, the priest said.

I repeated Ruth's theory about the mother-fixation of priests. The priest admitted that there could be psychological factors in his decision, "but this doesn't affect the validity of the decision —there are many ways by which God can bring one closer to him. But, I think there is still a specific experience in Christianity which cannot be found in any other form of religion. This central experience of Christianity—this is hard for a Jew to even understand." Father Stiassny spoke slowly, looking out of the window at the walls of the Old City. "I don't mean a mystic feeling or emotion, but a sense of being united with Christ. It is as if a seed were planted within, which gradually grows and transforms all the limbs of the body and the being—this is what we mean by being reborn in Christ."

"But my ambition in Israel," said Father Stiassny, "is to have more priests come here and study their religion in the language and in the land where it all began to flower. I think they would have a deeper and a more correct understanding of it."

"So you too are one of the Judaizers in the church," I said. I explained to the startled priest that many priests and ministers I had been meeting in Israel had expressed attitudes which if heard during the days of the Inquisition would have caused them to be burned as Judaizers.

Father Stiassny paused before answering. "Let me tell you my theory. You have heard about Jungian archetypes. Well, I have come to believe that there are such archetypes within the church. I have often thought that a person living in the fourth century would also have felt at home in the church of the ninth century. But a person in the eleventh or twelfth century would have had difficulty recognizing the church of the ninth century. It was during those centuries that we took in the great barbarian masses of Europe, and with them we took in the pagan archetypes within their souls. And always there is a struggle between these archetypes."

"You mean, for example, that when the Russian nation was

converted in the tenth century, it was done by a decree which changed very little within the soul of the masses of people, who brought into the church most of what they had been believing and feeling in the past?"

I found myself responding with enthusiasm to the priest's explanation; in fact, taking over his theory and using it to express the thoughts which had been crystallizing in my own mind as a result of the meetings with Israel's missionaries and Christian leaders.

"Would you say then that the type of struggle which took place in Spain during the Inquisition was a struggle not so much between the church and the Judaizers within it, as a conflict between the Christian and pagan archetype? For wasn't the Mithraic cult of the Bull, and the ritual of its killing, which existed for so many centuries along the Mediterranean, taken right into Spanish-Christian culture? Could the cluster of feelings which surrounded this essential paganism be called an archetype, which found itself in conflict with what you would call the real Christian archetype?"

Father Stiassny didn't answer, and I couldn't see his face because darkness had fallen in the room. A bell rang in the monastery and the priest told me he had to leave. He accompanied me down the stairs. In the hall we passed a large painting of the Crucifixion scene, faces contorted in sadness, the bloodied, agonized figure of Jesus on the Cross. The red drops of blood were not as bright as the red which one saw on Spanish crucifixes. There, in Spain, where the churches were often dark and the crosses sometimes made of black wood, the red droplets of blood oozing out of the skin of the crucified Christ were reminiscent in a shuddering sense of the red streams which gushed out of the black bull when the picadores inserted their barbs. And the awed faces of the people at the bullfight, watching the "moment of truth," have been likened to the hushed, reverent expression on the faces depicted in the Crucifixion painting, except that in the painting the ecstatic awe was mingled with compassion. Was this also the mingling of the archetypes that Father Stiassny had spoken about?

109

A Speculation

Father Stiassny's theory of the archetype in the church is reminiscent of a similar thesis advanced by the late German rabbi Leo Baeck. This brave and learned survivor of Hitler's concentration camps tried to trace what he called "a history of Jewish ideas within the church." The Jewish syndrome of ideas which the church inherited from the Old Testament consisted essentially of an "active, ethical, life-affirming faith, a conviction that history was real and that man could through his own efforts achieve a better world. There was also what Baeck called a non-Jewish syndrome within the church. This was a cluster of beliefs which expressed despair in man's goodness, or in the possibility of achieving salvation through human efforts. It emphasized grace and the importance of passively accepted magico-sacramental rites rather than human deeds. These contradictory syndromes, claims Baeck, were both included within the church. It was the genius of the church that it tried to hold them together within an all-inclusive structure. Only when there was open conflict, and one or the other syndrome sought to dominate alone, did the church act. For example, in the early centuries the church expelled Marcion, who openly fought the "evil Jewish God of the Old Testament." On the other side, when Pelagianism with its Judaic faith in the sufficiency of man's will and freedom wanted complete control, it too was banned.

The church was helped in this attempt to combine its opposing syndromes by the example of Paul, who was Jew and anti-Jew in one—"who quoted the Law only to prove that it could be broken." Baeck sees much of the historic conflict in the Christian church as a conflict of Jewish and pagan syndromes. On the Jewish side Baeck could list movements like Pelagianism and Socianism. The non-Jewish syndrome was expressed through the schools who followed Marcion, Augustine, and Luther.

Wasn't Baeck's thesis similar to Father Stiassny's "battle of the archetypes?" To be sure, the Jesuit priest thought in terms of Christian and anti-Christian archetypes rather than of Jewish and pagan syndromes. And at the center of the priest's Christian

110

archetype is the unique Christian experience centering about the person of Christ. But our question is—if there are different syndromes or archetypes within the church, what may happen to them today in the land of Israel?

Not long after my conversation with Father Stiassny I saw a number of my Christian friends in Jerusalem, at a conference where the major theme, it seemed to me, was related to this question. The occasion for the conference was a World Congress for Jewish Studies. It was opened by Prime Minister Ben Gurion, who suggested to the scholars that they re-examine their conception of Jewish and Christian history, for just as "the past undoubtedly sheds light on the present, so to no small extent, can the present help us to understand the past."

The point made by the Prime Minister was that modern Israelis were living in the same geographic habitat, speaking the same language, even facing the same general configuration of enemies as their biblical ancestors. They were therefore able to understand the meaning of the Bible, the character of the early Israelites, the quality of their experiences in a way which was not open to the understanding of the powerless European ghetto Jew.

"I feel myself much closer to Isaiah, or King Uzziah, than to my more recent Diaspora ancestors," says Ben Gurion. This is part of the Prime Minister's controversial "Leap of Time" theory. His thesis is that Israeli Jews now read Jewish history through "biblical spectacles" which were not available to his recent ancestors, who lived in certain circumstances of life so different from the characters of the biblical Israeli past. It was the Prime Minister's suggestion that the existence of modern Israel should also help scholars to understand the meaning and quality of past Jewish history in this land in a new light.

Actually, the scholarly discussions in the Congress did proceed to reveal how the past was being illuminated not only by current Israeli life, but by new scholarly discoveries. The discovery which attracted the most attention in the discussions was the Dead Sea Scrolls. All agreed that the full implications for history of the Dead Sea Scrolls were still uncertain. Most of the fragments found in the cave along the Dead Sea had not yet been put

111

together and translated. Yet there did seem to be one conclusion emerging out of the research so far. Jewish history of the pre-exilic period was not what we had thought it to be. "Judaism, the Dead Sea Scrolls show us, was much richer at one time in variety of sect than we had thought," was the expression of one noted scholar. Others went further, saying that what previously were thought to have been foreign importations into Judaism or pagan accretions, were now thought to have their origins within Jewish thought and life. For example, monasticism, doctrines about "salvation by faith" or salvation through the death of a "righteous man," might, in the light of the Dead Sea Scrolls, now be considered Jewish. A distinguished authority on Jewish mysticism, Gershom Scholem, declared that in his research on the origin of Gnostic theories he was now entertaining more strongly the possibility that these theories were not imported. Goodenough, a charming Yankee scholar from Yale, said that his research on Jewish symbolism also revealed that a limited picture of life in the Holy Land had been passed on to us by the Pharisaic scribes of the Talmud. They seemed to have simply censored the descriptions of the forms of Jewish life other than their own.

With or without Ben Gurion's advice there seemed to be a definite tendency on the part of the scholars to see pre-exilic life—especially that moment before the birth of Christianity—in a different light as a result of present-day research and understanding.

The second theme which Ben Gurion suggested to the scholarly conference was what he called "The riddle of Jewish survival."

Why, of all the peoples in the Near East, nothing has survived but inscriptions, *tels,* ruins, and temple remains; and their languages, literatures, and religions have vanished from the face of the earth—why the Jewish people alone has preserved its historic identity and preserved the power after thousands of years to ingather its scattered sons and help them strike new roots in its ancient homeland while maintaining its bond with modern culture—this was Ben Gurion's "riddle." The church would call it the mystery of Israel.

Seeing Bruno, Stiassny, and Roget chatting in the hallway

112

with some of the Little Sisters, I wondered again if they had ever thought of the history of Christianity in the land of Israel as a riddle or mystery. Why should a Christian find that what he sees in the Holy Land is a "needle to his faith?" Why, out of so many Carmelite monasteries, is the one on Mount Carmel seemingly the least attractive even to Carmelite monks? And the Benedictine monastery of Mount Zion, and the Church of the Holy Sepulchre, and the quality and commitment of religious life among the various Christian groups—why are they all so much less attractive here than in other lands?

The question may be broadened to include the past. Why, even when the dominant powers in this land were Christian, was the church too sterile to even produce a church historian? Why were the Crusades "a desecration of the Holy Spirit in God's name?" It is a riddle not easily resolved by claiming that the centers of culture after the birth of Christianity moved westward or that the Holy Land was impoverished by war and pushed to the byroads of civilization. Religious creativity has at times flourished in precisely such negative conditions, as the very birth of Christianity itself will testify. Nor is it to be resolved by pointing to a similar sterility in Moslem and Jewish associations with the Holy Land over the past two thousand years. These are also riddles.

To pose a riddle is to tempt an answer, though an answer to this kind of riddle can produce little more than a speculation—like the thought that historic Christianity did engage in a remarkably hasty "flight from origin."

The early Christian church did try to rid itself of its Jewish origin deliberately and swiftly. The language of Jesus was quickly replaced by Greek and Latin. The holidays celebrated by the Jew from Nazareth and the early Christians were changed— Saturday to Sunday, Shabuoth to Pentecost—and the reason openly stated: to distinguish the new faith from Judaism. Even the pictorial art of the church undertook to alter the physiognomy of Jesus and the Apostles, so that they no longer resembled the flesh-and-blood community from which they came. It was a conscious breaking out of the local, national envelope in which the Christian faith was born—a process not denied

113

by Christian historians. On the contrary, many of them would say the Christian faith had to burst from its parochial, local lineaments and appear to the world as a truly universal religion.

"When Paul did not desire to know Christ after the flesh," writes Albert Schweitzer, author of a historical biography of Jesus, "that was the first expression of the impulse of self-preservation by which Christianity continued to be guided for centuries—we have reason to be grateful to the early Christians that they handed down to us not biography, but Gospels."

Necessary or not, it was a flight from origin. And the question has often been asked even within the Christian church—how much of this flight from origin was also a flight from Jesus and his essential teachings, a flight from the primal Christian archetype?

But we ask something else. What can happen to Christianity when it, in a sense, returns to its origin? That, after all, is what does happen to Christians and Christianity in the Holy Land. It is, in many ways, a return to its original, local lineaments, to the original "envelope." In modern Israel a Christian cannot help but confront the physical features, the language, the landscape in which his faith was first clothed. The New Testament comes to life for him, just as the words of Isaiah or Joshua come to life for Ben Gurion.

Something else comes to life for a Christian in Israel—the Jewish people—and this is a phenomenon which can have disturbing implications for some Christian doctrines. The historic view of official Christianity toward the "Israel of the flesh," even as toward the land of Israel, is that they have served their historic purpose. The seed has given its flower. Why then need it blossom again? There is something disturbing in such a coming to life, for this Christian view. Hence the attempt to see the new Jewish State as an "historic anachronism," to quote Toynbee; for "a fossilized remnant of Syriac civilization," as Toynbee defines Judaism, is not supposed to show signs of vigorous creativity.

There is a Christianity which does prefer "graves to life," in the Holy Land. But is it only a Judaism "come to life" that bothers this kind of Christianity? May not the Christian's leap backward through time in modern Israel confront him with some-

114

thing in his own Christianity to which he may respond with anger? May there not be involved here something of Father Stiassny's theory of the archetype?

"Life for a Christian in the Holy Land makes him for Jesus and against Paul," says Martin Buber. Could we not add that it makes him "for Pelagius and against Augustine; for the Way of Nazareth followed by the Little Brothers and Sisters or the Protestant Darmstadt nuns, and against the lifeless, imported, cluttered Christianity of Nazareth's twenty-four churches; for the Messianic dream of a mankind and world utterly reborn and utterly new, and against the tired Levantine adjustment to life as it is and always has been. For it is not only Jews who take a "leap backward through time" in modern Israel. Is it too much to see such a leap through time also in the desire of priests to offer their missal in Hebrew, to celebrate Mass on the day Jesus called holy; on the part of Jewish converts to Christianity who insist that they remain Jews while believing in Jesus as the Messiah? And if the individuals we have spoken to succeed in attracting their brethren and colleagues to Israel from all over the world, where they can read the Bible and study the origins of their faith in its Jewish lineaments, what will be the effect on them of their new understanding of Christianity? It will, after all, be a Christianity again enveloped in its Jewish matrix. Some may call it a Judaization of Christianity. Others will insist that it is a Christianization, a strengthening of the historic Christian archetype as it reroots itself in the language, climate, and dust of its cradle soil.

There are, then, vital and fascinating currents of Christian ferment and thought beneath the seemingly barren surface of Israel's spiritual landscape. Perhaps even that religious dialogue for which Monsignor Vergani and others have yearned is also in process. But it is not a dialogue of words. Certainly, it has very little to do with the raucous exchanges between one and another Christian sect, or the charges and countercharges between government authorities and missionaries, or even the much publicized issues of church and state. It might better be described as a dialogue between a historic faith and a landscape.

"There are some landscapes," says an American teacher of religious philosophy, Henry Slonimsky, "which can evoke in an

115

observer the equivalent of the emotions that have been spilled out on their soil." They are "spatialized souls," so to speak, having the power to converse with us. Zion is certainly such a spatialized soul for Christians, and today it speaks in accents and sights which can engage Christianity in a dialogue with intriguing possibilities, in terms of its own self-understanding and vis-à-vis Judaism. Of course, a Christian may want to point out, Ben Gurion's "leap of time" would also bring back Jews to a point in history when Judaism was not yet separated from Christianity—or concerned about proving how different it was from Christianity, a concern it has had for the last two thousand years. But this is one of the thoughts we will save for our "digs" into the Jewish community of the new Israel.

CHAPTER VII

The Family that Never Returned

Quite frequently these days tourists visit the picturesque village of Pekiin, located high on a rocky slope of the barren Western Galilee hills. It is an ideal locale for those who seek authentic biblical scenery. They may stroll through its winding narrow streets, past courtyards where chickens, donkeys, and cows live comfortably with the human members of the household. On the roofs of the stone houses snuggled against the side of the mountain, oxen make interminable circles around ancient grindstones. Farmers pitch wheat against brisk mountain breezes with an art that not only permits the chaff to be blown away, but drops the remaining grain into carefully differentiated heaps. Besides biblical scenery, there is another reason for visiting Pekiin these days. We can meet there a Jewish family which claims never to have gone into exile. The fact that Joseph Zenati and his family never had to "return" to the land of their ancestors is a matter of pride both to Zenati and Israelis. It is a reminder that the thread of physical connection between the Jew and the land of Israel was at no time completely severed. There were centuries when this connection was quite tenuous, for example, the thirteenth century, when the Great Spanish rabbi Nachmonides reports, upon coming to the Holy Land, that only two or three Jewish families remain in Jerusalem. But during most of the two thousand years following the destruction of the Jewish state, rather substantial Jewish communities continued to live here. The elaborately carved pillars and stones of synagogues like the one at Capernaum are testimony that Jewish religious life in the Holy Land remained strong through the Byzantine period. After the Moslem conquest of Palestine in 636, the Jewish community enjoyed an even greater measure of religious toleration. The

117

sixteenth and seventeenth centuries saw an efflorescence of Jewish religious life in the Holy Land brought about by the influx of refugees from the Spanish Inquisition. During the eighteenth and nineteenth centuries the four holy cities, Safed, Tiberias, Jerusalem, and Hebron, contained substantial numbers of Jews. The thought that Jewish physical roots in the Holy Land were never completely severed is obviously important to a community which while asserting its belongingness in the land of Israel is, for the most part, made up of immigrants or the children of immigrants who have lived in other lands for almost two thousand years. Hence, the Zenati family of Pekiin, whose ancestors never left the Holy Land, is something of a museum piece which the Israeli government proudly presents to both Israelis and tourists.

Joseph Zenati is an elderly man, dark-visaged, short of stature, and scarcely distinguishable in appearance or dress from his Druse neighbors. An observer eager to find some particular characteristics in his face would have to settle for "something" about the old man's eyes. It is this something about the eyes, sadness, or perhaps a kind of pigmentation, to which researchers into the characteristics of Jewish physiognomy have been forced to resort after fruitless scientific measurements of skulls, noses, etc.

I too thought there might be something in the eyes of Zenati and his wife, but it may have been that they were simply old and in poor health. Not long after the old man had greeted me, he complained about his wife's dizzy spells, and asked if I had any pills which might help her. He told me this while taking me to the little synagogue for his usual lecture.

The village of Pekiin, he said, was mentioned in talmudic sources of the second and third centuries. Several famous rabbis were known to have come from it, and a small cave nearby was associated with the illustrious second-century rabbi Shimon Bar Yochai, to whom Cabalists attribute the authorship of the famous mystical treatise called the Zohar. Until the early 1930s, the old man explained, a number of Jewish families had lived in this village. The Druse had come here less than a hundred years ago, but during the Arab riots under the British Mandate

118

in the late twenties and thirties, most of the Jews had left. Apologetically, Zenati admitted that he too had left. But after the Israeli war, with the help of the government, he had returned.

"We must cling to every Jewish point in our land with our very teeth," the old man said with rhetorical passion. His son and daughter, though they worked in other places, still lived in Pekiin, and would continue to live there.

Zenati pointed to some granite blocks mounted in the walls of the synagogue. On them, carved in relief, were traditional Jewish symbols—the Holy Ark of the Temple, the citrus fruit, Esrog, and Lulav, palms for the festival of Sukkoth, and the Lion of Judah.

"When the first Temple was destroyed," explained Zenati, "the Jews fled to all corners of the land, and some came here. When the second Temple was destroyed, these stones fell to the ground. They remained on the ground until the establishment of the Jewish state. Now they have been put upright again." The synagogue itself was rebuilt in the nineteenth century with the help of wealthy Lebanese Jews, but it was on the site of a more ancient structure.

While Zenati was speaking to us, a gray-bearded old man in a torn, nondescript jacket and gray cap appeared at the door. He stood there for a moment, pressed his fingers on the mezuzah scroll in the frame of the doorway, then hobbled slowly toward the Ark in front of the little synagogue.

"My brother-in-law from Haifa," Zenati said. The old man stood quietly in front of the Ark for a few minutes, bowed, then walked out. He was still in the courtyard when I came out. His eyes, I noticed, were half blinded by cataracts. I asked him what prayer he had briefly offered before the Ark. The old man bowed his head gracefully.

"I prayed first for peace in Israel, and second, that He might return us with a complete returning."

"Return" is a key word in any delineation of Israel's contemporary spiritual physiognomy. The question as to whether the present-day physical return of Jews to Israel is the return envisaged by the Old and New Testaments, is the problem which agitates Christians who concern themselves with the mystery of

119

Israel. But it is also the same question which divides the Jewish community in modern Israel along religious and spiritual lines.

The classical or biblical definition of the word may be illustrated from the book of Deuteronomy.

"And thou shalt return unto the Lord thy God, and thou shalt listen to his voice, and all that I command you this day, you and your children with all of your heart and all of your soul. And the Lord shall return your exile and have mercy upon you, and return and gather you from among all peoples among whom God has scattered you. . . ."

This association of the physical return to the land with the spiritual return to God is constant through most of Jewish history—though the proportion of each element in the combination varied from time to time. When the Jews of fourth-century Jerusalem wrote to their brethren in Alexandria asking them to return, they were inviting them to move to the land of Zion. But the Cabalists of the fourteenth century, who tried to return through esoteric formulas, fasts, and mystical studies, had in mind a mystical Zion. From time to time, depending often on actual immigration possibilities, the proportion of earthly and heavenly Zion involved in the idea of return varied. But the essential connection between the two elements was never broken.

It was modern Zionism which in the nineteenth century suggested a break.

The full meaning of this radical change in meaning was disguised at first by a blurring of terminology. For example, Achad Haam (the pen name of Asher Ginzberg, influential nineteenth-century Zionist essayist) held that the purpose of the Jewish homeland in Palestine ought to be the creation of a Jewish spiritual center. But the spiritual center he had in mind was but vaguely connected with the holy laws and religious faith which was part of the traditional concept of return. Theodore Herzl, the founder of modern Zionism, plainly stated the reason that motivated modern Zionism—a reason which had little to do with God's covenant. It was to "solve the Jewish problem," namely, anti-Semitism. A Zionist philosopher like Jacob Klatzkin made the change which Zionism had brought about in the classical definition of return quite plain. "What is really new in Zionism

120

is its territorial-political definition of Jewish nationalism. Strip Zionism of the territorial principle, and you have destroyed its character and erased the distinction between it and the preceding periods. . . . In longing for our land, we do not desire to create there a base for the spiritual values of Judaism. To regain our land is for us an end in itself. . . ."

Actually, the motivations which brought the Jewish pioneers of the 1890s and the early twentieth century to Palestine were not as sharply different from previous immigrations as Klatzkin suggests. But there were religious Jews, including those who had come to settle in Palestine long before the launching of the Zionist movement in 1897, who saw little similarity between the return envisaged by modern Zionist pioneers and the "complete return" for which they had been praying. These Jews, who insisted on the old concept of return, were called by the new settlers the "old Yishuv," the old community. In the eyes of the newcomers, the members of the old Yishuv were indeed *B'nai Mata*—children of death, as the Arabs called them, seeing that their main concern in the Holy Land was to wail at the graves of their ancestors, and to be themselves buried there.

In the eyes of the old Yishuv the new settlers, the "new Yishuv," were not only perverting the traditional meaning of the return to Zion, but by their ideas and way of life even preventing this complete return from coming about.

Basically, this difference of opinion still divides Israel's modern Jewish community. The old Yishuv insists that a return to the land of Israel must involve a return to God and the sacred Law. The leaders of the new Yishuv, though no longer young, are still loyal to the definition of a return envisioned by Achad Haam and Theodore Herzl. During the last forty or fifty years another point of view toward the meaning of return has become popular, especially among the sabras, who themselves never had to think of returning. This latter group finds the whole discussion over the meaning of the return quite pointless. It is into these three groups that we will divide the present-day community of Israel for our proposed "digs."

CHAPTER VIII

The Old Yishuv: A Look from Within

> We have been told that there is a "present world" and a
> "world to come." That there is a "world to come" we must
> believe, for that is our faith. And maybe someplace there
> is a "present world,"—though I am sure it could not be
> this hell we are living in now.
>
> —*Rabbi Nachman of Bratzlav*

Meah Shearim and the Dead Hasidim

The stronghold of the old Yishuv, the pre-Herzlian section of
the Jewish community, is a narrow, winding street called Meah
Shearim, the Hundred Portions, after a phrase in the Bible which
was read in the synagogue in the week when the foundations for
its first houses were laid almost one hundred years ago. Meah
Shearim is a standard stop in any Holy Land tour, I assured a
group of American tourists one summer afternoon. Its three or
four thousand inhabitants offered a visitor a glimpse of what was
probably the most intense concentration of Jewish Orthodoxy in
the world. The particular group we were going to visit on the
street was especially interesting because of their devotion to a
man whose thought was an example in its most extreme form, of
the classical religious attitude toward the Holy Land. Rabbi Nachman, whose followers we were going to meet, died 150 years ago,
in the Ukrainian town of Uman. "In the land of Israel," he
taught, "even the direction of a stick lying on the ground has
significance." A few years before his death Rabbi Nachman
made a pilgrimage to the land of Israel, a visit replete with
strange episodes which were faithfully recorded by his disciples.

123

The descendants of these disciples are today called the "Dead Hasidim."

Hasidism is a mystical movement which originated in eighteenth-century Eastern Europe, and emphasized the importance of the spiritual leader, whom they called the rebbe. To his followers, the rebbe was their guide, their counselor, ultimate authority and living embodiment of the Torah—the sacred teachings by which they lived. What makes the followers of Rabbi Nachman, Dead Hasidim is that they have had no rebbes since Rabbi Nachman. Before his death Nachman had told them: "My light will glow till the days of the Messiah," a statement which they interpreted to mean that they would never have to appoint another rebbe. Today, these Hasidim still speak of Rabbi Nachman in the present tense, read and reread his writings and stories with ever-deepening sighs of astonishment and admiration, and believe that their dead leader is "present" when they pray or study together. In the synagogue we were about to visit was a black wooden chair, whose intricate carvings are marred by scratches and cracks. Some years ago this chair was broken into little pieces and smuggled over the borders of Russia into Israel by followers of the dead but "present" rebbe.

I wanted to say something more to the tourists about the particular group we were going to visit in Meah Shearim, but through the revolving glass doors of the King David Hotel I could see our guide Arele waiting. Arele was about seventeen years old, and the earlocks which descended from under his round black hat reached down to his shoulders. Seeing him there carefully averting his eyes from the female passers-by, I reminded the ladies that the synagogues of Meah Shearim were male domains. Some of them had balconies or sections where women could sit and not be seen by the men, but this might not be the case in the synagogue where we were going, and they might have to wait outside.

"Don't worry," the women assured me. They would take it all in good fun. Besides, they had prepared themselves by putting on long-sleeved dresses and covering their hair with kerchiefs.

It was late afternoon and the sunlight, so blinding during most of the summer day, was beginning to mellow and bring out

124

golden and pink tints in the granite stone of Jerusalem's buildings. Against the houses we were passing, the walls of the Old City of Jerusalem appeared in sharp outline. To the right, near Mount Zion, the geometrically squared walls ended and we could see the undulating, gray-white hills of the Judean desert, frozen in barrenness. Beyond them was the high purple mass of Moab, on the other side of the Jordan River.

Arele saw me looking toward the desert. Rabbi Nachman, he told me, had taught his followers to make a special place in their spiritual life for the desert.

"Often after prayer we go out in groups to waste places as our rebbe—our spiritual leader—instructed us. We keep at least twenty paces from each other and have a *schmoos*—a discussion with God. You know—he asks us what we have done, whether we have been honorable Jews, and we make an accounting of soul." Arele's eyes shone happily as he told about one man in the Yeshiva—the House of Study—who got up every morning at three o'clock and stood for hours in *hitbod'dut*—in solitude. "We can hear his groans and sighs for hours. Or sometimes, we pray near fields. Our rebbe told us "it is good to be pious among them—the grass and trees."

I transmitted the information I had just received to my tourist friends, who did not seem overimpressed. Meditation alone or in the presence of nature is, after all, not an unusual religious expression in Western civilization. But against the background of Orthodox Judaism, as Arele knew, it represented a revolutionary departure from tradition.

"He who rises at night to walk alone is guilty with his soul" warns a basic rabbinic text. Jewish tradition fears the destructive or self-indulgent possibilities of monastic religiosity.

Bialik, a modern Hebrew poet, himself somewhat rebellious against the tendency of rabbinic Judaism to discourage direct connections with the world of nature, tries to explain that once the Jew had lost his natural habitat of survival, that is, his own land, all that he could count on to preserve his group entity was the "four corners of the Law"—his sacred books. These became his portable land and government, his central instrument for historic survival. The temptation to leave this artificial source of national life and become rooted in the actual space dimensions of the land in which he lived was always a strong pull, and surrender to this attraction would have meant assimilation. Consequently even the language of the Jew in the Diaspora became "denaturized." Loose generic appellations like "tree" or "bird" take the place of the sharp, concrete terminology of nature found in the Bible. Only the sacred Law is clear, meticulously defined. Everything else—the physical world of nature, the non-Jewish population—is pushed into a rather blurred periphery.

Rabbi Nachman's insistence, therefore, on the necessity of periods of religious solitude among trees and grass was somewhat at variance with the Orthodox world into which he was born. But this rapport with nature was in the tradition of his great-grandfather, the Baal Shem-Tov, who is recognized as the founder of Hasidism. The Baal Shem-Tov was born Israel, the son of Eliezer. As a child, he was said to have often fled the little schoolhouse where he studied, in order to meditate alone in the forest. This attachment to nature was felt by his great-grandson, Rabbi Nachman, though the latter's relationship to nature and to life in general was quite complex. Though, like the Baal Shem-Tov, Nachman spoke often about the importance of joy, he was personally drawn from his youth to a morbid kind of mysticism which at one time expressed itself in an attempt to eat in such a fashion as to avoid tasting his food. Rabbi Nachman, when searching for the holy joy which was the central teaching of Hasidism, had to overcome the involutions of a character which nowadays might be called manic-depressive. Paradox was the essence of Nachman's mystical teaching—joy through despair, wisdom through the attainment of a "cow-like" simple faith.

I would have liked to discuss the paradoxes of Rabbi Nachman's faith with Arele, but we were soon approaching Meah Shearim. To tourists, Meah Shearim appears to be a thoroughly homogeneous community. Most of the men there wear broad-brimmed hats, sometimes trimmed with fur, and all the ladies are clothed in uniform-like loose-fitting dresses with long sleeves and their heads are covered with either wigs or kerchiefs. The lives of its inhabitants are homogeneous in the sense that all

Orthodox Jews submit their lives to a pattern outlined by 613 commandments derived from the Bible, and hundreds of other laws and customs authorized by rabbinic authorities of later generations. To the sophisticated eyes of an insider like Arele, however, this apparently homogeneous Orthodox world of the old Yishuv dissolves into dozens of sub-worlds, each of them vastly different in historic origin, religious custom, even dress and facial feature. There is, first of all, here as in all Israel, the major division between Ashkenazim, meaning communities of European origin, and Sephardim, Jews who originate from lands about the Mediterranean. The latter group are, as might be expected, usually of darker complexion and their Hebrew pronunciation reflects the Arabic environment. After only a few moments of observation it is apparent that these broad divisions are themselves broken down into communities easily distinguished from each other. The Jew from Turkey and the recent immigrant from the Atlas mountains of Morocco are both classed as Sephardim, but they clearly reflect the separation of geography, language, local custom, and even racial admixture. Another way of categorizing the Jews who come from the Near East is "Oriental," but actually the small-bodied, fine-featured Yemenite has little in common with the husky Kurd whose wife still bears the tattoo marks popular in her native Iraquian village. In the European Ashkenazic community, there are also differences stemming from diverse geographic orientations—Polish, Hungarian, Russian, etc. A further fragmentation within each of the geographic communities occurs along religious lines. For example, a black silk cord tied around a long frock coat immediately informs Arele that the wearer is a Hasid. That is, a follower of the mystical movement which originated during the eighteenth and nineteenth centuries in the villages of the Ukraine. If the wearer of this belt or *gartel,* as Hasidim call it, has pushed the cuffs of his pants into white stockings, chances are that he is not only a Hasid but a follower of the Gerer rebbe—a specific group of Hasidim famous for their military-like discipline. Gerer Hasidim line up in ranks like soldiers for inspection by their rebbe. Occasionally some bearded Jew who may or may not be a Hasid is recognized by Arele as a member of the Neturai Karta, the

"Guardians of the Wall," a group famous for their aggressively antagonistic attitude toward the Israeli government, which they look upon as an "abomination."

As we walked through Meah Shearim, evidence of the war constantly going on between the more fanatic Orthodox groups and the rest of Israel appeared all about us. A large banner strung across the street had shrieking black letters which I translated for our group: "Daughter of Israel, dress modestly, do not desecrate the Holy Law." The ladies smiled and pulled their shawls tighter about their shoulders. There were other black signs in the street, pasted along the walls of the houses, but they used less gentle language, and I didn't translate them. Some called out anathemas upon members of the female sex who "dressed like men" or "harlots" with low-cut clinging dresses. One recently pasted poster put up by the followers of the Gerer rebbe directed dire threats at Benjamin Mintz, a former follower of the Gerer rebbe who dared to ignore his spiritual leader's command and joined the government of "that cursed one" whose name the sign would not even deign to mention. The "cursed one" was, of course, Ben Gurion, the "reviler of the Torah," and other juicy epithets according to the sign. Another large placard signed by the Society of Sephardic Jews wanted to tell everybody of their contempt for Rabbi Nissim, the Chief Rabbi of the Sephardic community, who was then engaged in a struggle for power with the late Rabbi Toledano, also a Sephardic Jew and the Minister for Religion at that time.

I asked Arele if he was troubled by all the controversy. He smiled cheerfully. "We are used to *machloket*—controversy," Arele said, his eyes twinkling. "Our rebbe used to say, 'Out of the stones that are thrown at us, we will build houses.'"

No doubt to young lads like Arele in Meah Shearim the nightly rush to paste placards on the walls was exciting, offering them the emotional equivalent of the bravery and tension which other Israeli lads enjoyed on border patrols. To visitors, however, the exchange of insults and anathemas emanating from this section of Jerusalem appeared to do anything but "sanctify the Name." I was glad that my own American friends were unable to read the placards we were passing. I wanted them to see some-

128

thing of Meah Shearim other than the well-publicized religious struggles.

The synagogue to which Arele led us was at the end of the famous street, only a few yards away from the Jordanian border. It was a rather large, concrete structure, seemingly unfinished. The women in the group waited outside, while the men entered with Arele. Within, the unpainted walls were bare except for some cards with different Hebrew inscriptions, each beginning with the word *shiviti,* from Psalm 16:8 ("I have placed the Lord always before me"). This is a traditional bit of synagogue decoration, but of special significance for Hasidim. The pseudepigraphic "will of the Baal Shem-Tov" opens with an interpretation of the word *shiviti.* It comes, says the author, from the Hebrew word *hishtachavut,* which connotes the quality of equanimity. He who can rise to the level of always placing the Lord before him will find that all other matters in the world are relatively unimportant. Health and sickness, richness and poverty would become as equal from the perspective of the only true reality of the world, God.

From the perspective of American tourists, however, there seemed to be very little equanimity in the mood of these men praying in the synagogue. Everyone seemed to be in motion, either nodding rhythmically as they sat on benches near long tables, walking about, or rocking back and forth near a pillar or corner. Diversity of dress, posture, and even rate of prayer seemed to be the rule. Some of the children had crewcuts under their little black skull caps, with long side locks emerging incongruously in front of the ears of their bare heads and reaching down to their shoulders. A few of the older boys were dressed in miniature imitation of their fathers, long frock coats and heavy fur-brimmed hats. What confused the tourists most was the apparent disorder of prayers. Everybody seemed to be working on his own, some chanting, others mumbling, whispering, or shouting forth their words. An outburst of protracted clapping from one corner of the synagogue brought further bewilderment to the eyes of the visitors. Interspersed among the jumbled murmur of prayers were deep groans and sighs. A sudden shriek as if of

129

pain came from a man rocking back and forth near a concrete pillar.

"I thought he had hit his head against the pillar," one of the Americans whispered with relief when he saw that the man who had uttered the scream was continuing his prayer. "Why," asked the tourist, looking at the motley dress of the Hasidim, the unpainted walls of the synagogue, and the books lying in disarray on the rough wooden tables, "does holiness have to be associated with dirt?"

Unexpectedly the disordered variety of prayers merged into a common silence as everyone in the room rose for the standing prayer. All was quiet now in the synagogue, though from time to time the clapper in the corner would burst forth in a new swell of emotion. Occasionally there was a bit of hand-clapping from other corners, but more moderate in sound and of briefer duration.

When the silent prayer was finished, Arele came over. "You see how prayer is here." His eyes glowed happily. "A man starts talking with the Master of the Universe and the One Above asks him what he did this week, and what he didn't do. The man remembers, groans, stretches out his hands, and asks God to forgive him and bring him close again—you see how it is here?"

One of the tourists tugged my sleeve. His son had just come into the synagogue with an urgent message from the ladies outside. We were to come out immediately. We walked out to find the women drawn up as if in battle array, their faces cold with fury and disgust. Gone was the good-natured tolerance and sportsmanship they had taken into Meah Shearim. In a controlled but thoroughly angry voice, one of the women related what had happened. After standing a few minutes outside of the synagogue, one of their group had suggested that they enter through a side door into a corner of the synagogue, which was shut off by wooden partitions from the rest of the room and was apparently meant for women. The ladies had followed her into this section of the room. In a few minutes another of the ladies had decided that there could be no harm in opening the door a crack so that they could peek into the synagogue and at least see the famous chair of Rabbi Nachman. She had swung the

130

door open a bit, and it had been slammed back in her face by one of the Hasidim on the other side. Indignantly she had opened it again, whereupon the man on the other side had spat on her. The women had seen enough of Meah Shearim and wanted to leave immediately, they informed their husbands. Judging by the expression on their faces, they were not going to be appeased. The spitting incident had brought to the surface historical resentments which were no laughing matter. The cover had been ripped from the male arrogance of a religion which legally categorized women with idiots and fools, segregated them as unclean during their periods of menstruation, put them behind curtains in the synagogue, and commanded a man to say a blessing every day over the fact that he was not born a woman. It was actually a form of reverse lewdness, one of the ladies suggested. Rather ungallantly one of the husbands began to laugh—a mistake, for his wife proceeded to march away toward the border. For a moment the ranks of the men held, then they broke, and followed the women into the more "civilized" area of Jerusalem. I was left alone with Arele, who had not followed the English exchange but sensed what had happened.

"We have some *takiffin*—some strong ones—here," he agreed, shaking his head. "But stay a bit more, soon we are going to study the writings of the rebbe," he promised. Have you ever heard prayer like this before, prayer with sweetness and *hitlavut*— flame?"

When I returned to the synagogue with Arele the men were already seated around a long wooden table, waiting while a black-bearded man with thick-lensed glasses leafed through the pages of a large folio. On either side of him sat white-bearded men, one of them with most delicate, translucent features, eyes closed as in contemplation. Now, at closer range, faces which had previously seemed like anonymous blurs behind their beards and under their large hats began to appear in concrete outline. They were strong faces, individual, and intelligent most of them, often with a humorous glint in the eye. Room was made for me on one of the benches, and somebody brought me a book. A black-bearded elder was turning the pages of a book and humming. He had come out of Russia just two years ago, Arele

131

whispered to me. The reader sighed twice and began to read the Hebrew text of a collection of laws compiled by Nathan, a pupil of Rabbi Nachman. I was sorry that the tourists had left, for the fading light of the Sabbath, the rapt expression on the faces of the listeners, and the gentle chant of the reading combined to produce an air of spirituality which even a visitor from abroad could sense. On the other hand, I was glad that no American friends were present to understand the subject of the reading, which dealt with the dangers of *nieuf*, a term that technically means adultery, but in rabbinic literature is extended to all kinds of illicit sexuality.

"The root of all sins," went the passage we were reading, was *nieuf*. And it went on to talk about the danger of salacious talk and nocturnal seminal emissions. At one point the reader paused to make a comment about the dangers which beset religious Jews these days.

"When a person goes to war he trains himself how to avoid a wound or a blow, but there can be a blow also to the sight, a wound in the soul resulting from what one sees. Today when one goes to a market place and sees the way women dress, we expose ourselves to such blows. Therefore we have to prepare ourselves as carefully as those who go to war."

Was it possible that he had selected this passage deliberately because of what had happened in the synagogue with the American women? But no, the Sabbath discussions followed a previously arranged order. The image of Orthodox Jews fighting a battle was fitting to the predicament of Meah Shearim. They were, after all, an island of life and ideas surrounded by standards of morality and secularism which could, unless a wall were raised against them, quickly inundate their community. As to the subject of *nieuf*—fornication—a large part of the Cabala, the Jewish mystical teaching, from which Hasidism draws deeply, was concerned with sex. Of course, the sex act like all earthly events was but an allusion to great cosmic acts of unity and creation.

Since acts "below" were not only allusions to what was happening above but also affected these happenings, a man's seminal emission was not therefore to be considered an unimportant

132

event. Just as the act of physical union must be preceded by certain kinds of thoughts, so must the act of emission also have origin in thoughts—the wrong kind—and a man is responsible for his thoughts as for his deeds, according to Rabbi Nachman. A man's thoughts are in turn stimulated by what he sees and does, therefore he ought to keep his eyes averted from women.

I wondered if the women would have felt less insulted if they had known that the Hasid who spat at them had something much bigger in mind than thwarting their curiosity.

The reader finally left the subject of *nieuf* and went on to an entirely different theme—one also frequently discussed in the Cabala—the connection between the "fruit and the shell." In Jewish mystical terminology the shell refers to the external, the rigid and harsh. It may be the external form of the law, the necessity of saying no in order to achieve a structure in life, the act of limitation which must accompany the "giving" act if there is to be a lasting form. The point Rabbi Nachman wanted to make was that those who think they can "eat the fruit" without encountering the external *klipah*—shell—will miss both the fruit and the shell. Those who looked upon the structured life of the Jews in Meah Shearim, the "yoke" of 613 commandments, the negative prohibition of Judaism as needless "externals" unnecessary for "inner" spiritual life were making the mistake of trying to find a fruit which did not have a surrounding shell.

The Sabbath was over by now, but Hasidim, reluctant to part with "the Queen," stretch out its holiness by saying the concluding prayer as late as possible. I told Arele I would have to go now.

"Still," he insisted, "you must say the concluding prayers of the Sabbath. Here, I will take you to a place where you won't have to wait."

There was no refusing Arele, and we walked through the streets of Meah Shearim alongside houses still dark, whose occupants were also stretching out the Sabbath, refusing to put on electric lights. From within one house completely without lights we heard voices in prayer and song.

"He has seventeen children," explained Arele, "and can form

his own minyan [quorum of ten], so that he doesn't have to go to a synagogue."

We turned into a small alley where two small synagogues faced each other.

"Come in—the next minyan is now forming," called out a young man from one of them. Within two minutes a dozen men had joined us. The Sabbath prayers were quickly recited. As I walked out, the next prayer quorum started forming.

Arele explained that anyone in Meah Shearim who needed to say their prayers in a hurry could come to this synagogue. It was, so to speak, set aside for a quick spiritual ascent and indeed I had the feeling of having just left an elevator.

Arele insisted on walking with me up the hilly street toward the center of Jerusalem. We passed a black station wagon standing in a side street.

"Do you know what that is?" Arele asked cheerfully. "That's the hearse of the Chevra Kedisha—the burial society. At the end of the Sabbath they come around and take out all the bodies that have died during the Sabbath." Without altering his pleasant expression, Arele regaled me with a story about a member of the Chevra Kedisha who had once remained at the cemetery at night after having buried somebody. There he had seen the way the *shadim*—devils—had come and beaten the dead man with iron chains and whips for his sins.

"The sight was terrible," said Arele happily.

Incidentally, Thursday night I could come with the Hasidim, if I would, to visit the grave of King David on Mount Zion. Bratzlaver Hasidim were always visiting the graves of Jewish saints, Arele told me.

"Once a year we hire a bus to make the graves of all the holy ones in Israel. Of course, in Europe we visited the grave of the rebbe, as he commanded us. Do you know what he said? 'If you come to me and say prayers over my grave, I will stretch myself this way and that way, and pull you out by your very earlocks from the gates of sin.' Ah, he was *gewaldig*, a tremendous man. You know what he always used to say? '*Gewald* —Jews—do not despair.' And he used to stretch out the word *gewald* so that it would include future generations."

134

Gewaldig might be translated as powerful, enormous, vehemently forceful, even ferocious. It is this kind of power one senses in Rabbi Nachman, strangely coupled with the most exquisite and delicate spirituality. Power and gentle delicacy—additional extremes which can be added to the long list of opposites that consorted in the soul of this spiritual genius—a genius in whom the traditional mystic yearnings of Judaism for the land of Israel reached their apogee.

He was born in 1772 in the city of Miedzbosz, where his famous great-grandfather died. Even as a child, writes Buber, Nachman was already engaged in "strenuous seeking and searching." He would visit the grave of the Baal Shem-Tov and lie there for hours. He sometimes engaged in long fasts.

This is Nachman's essential teaching—a constant insistence that the "troughs" of life are given us in order that we may utilize them for new liftings of the spirit, and the conviction that in this constant effort we find our fulfillment and connect up with the deepest will of the universe, for even nature has its periods both of barrenness and flowering.

As Nachman himself says, there is nothing original about his teaching. What gives it power in the lives of his followers is its life embodiment in Nachman, who struggled all his life with his own "fallings."

There is, Nachman says, a kind of man whose soul must wax and wane like the moon. He himself was such a "moon" personality, fated forever to alternate between periods of contraction and growth. This rhythmic experience with a contraction verging on self-annihilation comes to its most extreme manifestation in Nachman's life with an experience that he considers to be the climax of his days, his trip to the Holy Land.

Rabbi Nachman's attachment to the land of Israel is also *gewaldig*—fierce—expressing in its most extreme form the feelings of historic Judaism for its ancestral homeland.

"The virtue of the land of Israel is great and wondrous beyond grasping, and the praise of its holiness we can see in all of Torah from beginning to end. . . . And every blessing which the Name, be it blessed, made to our Fathers, to Abraham, Isaac and Jacob, was at its center a promise of inheriting the land. The redemption from Egypt, led by Moses our teacher, was to grant us the privilege of coming to Israel. Our Sages, too, have expressed in great detail their opinion about the high level which occurs to one who dwells there, or even walks four paces there. Hence, if a man believe in truth and the holiness of the law, even in the smallest part of what it really is, he would certainly run and fly to the land of Israel and permit no obstacle to stand in his way."

When Rabbi Nachman hinted to his followers that he had determined to actually go to Israel, they tried to dissuade him. The way was dangerous and long. There was no money for the journey, nor for the sustenance of his family while he was gone. "And who will be our rabbi?" they pleaded. Nachman would not be deterred.

"Because of my love for you, I will be even closer to you there than here," he told his Hasidim. When his wife heard of his decision, she sent one of their daughters to cry to her father, "Who will support us?"

"You will go to your in-laws," replied the Rabbi, who taught that the world is sustained by the quality of mercy. "Your older sister will be a servant, your younger sister will receive charity, and your mother will be a cook. Everything in the house I will sell to get money for the journey." His answer was received with fresh outbursts of tears. All that Nachman would reply was, "It cannot be otherwise. The greatest part of me is already there—and according to law, the minority must follow the majority."

For a man who claimed that the world was sustained by mercy, it seemed like a ruthless attitude. But many a modern pioneer to Israel remembers the "ruthlessness" which preceded his decision to separate himself from his family and follow his inner compulsion to go to the land of Israel.

Ostensibly, Theodore Herzl's reasons for a Jewish state also had little to do with religious or spiritual goals. He presented his

136

Zionism as an opportunity for counteracting anti-Semitism by "normalizing" the condition of the Jewish people and providing a place of refuge for those who had no home elsewhere. Many of those who came to the first collective settlements during the early part of this century used revisionist-Marxist ideology to explain their "ascent." Israel was going to give them an opportunity to correct the topsy-turvy economic pyramid of the Jewish people and create a genuine proletariat which could then contribute to the march of world socialism. But underneath all these pseudo-historic explanations pulsed ideas which have been at the center of the Jewish religion since its inception.

"We have come to the land to build and be rebuilt," sang the early pioneers of the famous Second Aliyah in 1904–05. At heart the singers believed that the coming together of the land of Israel and the people of Israel was not to be an ordinary historic happening similar to the meeting of other peoples with new lands of residence. It was involved with a spiritual and cosmic mystery as well as with current historic problems of anti-Semitism. In essence the belief was that the coming together of Jews and Israel meant a releasing of life springs in the land and the Jewish people, and even in the world, which were otherwise fated to be sealed. It was, in fact, the old Messianic faith in modern garb, the belief that when they returned to their land, life was not going to be as it had been in the past. Great changes were to be effected, in the personal life of each individual, in the life of the Jewish community, and through their example in the life of the world.

In a sense the land of Israel was supposed to do for the self-proclaimed secular Jews of the modern Zionist era what the Tsaddik, according to Rabbi Nachman, was to do for his followers. It was to give them the proper *tikkun*, the "fixing up" which each soul needed for its fulfillment. Like the Tsaddik, the land of Israel was going to bring each life an increase of truth, a clarification of purpose, and a higher quality of interior life and human relations. It was to remake the Jewish community so that it would fulfill the prophetic dream of being a "light to the Gentiles." One does not have to dig very far below the speeches and thought of

137

the pioneer ideologies to detect these old Jewish ideas. But for many of them, as for Rabbi Nachman, there came a time when their dreams had to face realities.

It is always a painful struggle, this confrontation of one's dream with the reality. It was painful for the Hasidim of Nachman's day when they came to Israel. It was painful for the immigrants who came in 1905 and in the early years of the 1920s. It remains a painful adjustment for today's immigrant. Somehow the actual smell of perspiration in a hot climate—or the appearance of the Jordan river, or the visits to the holy tombs—are not what was expected. Often the reality of life in the Holy Land appears to be less spiritual, more prosaic even than life in the Exile. The battle which has to be waged by each person is how to meet this apparent contradiction and not be broken by it.

Nachman's pilgrimage to the Holy Land is a strange experience, filled from beginning to end with phenomena which astound his followers, and which he himself never fully explains. Yet there is something about Nachman's aliyah, his ascent to the Holy Land, which may express though in different terminology and through the psychological spectrum of a mystical "moon" personality, the adjustment problems of even modern immigrants to Israel.

While passing through Constantinople, he shocked the Jewish community by removing his outer rabbinic garb and running barefooted in the streets, where he played with little children at a game of cops and robbers. On another occasion he disguised his identity to questioners. When after many harrowing incidents he finally arrived in Haifa, his first steps on holy soil were accompanied by a "joy beyond description," but a few hours later he announced to the Hasidim who had come to greet the great-grandson of the Baal Shem-Tov, "I have accomplished that for which I came," and said that he wished to leave the Holy Land immediately. He even refused to visit the holy tombs or to journey to Jerusalem, and it was only the anguished pleading of the Palestine Hasidim that persuaded him to stay. He began traveling about the land, but still avoided Jerusalem. Despite

138

the repeated requests of the Hasidim who flocked to greet him, he would not—or could not—teach. Once in Tiberias he was about to reveal a great mystery concerning the phylacteries, but as he opened his mouth he began coughing blood and was unable to go on. Before a year had passed he left Palestine, on a return voyage also filled with great difficulties.

For some time after his return to Bratzlav, Nachman hardly mentioned his trip. Later, he said, "Everything I learned before my visit to the land of Israel was as nothing," and, on another occasion, "Wherever I travel, I still travel to Israel." But soon after his return Nachman's illness—probably consumption—became more severe. There were more periods of "smallness" and "falling," but there were also new beginnings and ascents.

Nachman was forty years old when he died in 1812—truly a *gewaldige* man. A few years before his death he suddenly announced to his followers, "And now, I will begin to tell stories."

The stories of Rabbi Nachman of Bratzlav, Buber has suggested, are a new kind of literary genre. They have been compared with Kafka's literary creations. The plots and characters move on a human plane but at all times involve several levels of meaning. Poetry, ethical observations, shrewd psychological insights and Cabalistic formulas are blended with a skill and structure quite amazing in view of the fact that these stories were told orally and often on spontaneous impulse.

The stories—only thirteen were preserved in print—were recorded by Nachman's famous disciple, Nathan of Nemiroff. Their themes are rather similar. They deal with something which is lost, not in its proper place, stolen or captured. Children go astray in the forest, a king's daughter is kept prisoner in a mountain fortress, two birds who are meant for each other live at opposite ends of the world—and the plot evolves out of the search to adjust what has been put out of place, to redeem what has been lost—the theme of redemption, the search for the "adjustment" which in Hasidic terminology is called the *tikkun*. There is also a similarity in the characters. There are usually opposites, like the wise man and the simpleton or the weak beggar and the powerful hero. A poetic passage from the famous story "The Seven Beggars" has often been translated:

139

And there is a mountain
And on the mountain is a stone
And from the stone there goes forth a well,
And everything has a heart.
The world as a whole too has a heart. . . .
And this mountain on which rests the stone
From which goes forth the well,
Stands on one side of the world.
But the heart of the world
Is placed on the other side of the world.
And the heart which is placed opposite the well
Is drawn towards and yearns greatly
To come to the well.
The well also greatly desires the heart. . . .

This passage like most others in Nachman's stories cannot be understood without knowledge of the Cabalistic symbols referred to by "heart" and "mountain" and "well." But Nachman warns against interpreting the tales, though his disciple Nathan does offer some hints of their Cabalistic meaning. The stories are profounder than all the interpretations, on the level almost of Scripture, whose depths can never be drained. Better to read them without interpretations, say Bratzlaver Hasidim. But, as I discovered on Sabbath morning, they do not take their own advice.

When I came to the synagogue in Meah Shearim that Sabbath morning, the service was well along. Everyone was doing their "work of the heart"—prayer—in their own individualistic ways. Again there were the occasional outbursts of hand-clapping and groans, but this time I did not find it disturbing to the subdued yet bright mood of the Sabbath service. By 10 A.M. the prayers had ended and the men began to fold their prayer shawls. A lad with shaved head and long earlocks walked about and gave out some small books which the congregants immediately opened and began reading. The book was called a *tikkun*—the word we have before translated as a "fixing up" or "adjustment." The title page explained that this particular *tikkun* was designed for the "covenant"—a euphemistic term referring to the male sex organ.

The introduction to the Psalms reminded the readers that the "thought was also a deed" and sinful thoughts of concupiscence were not to be regarded lightly, "since man can, if he wishes, control his thoughts by deliberate effort." If then he has had a seminal emission during the night, though it may sometimes be a meaningless accident like one who urinates, chances were that it was really preceded by some impure thoughts. In any case, whatever evil thoughts slipped by the effort of a human being to turn from them could be "fixed up" by the heartfelt recital of these ten Psalms. They were to be spoken as "one speaks his heart to a dear friend." About me I could hear the Hasidim quietly chanting the Psalms, which Rabbi Nachman had chosen and which were among the most beautiful in the Bible. Again I thought of the skin-and-fruit problem. There did seem to be an almost perverse juxtaposition of elements here—high and low—deeply spiritual outpourings and seminal emissions.

Following the reading of the *tikkun,* some of the men left the synagogue. One tall young Hasid with a full black beard and dark, expressive eyes walked to the door, saw me, and walked back to wish me a good Sabbath. About twenty men remained and sat down about a wooden table near the Ark. Wine and bread were passed about, first to the man with the thick eye-glasses who was evidently going to read, then to others. Some of the little children in the synagogue were called over by their fathers to participate in the Blessing. It occurred to me that the scene of men sitting about the table breaking bread and wine could not be much different in appearance from the actual Last Supper of Jesus and his Disciples, though it would be hard to recognize the resemblance from the pictures of this scene as it has been recorded by Christian artists. Again, the black-bearded leader preceded his reading with sighs. They were sighs not of sadness, of course, but of joy—the joy of meeting again with that which is so good, so "sweet," as Arele would say.

The special prayer ordered for those about to read the stories of Rabbi Nachman was, I assumed, said quietly by each person. Then the reader began in the middle of a story—the tales of Rabbi Nachman were obviously read in sequence. It was the tale about a Master of Prayer, and there was no need to re-

141

capitulate what had gone before to the Hasidim, who sat now quietly attentive.

The portion being read this Sabbath told about the encounter of this "Baal T'Filah," this Master of Prayer (a term Nachman uses to describe the Tsaddik or rebbe), with groups of people who had decided to choose kings for themselves. The logical way to choose a king, they had decided, would be to find one who, by personal example, exemplified the *tachlit,* the main good of life.

"One group," read the man with the thick glasses in Hebrew, "decided that the *tachlit* of life was to get honor . . . for not only during his life, but even after his death, a man cares for his honor and reputation." The Hasidim around the table nodded and the reader interrupted himself to quote the talmudic axiom "He who pursues honor—honor flees from him."

"A second group," he went on, "held that killing was the main purpose of existence." Proof for their view was the fact that everything, "people, animals, plants, grass were finally annihilated—hence the end of everything was destruction."

"There are lands today like that," an elderly man who had recently arrived from Russia said cheerfully.

In this way, with occasional interruptions and meaningful sighs, the reader managed to get through a few more paragraphs of the story, telling about other groups, who tried to pick for their kings exemplars of wisdom, of beauty, of the ability ". . . to talk a lot, even of joy. The latter group settled on a foolish drunkard and went to settle in a country where they had five vineyards. Despite their efforts, they had a hard time rejoicing because they didn't have much about which to rejoice."

"Of course," pointed out the reader, "if one wants to know to which kingdom he belongs, he need only ask himself, 'What do I consider an important day?' If it is a day on which he has made a lot of money, then he belongs to the kingdom of wealth. If his important day means an occasion when he received plaudits and honors, then his kingdom is the one of honor. If, on the other hand, his great day is one which was filled with prayer and good deeds, then he belongs to still another kingdom. But the point of what we have been reading is to tell us that the Master of Prayer was able to come to each of these various

142

kingdoms and through his prayer show them how to bring their conception of truth to a higher level. For there is a truth in each of the conceptions held by the people of these kingdoms, only it is not the whole truth. A real Master of Prayer is one who does not deny the truth that a person sees, but shows him a way of including it within the larger and greater truth. This was Rabbi Nachman's way," concluded the reader. "He thought that it was a mistake to insist that everybody follow the same way in serving the king."

"What does it mean when a person wants another to follow only his way," the young man near me asked even as the others were getting up, and answered his own question. "Not so much that he believes his way to be the only way, but he simply wants to make nothing of the other person."

One of the elders began singing a quick little tune, "Sing to Him, Rejoice in Him." A few voices joined in the song. Soon everybody in the room, including the children, had formed a circle, a kind of chain with hands held in front and in back. This was the Bratzlaver dance I had heard about—a simple kind of quick step in the rhythm of the sprightly tune which all were now singing. Some of them simply walked about rhythmically, while others hopped a bit. Both the singing and the dance were rather quiet. A few of the Hasidim had smiles on their faces, and others were simply relaxed, peaceful. It was a mood quite different from the husky outburst of the modern Israeli circle dance, or even the hypnotically stimulated emotion worked up in the dance of other Hasidic groups. The Bratzlaver dance is inner-directed, soft. In a few moments it was over and everyone left the synagogue to return home for breakfast and the Sabbath nap, which if missed is supposed to leave an Orthodox Jew tired all week. I walked back through the quiet streets thinking about religion, dancing, and Hasidism.

I was sorry that the tourists I had brought here the week before had not seen the quiet joy on the faces of the old men and children as they circled about singing snatches of the Psalms, or heard the story of the Master of Prayer interrupted by gentle sighs of joy expressing the wonderment of the Hasidim at the rich heritage they had inherited from their dead rebbe. They

143

would have sensed not only the spirituality of the mood, but have realized that these men and children in Meah Shearim were exposed to a remarkably rich pattern of life. Whatever one may believe about the presence or lack of the inspiration in the 613 commandments of the law which an Orthodox Jew fulfills, this "yoke" of prayer, study, and performance of the commandments brings him into daily contact with a remarkable range of literary and spiritual creativity ranging from Psalms through the philosophical and legal tomes of Maimonides, and including the stories of Rabbi Nachman. The people in the Bratzlaver synagogue were almost all of them simple workmen, poor and uneducated by worldly standards. Yet even the children among them had a relationship with the universe suffused with a sense of purpose and mystery. The simplest worker sitting around that wooden table was feeding his mind and emotions on a fare of imagination, moral insights, and poetic imagery which comes the way of only a very few in the outside world despite the abundance of television sets and public libraries in that world.

But perhaps I was wrong in assuming that my tourist friends would have tasted the spiritual fruit which I thought was here. After all, the shell was also still here—the strange outbursts of clapping, the fur-trimmed hats, high style during the seventeenth century in Europe but so grotesque in semitropical Israel. The wine cup which had been passed from mouth to mouth for the blessing of sanctification after services had been quite dirty. My American friend could well have asked again, "Why does holiness have to be associated with dirt?" It is a question which, in various forms, has been asked throughout the history of religion. Why not separate the higher elements of life from the lower; lofty spiritual insight from petty legalisms? Why not separate?—this is the "characteristic" approach to life expressed not only in Plato and the church fathers, but, at times in Judaism. Only in Judaism it met with a primary biblical monism, a refusal to separate body and spirit, the "essential" from the "detail."

And the classical Jewish faith in resurrection means the renewal of body as well as spirit, not just immortality for an abstract soul. Similarly, Orthodox Judaism refuses to recognize any distinction between the high and low. The lofty commandment to love thy neighbor as thyself is given no more attention in the biblical chapter then the wool and linen admixture of cloth which a Jew is forbidden to wear, or the food he cannot eat. It may seem wrong—it has seemed wrong—to some of the prophets that essentials and details should be given equal importance. But even if it is wrong, it is a fact of life that the malfunction of a small cell can destroy the loftiest dreams and spiritual potential. The tremendous is mysteriously interwoven with the trivial in actual life. Instead of trying to deny this fact, suggests classical Judaism, particularly in its mystical expressions, why not try to understand the trivial incident also as a mystery beyond our comprehension. If the malfunctioning of a single cell may give or take life, who knows what the effect of clothing or food is on the ability to love one's neighbor as oneself, in the mysteries of the divine arrangement?

That the Jewish people are included in a divine arrangement, whose mysterious details cannot be comprehended by the human mind, is a basic article of faith in Meah Shearim. That a Jew's part in this plan is outlined for him by the Torah, the Holy Bible as it is interpreted by the rabbinic sages, is also part of this faith. And that one may not speak of a Jewish return to the Holy Land outside the framework of this Orthodox religious outline is the basic point of difference between the new and the old Yishuv—a difference which is expressed in its sharpest and, as far as most Israelis are concerned, most repulsive form by the "Neturai Karta"—"the Guardians of the Wall."

Guardians of the Wall

Rabbi Amram Blau, leader of the Neturai Karta, the Guardians of the Wall, has never permitted the money of the state of Israel to touch his hands. Apart from the fact that he disapproves of the images sometimes printed on this money, its very handling might imply recognition on his part of the Jewish state's legitimate existence. Such recognition Blau and his followers refuse to give. As far as they're concerned, the return to Zion for which they still offer daily prayers has not yet taken place. What has occurred, they say, is the establishment of a government contrary to the will of God and to the laws of the Holy Torah.

The core membership of the Neturai Karta is probably not more than a few hundred families. Their activities, however, generate an interest on the part of both Israelis and Jews living outside of Israel, far out of proportion to their small numbers. Most people know of them through newspaper reports which describe their assaults on cars that dare invade the Orthodox quarters of Jerusalem on the Sabbath. Israelis have read posters signed by the Neturai Karta protesting the drafting of girls into the "brothel-like" atmosphere of the Israeli Army, or objecting to the "lewd" public swimming pool in Jerusalem where members of both sexes may bathe at the same time. There is also a rumor that during the War for Independence a band of Neturai Karta started marching toward the Jordanian border carrying the white flag of surrender. It is even said that some years ago they addressed a public appeal to the pope, asking him to save them from religious persecution at the hands of Jewish governmental authorities. Most Israelis, even the religious Orthodox, can only speak of Neturai Karta or their leader, Amram Blau, with disgust.

I was fully prepared, I confess, to share this feeling when I set out one Sabbath morning to find Blau in the little synagogue, the House of Joseph, off the main street of Meah Shearim. It is a small decrepit building like many others on that street, and the congregation of men and boys joyously chanting their prayers that morning appeared like dozens of other congregations in the vicinity. One young man wearing a fur hat and the yellow robes which old-time Jerusalem families favored offered me a coverless prayer book without comment and pushed some children together on a bench so that I might be seated. After a moment I asked another young man, with whom I was sharing the bench and long prayer desk, if Amram Blau were present. He pointed to the back of a tall figure leading the prayers at a stand near the Ark in the center of the room. A glass case on the top of the prayer stand framed the *shiviti* psalm and reflected Blau's long face with its wisps of blond hair straggling out from under the white prayer shawl which covered his head. His eyes

146

appeared to be closed as he rocked back and forth and led the prayers in a slightly hoarse chant.

This was a special Sabbath in the life of the Blau family, my neighbor informed me. A grandson of the Neturai Karta leader —he pointed to a straight-backed lad with a sparse dark beard standing on the other side of the Ark, facing the congregation —was going to be called to the Torah, for it was the Sabbath before his wedding. When, later in the service, the bridegroom chanted the final blessing over the Torah, thanking God for having "planted eternal life in our midst," a shower of peanuts and sunflower seeds poured down from the thickly curtained women's gallery above. Youngsters scrambled about the room filling their pockets. An altercation between several children was providentially stopped by one bearded elder with the admonition, "Nevertheless he is a Jew, and Jews don't hurt other Jews." It was not the kind of philosophy I had expected to hear among the Neturai Karta.

In answer to questions whispered between sections of the Bible reading my neighbor told me that the Neturai Karta were not actually an organized group, but drew their support from various elements of the old Yishuv. Their numbers varied according to the interest evoked by a particular demonstration or "activity." Blau and the congregation where he prayed were Hasidic in their ritual, but at present had no rebbe. At one time they had been the followers of the Tsanzer rebbe from Hungary. They still maintained a special relationship with his descendants, one of whom lived in the Williamsburg section of Brooklyn and was called the Satmer rebbe. Another descendant of the Tsanzer rebbe, the Klausenberger rebbe, had recently come to Israel with his followers, but their relationship with him was clouded these days because of his pro-Zionist sentiments.

"Actually, if we have a rebbe today, it's Blau," my neighbor concluded. "That is one of his sons." He nodded at a blond young man sitting at his side, whose severely bitten fingernails had caught my eye when we were sharing the Bible. "He has been in jail too," he told me proudly.

After the conclusion of the service, as the men were folding

147

their prayer shawls, I introduced myself to Blau as a visitor from America. His blue eyes smiled warmly.

"Blessed be he who comes." He extended his hand in the usual limp handshake of the Orthodox Jew. There was to be a kiddush, a little celebration, he said, at the home of his grandson's future father-in-law.

"Come. I can't guarantee that you will get some food, but come anyway," he urged.

After leaving the synagogue most of the congregation began walking behind the bridegroom, who was accompanied on one side by his future father-in-law, and on the other by his famous grandfather. Somebody started a *niggun*—a melody without words—and soon it was taken up by the rest of the group. On either side of the narrow street bearded men returning from synagogue with their prayer shawls and books stopped to smile greetings at our party, some of them coming up to congratulate the wedding party. Groups of women standing on the corners with baby carriages also looked up with friendly curiosity at the group of men and boys walking slowly through the narrow streets, singing a melody which was obviously of Slavic origin and in a three-quarter waltz rhythm. I asked a black-bearded young man walking beside me about the song.

"Better just call it a Jerusalem *niggun*. They sang it to my grandfather when he walked home from the synagogue on the Sabbath before his marriage, and they sang it to me also. We are most of us descended from families who came here long before the Zionists."

I soon found myself humming the song along with the group. The warm Jerusalem sun lighted up the red and yellow hues in the Sabbath robes about and was reflected in the friendly eyes of the men and women we were passing. It would indeed be unpleasant, I caught myself thinking, were a motorcycle or car to burst in and break up this Meah Shearim scene.

The large congregation filled the small house of the bride's family to overflowing. Some of the women trying to get in had to wait until a corridor was formed which allowed them to go by quickly without touching the men. I waited near the entrance, and after a few moments Blau pushed through the crowd to offer

148

me a plate of *kugel* and a fork. Trying to cut the *kugel,* I broke the fork. Not knowing what to do with the embarrassing evidence of a Sabbath-law transgression, I decided to hide the parts of the fork in my pocket, fulfilling, I suppose, the talmudic warning that "one sin brings on another." I left soon with the black-bearded man who had told me about the Jerusalem *niggun.* He spoke about Amram Blau. "A saintly man, clean of hands—one can't buy him with money," he told me.

I asked what work Blau did.

"Why, he studies, of course."

"How does he make a living?" I asked more directly.

"Oh, his wife sews and sells *kapotes*" (the long robes that are favored by some Orthodox residents of Meah Shearim). "Yes, Blau is a saintly man. He has little money and he gives all of it away to the poor. There were a number of people present to-day who eat regularly at his table." I asked my companion if he could define the ideology of the Neturai Karta, but he suggested that I speak with Blau that evening. "He doesn't give interviews to Israeli newspapermen, but he will to you. The Israelis always falsify what he says." There was also a book in English which would provide a fuller explanation of the ideology.

"But briefly, why are you so opposed to the Jewish state?"

"Because it is not founded on Torah, but on laws which are got together from other lands and peoples and which have little to do with our Torah. How can we recognize it? I could show you an article in a paper in my house where the head of the state, Ben Gurion, is interviewed by a reporter after he had attended Yom Kippur services. Ben Gurion told the reporter, 'But don't think that I fasted on Yom Kippur.' I can show it to you in the paper. How can we recognize a state with such a leader?"

I accompanied my new friend to his home and he gave me the book he had spoken about, which he confessed he could not read because it was in English.

Later that afternoon I leafed through it. The author was an I. Domb. It was entitled, *The Transformation.* A foreword in the book admits that the ideas expressed in it would "startle and perhaps shock a considerable portion of readers." Yet the ideas

149

were far from new. "To most Jews in the 18th century, and to many in the 19th, they would have been so familiar that it might have seemed superfluous even to write them down. The very fact that they are now likely to surprise public opinion indicates the extent and the subtlety of the process of replacement of traditional conceptions by revolutionary slogans during the last two centuries. Today these ideas which were once commonplace in Jewish life are now heard only from a minority which has not mastered the techniques of modern publicity, and even if it had, it is hardly in a financial position to apply them. It is a rear guard action that is being fought by survivors of a holocaust of souls in the conviction that the trends of the past two centuries are due to be swept away and that with our arrival at the climax of defilement, an age of faith is once more due, a prelude to the fulfillment of the final destiny of the true Israel for the benefit of the whole world."

The author of the book is well aware that his group is considered a lunatic fringe. Yet, he says, the basic premise of the Neturai Karta is simply the traditional Jewish belief that the *raison d'être* of the Jewish people is its connection to the Holy Torah and its commandments. Like the Laws of the Torah, the destiny of the Jewish people is not to be comprehended by human reason or in terms of cause-and-effect laws which apply to other peoples.

The Neturai Karta grant that there is nothing inherently evil in a state—"indeed statehood may mean happiness to any other people—but we Jews have been destined for a higher and an essentially different purpose. . . . It manifestly is absurd to believe that we have been waiting two thousand years in so much anguish, with so high hopes and with so many heartfelt prayers merely in order to finish up by playing the same role in the world as an Albania or a Honduras." The basic goal of Jewish survival must be bound up with a supernatural plan, part of whose wisdom has been revealed through the Torah with the laws which provide Israel with the technique for "penetrating deeper and further into the treasures of holiness." The Jewish state which has been established not only ignores this purpose but militantly works against it, in the opinion of the Neturai Karta. For ex-

150

ample, pious simple Yemenite immigrants, claims the writer, are exposed to teachers who deliberately smoke before them on a Sabbath to show them that no physical harm can result from desecration of the Holy Law. Even the language "invented" by the Zionists, which the Neturai Karta called Ivrit—Hebrew—to distinguish it from the "holy tongue" of the Bible and prophets, reflects the non-Jewish and non-holy spirit of its inventors. An individual or people implants its character in its language. The "holy tongue" of the Bible and the sages developed a character and logic of its own. "Purity and holiness are its basis," but the creators of Ivrit were uninterested in the traditional connection between holiness and character. "They wanted to make the language fit the normal tendencies of a normal person, and in order to fulfill this end, they translated the expressions and phrases of different languages into new and artificial equivalents which have only a technical connection with the original holy tongue." The heresy of Zionism is implanted in the new tongue, says the writer, who adds, "It is perhaps worth mentioning that Ben Yehuda, the chief architect of Zionist Hebrew, died suddenly on the Sabbath, holding his pen in hand, and writing in Hebrew"— that is, desecrating the Sabbath, according to traditional concepts.

The writer saves his choicest invectives for the religious parties who, he claims have been "bought" by Zionist gold. Even the Agudas Israel, founded in the nineteenth century by great rabbinic sages to combat the Zionist heresy, has gradually surrendered to Zionist influence and methods. This surrender, he claims, was brought about by pressure on the part of its membership to equal the "achievements" of the Zionist movement. Striving to produce "results" in terms of members, meetings, buildings, it soon found itself adopting the methods of the Zionists. Soon, this originally anti-Zionist movement could see no harm in accepting some money from the Zionist organizations, ostensibly in order to further their religious purposes. On their side, the Zionist machine found it to their advantage to subsidize these religious elements in order to "show the world" the united Jewish front and to gradually seduce them into the Zionist goals. This is precisely what has happened, claim the Neturai Karta, and today the Agudas Israel and the avowedly religious Zionist parties can hardly be distinguished from each other.

The Neturai Karta have no goals in terms of buildings, publicity, or even results in terms of numbers. They have no office, no membership, no presidents. They do not have any plans for saving the Jewish people. Their only plan is that outlined by the divinely ordained Laws of the Torah, and the ultimate crucial events in this plan are decided by the Divine Power above rather than by the strategems from below. The real cause of Jewish suffering in history is not to be attributed to the "statelessness" of Jews, as Zionists think, in the opinion of the writer, nor even, in the ultimate sense, is it caused by their persecutors. The writer quotes a young rabbinical student in Auschwitz who once asked his SS torturer why he was behaving that way, and received the reply, "I don't know, I'm just obeying orders." When the rabbinic scholar asked what the purpose of these orders was, he received the reply, "They don't know themselves." After having received this reply, the rabbinic scholar said, "Then, I can no longer see SS and gas chambers in Auschwitz, but I can see only verses from the Bible moving in front of my eyes in the full living horror of their fulfillment. . . ." This is a view, says I. Domb, which will startle Jews today, but, he points out, it is not a new thought in Judaism. Indeed, it is the traditional analysis of Jewish suffering which past generations accepted as obvious.

Domb admits that the Neturai Karta have no hopes of convincing many today of this truth. They cannot compete, they say, with the propaganda apparatus of the Zionists, or with the powerful currents of modern thought that use "artificial and seductive expressions such as 'broad-minded,' 'factual,' 'realistic,' and 'moving with the times' for the purpose of justifying the expansion of appetites. Realizing their powerlessness in the terms of monetary or program approach, they "concentrate their efforts on the surviving remnant of the faithful and seek to secure that this remnant should remain unscathed by Zionism." Thus, they call themselves the Neturai Karta—the Guardians of the City—"who preserve the sacred flame from being extinguished."

"Nominal Jews have a saying to the effect that everything

goes with the times. This is the attitude of most people in our time. We shall for once make use of this motto, and although the present may be clouded by dark and threatening shadows, the time will pass and with it the darkness will vanish before the great revelation of the final transformation when the glory of the Lord will be revealed and all flesh together will see that it is the mouth of the Lord speaking." Thus the writer concludes his book. When that times comes "we wish to ascend to the Land of Israel with the future redemption which God has promised us. . . . We shall not go up to the strains of the Zionist Hatikvah, we will go up to the music of Divine Illumination of the whole creation. . . ."

That Saturday evening I visited Blau in his home, which is in the Hungarian quarter of Meah Shearim. Six or seven women were sitting on couches in a small empty room. Within, in a larger room, Blau, still dressed in the loose-fitting white Sabbath garments, was sitting by a table talking, or rather, listening to a young man. The latter, his gray felt hat pushed back on his forehead, was excitedly describing a visit he had made to the United States that fall—"to 770 Eastern Parkway," he informed me in broken but proud English. That was the central office of the Lubavitcher movement, a large Hasidic sect. A group of Lubavitcher Hasidim had chartered a plane in order to spend the High Holy Days with the rebbe—an enterprise which had exhausted them financially, but provided them with spiritual fare which they were still tasting many months later. "I tell you Reb Amram, I saw miracles there—with my own eyes I saw them." The young man affectionately grabbed the hand of the elderly Neturai Karta leader. "Oh, I know you don't agree with him in everything, Reb Amram, but you will someday." Blau chuckled at the enthusiasm of his young visitor and was about to say something, but the young Hasid continued his monologue. For the next half hour Blau and I were regaled with an example of the Lubavitcher rebbe's Torah. It revolved about an interpretation of the biblical Psalm, "Redeem from Egypt." The word for Egypt in Hebrew was *Mitzraim*—which the Rebbe had linked in meaning to the Hebrew word *mitzri,* meaning "narrow." The main point of the Torah was that narrowness was the real

153

Egypt which every Jew carried about in himself and from which he had to be redeemed. For the soul, which could abide no limitations, the body was its Egypt—the narrowness from which some day it would be released. But there are other spiritual Egypts to which even a religious person could be enslaved. "When a Jew comes home from synagogue on the Sabbath and looks with satisfaction at his food, and says his blessings and sings and feels that he is fulfilling all the Law—he too is in Egypt. He has settled for the meaning of the Law in its narrower terms. The true holiness of the Law is never completely fulfilled. One must strive to always expand its meaning and holiness, and never be satisfied with a limited observance." With glowing eyes and frequent sighs of admiration the young Hasid poured forth the Torah he had learned in America.

"You must understand that there are divine sparks everywhere, not only in the prayers, but even in nature and in food. And we must work with such things in order to redeem the divine sparks from their Egypt." The young man now was addressing me—the Lubavitcher movement is known for its missionary propensities.

"You see this table." The Hasid banged on the table, shaking the bottle of wine and silver kiddush cup lying on it. "It looks like a dead thing, but it isn't, not at all. It really is filled with divinity. It couldn't hold together and exist for a moment without such divinity for 'there is no place empty of Him.'" The Hasid quoted a talmudic phrase which was a central thought of Hasidism and which the opponents of the Hasidic movement in the eighteenth century criticized because of its pantheistic implications.

Reb Amram nodded smilingly at the enthusiasm of the young man and submitted to his handclasp. "Oh, he's a wonderful rebbe—you will see some day, he will come here."

"Let us hope the Messiah comes first," Blau said, laughing.

A sad-faced young man came into the room and greeted us. He had been pointed out to me at the synagogue as one of those who ate every Sabbath at Blau's table. He had come to recite the Havdalah blessings over the wine for the conclusion of the Sabbath. Blau poured a cup of wine for him and the young

154

Hasid stood up and held up two lighted matches in lieu of the candles which are usually used for this ceremony. Conversation ceased while the traditional words were chanted. "He is the God of my salvation, I shall not fear—blessed be He who separates light from darkness, the Sabbath from the ordinary, Israel from the other peoples. . . ."

"Amen," said Blau, after the conclusion of the Blessing.

I took advantage of the ensuing pause to launch the questions I had prepared. "Do you agree with the Lubavitcher rebbe?" The Lubavitcher rebbe was not a Zionist, but was known to cultivate close relationships with the nonreligious government officials in Israel.

"Why shouldn't he agree?" The Hasid again grabbed Blau's hand as if to forestall what he was afraid might soon be said.

"But a Lubavitcher Hasid once told me," I pressed, "that the best way to drive away darkness was not with a stick, but through light. Do you agree with his technique."

Blau finally managed to break through the stream of words which were still coming from the Lubavitcher Hasid.

"I respect the Lubavitcher rebbe. He is a good man and does good things. I have a letter from him. But we differ from him in two main points." The Lubavitcher Hasid leaned back a bit glumly, and Blau continued gently but firmly.

"First, we don't believe in taking money from the Zionists or the government here. You know the saying in Proverbs, "A bribe blinds the eyes." The taking of money enslaves the mind. Second, we do not believe that religious Jews should go to the polls. If they vote, they not only recognize the so-called state, but they become a minority in government and as such their influence is nullified by the majority. As it is, if we don't vote, we remain what we are."

The young Hasid tried to break in again, but I threw my question more quickly.

"But are the Neturai Karta opposed to Jewish immigration to Israel?"

Blau formulated his answer carefully. "We take our stand on the saying of the Gemara in the Talmud, which says three

155

things. First, 'It is forbidden to shake off the yoke of the nations.' This means," explained Blau, "it is forbidden to make a revolution in the existing scheme of things. Second, the Talmud says, 'It is forbidden to stand on the wall.' This, Rashi, the eleventh-century commentator, interpreted as meaning that it is wrong to organize mass immigration to the land of Israel before the coming of the Messiah. And third, 'It is forbidden to hasten the end.' That means to push the days of the Messiah before their time. This is our view."

What then did the demonstrations for which the Neturai Karta were so famous hope to accomplish. Did they not in fact repel rather than attract Jews to Torah?

Blau shook his head.

"We are not concerned whether they repel or attract. There are two reasons for the demonstrations. First, there is the simple response to the commandment 'to hate evil.' Thus we are bound to react whenever we feel that the name of God is being desecrated in the Holy City. Second, we want to show that the so-called religious parties do not speak for Judaism. There is another voice, and the only way we can show it is through such demonstrations. It is interesting, is it not. Despite our smallness in numbers, so many people in all parts of the world are irritated and have to pay attention to what we say."

The young Hasid, I saw, was not going to be restrained much longer, so I quickly asked my last questions. "What about the stories which have been spread about the Neturai Karta and which make them so repugnant in the eyes of most Israelis. For example, is it true that the Neturai Karta walked toward the Arab lines with a white flag during the war." Blau cleared his throat.

"We cannot help what the Zionist papers write about us. Nor am I concerned with denying the story about the white flag. It is possible that under some circumstances it might be right to walk with a white flag in this way. But what happened was actually as follows. We had just seen the Jewish section of the Old City destroyed, even the Churvah, the ancient synagogue, all of it wiped out. We saw the possibility of the same thing happening

156

here and so we held a meeting. After the meeting we took a sign and wrote on it, 'We are for peace.' We walked with it toward the Geula area—not to the Arabs but to the Jews. We were met by guns and sticks and that was the end of it."

"There was no white flag then?"

"No, but we are not interested in denying the story."

The young Hasid added, "You should know that during the war Reb Amram stayed in this part of Jerusalem, which was the most dangerous part, even when the others, the Zionists, had fled."

"One last question: Is it true that the Neturai Karta once sent a petition to the pope asking him to rescue them from the Jewish government?"

For the first time it seemed to me that Blau's voice wavered. "I cannot remember now all the details of what has happened in the past."

I did not press the point and a few minutes later rose to take my leave. Blau accompanied me to the door with a warm blessing.

"When you get back to America, visit 770 Eastern Parkway—don't forget," the young Hasid called out as I left.

The day after my visit with Amram Blau I spoke to another rabbi in the Meah Shearim area about the Neturai Karta. He reached for a book containing a letter written by a Hasidic rebbe, Mendel of Vitebsk, who in the early nineteenth century was one of the founders of the old Yishuv. "It is obvious and crystal clear to me," wrote Rabbi Mendel, "that the essential reason for our people's lowered condition is the disrespect shown by those who uphold the Torah toward those who abandon it. It is the person who mocks the one who leaves the Torah, and not the latter, who withdraws himself from the community of Israel and Divine Grace."

The man who showed me the passage was Zvi Yehudah Kook, son of the first Chief Rabbi of Palestine. The Neturai Karta, said Zvi Yehudah, speak of a "transformation," but they are unaware of how they have transformed Judaism. Have they not, asks Zvi Yehudah, forgotten the essentials of their faith—the simple commandment to love the people of Israel, to love one's fellow man. They have forgotten how to look upon what goes on in the land "from the roots on high." From this perspective, claims Zvi Yehudah, Ben Gurion and Amram Blau are not as separated from each other as each may think.

CHAPTER IX

Another View of the Old Yishuv: From the Roots on High

All definition is spiritual idolatry. . . . Man is repelled by the assumption of the insensitive that words and letters in themselves contain the divine essence, and "God-denial" comes as a cry arising from the painful effort to lift and redeem man from this strange and narrow pit and raise him above the darkness of letters and formulae to the fuller light of the idea and the emotions, and to the dimension of ethics. *Atheism has a provisional right to existence.* . . . Let the violent winds of "God-denial" purify all the refuse which has accumulated about the lower levels of the spirit of faith; in this way the heavens shall be cleansed and the clear light of God that is the source of higher faith shall become visible.

—*Abraham Isaac Kook* (*Chief Rabbi of Palestine, 1921–35*)

One man there was, of the old Yishuv, an important man— indeed, the first Chief Rabbi of Palestine—who believed that modern Jewish resettlement in Israel was the beginning of the complete return envisioned by the prophets. Not that Abraham Isaac Kook was oblivious to the phenomena which disturbed the Orthodox religious elements of the old Yishuv. He was well aware that many of the halutzim—the Jewish pioneers who came to Palestine in the early 1900s—had an attitude toward the Holy Laws of the Torah and toward pious Jewry which could only be described by the Hebrew word *chutzpah*—brazenness. He sensed their reverence for labor of the hands, and their

159

contempt for those who directed all their energies to prayer and sacred studies. But he visited them in their settlements, joined hands with them as they danced the hora. To those of his own religious community who pointed out that it was unbecoming for a Chief Rabbi to publicly embrace desecrators of the Sabbath, he replied not apologetically but with words that shocked them even further. Yes, there was *chutzpah* here among the new settlers but it was nothing less than the brazenness which the Talmud said had to precede the coming of the Messiah. As for the seeming disrespect of the pioneers for matters of the spirit, said the bearded mystic, the Jewish people had in the last centuries almost perished from excessive spiritualization. It was time now for them to become "animalized," so to speak, to recover the gross qualities of life. "The vessels must be thickened before they can become proper receptacles for the highest and the most intense illuminations."

When the rabbis of Meah Shearim and the old Yishuv reminded him that Judaism made distinctions between the holy and the profane, and that he ought to distinguish between those who reverenced and those who were indifferent to the Holy Laws of traditional Judaism, he replied with a parable.

"In the Temple there was a Holy of Holies, into which only one man, the High Priest, could enter, and then only at one time of the year, on Yom Kippur. But," he reminded his listeners, "what was the situation when the Holy of Holies was being built? Was it then built only by the High Priest, or even by the priests? Did not the ordinary carpenters and the hewers of stone also enter freely and contribute their offering to the total structure? We are building today, and we have not yet completed our 'Holy of Holies.' All . . . all have a portion to offer in this building, and one no more right than another in bringing their offering."

Rabbi Kook's views were far more than an expression of tolerance. They were rooted in the very core of his paradoxical personality, and in a philosophy of religion and life which today, more than twenty-five years after his death in 1935, is recognized as one of the profoundest and most original spiritual expressions. Against the background of today's religious quarrels in the Holy

Land, the figure of Rabbi Kook is assuming legendary proportions in the eyes of religious and nonreligious. But it was still possible, I thought, to meet the real man, if not in person, at least through the eyes of his only son, Zvi Yehudah Kook, who teaches at the Universal Yeshiva which was founded by his illustrious father.

There are plans now for a new building, but when I visited there, the Yeshiva was still located on the "Street of Rav Kook" in the center of Jerusalem. Its approach is through a courtyard, past an eye clinic which occupies the first floor, and up some stairs in the back. Though the stone courtyard and stairs are well scrubbed, the air is slightly tinged with the odors from the poor sewage system of that section. A long corridor runs the length of the second floor, leading at one end to the Yeshiva proper, which consists of a large classroom and a small chapel. Toward the center of the corridor is an office and then some rooms which are occupied by the family of Rav Kook's daughter and her husband, who is today the acting head of the Yeshiva.

The Yeshiva seemed deserted as I entered. I glanced into the main room and saw two students, hats pushed back on their heads and engrossed in conversation. In the small office, a bearded man, evidently the secretary or administrator, greeted me in a friendly fashion, saying that Zvi Yehudah Kook would soon return. He offered me an English pamphlet to read, which described the program and hopes of the "Center of the Rav," and appealed for funds.

After a while I went into the large classroom, where the two young men glanced at me with polite curiosity and continued their conversation. On the wall near the window was a picture of Rav Kook taken when he was Chief Rabbi, his black beard streaked with gray, and a large fur hat on his head. Directly below the picture a quotation from the *Ethics of the Fathers* was framed: "Be ye of the disciples of Aaron, loving and pursuing peace, loving mankind, and drawing them close to the Torah." On the other side of the window was a picture of a man wearing a medieval-style Arabic turban. It was a portrait of Maimonides, and it was somewhat surprising to find the picture

161

of that great legal authority and rationalist in this Yeshiva, Rav Kook being, I had considered, far closer in spirit to the poetic and mystic philosophy of Judah Halevi. In a way, though, the medieval physician and philosopher did express Rav Kook's hopes for his own Yeshiva. Though he asked his students to set aside time for the study of the minutiae of the animal sacrifices which would have to be offered by the priests when the Temple should be rebuilt, he also urged that the curriculum of his Yeshiva include secular and scientific studies. "For how," he wrote, "can a teacher communicate with and improve his people unless he be acquainted with the ideas that set the style of the generation?" Above all, Kook constantly insisted that only when Judaism was made fertile by true genius of mind and heart, could it reveal its full light to the world. This thought of combining great minds with Torah remained with him, literally to the end of his life. On the very day of his death, Dr. Zondek of the Hebrew University visited him. When he had finished his examination, the people standing around the bed heard Rav Kook whisper to the distinguished but not particularly religious scientist, "May the day come when the great of the Jews will also be Jewishly great."

I was looking at the picture on the wall when the secretary came in to tell me that Rabbi Kook had arrived, and I could see him in his office. Zvi Yehudah Kook is quite different in appearance from his father. His eyes are small and twinkling, and a short white beard covers his rather fair skin. He took my hand in warm greeting, and asked how he could help me. I said something about being interested in learning more about Ha-Rav, *the* Rabbi, as he is called in Israel. Smiling, he nodded his head in eager assent: "Yes, he was unusual. He combined all levels together . . . the mystic and the legal; deep poetical feelings with clear logic and practical judgment . . . all together."

He agreed readily to set aside some hours for discussion of his father's teachings. Taking me by the arm, he walked with me into the corridor and out to the stairway. There, still holding my hand, he inquired as to my first name and my work, and invited me to visit him the coming Sabbath at home.

162

That Saturday afternoon, making sure I had a *yarmelke* in my pocket, I set out for the Vineyard of Abraham quarter of Jerusalem, where Zvi Yehudah Kook lives. "The son of Rav Kook"—this is what everybody calls him. I decided to add a question, if the mood permitted, about how it felt to go through life known mainly as the son of somebody else. Before such questions, however, the obvious topic to discuss was the present religious crisis in Israel.

As I walked along the streets toward the Orthodox quarter of the city, the symptoms of the crisis were evident. This area of town was quiet, for the taxis bustling about in other streets would not take the chance of driving here: too many had been over-turned on the Sabbath. But it was a tense sort of quiet.

Not far from the corner of Herzl Street, a young boy, his fists clenched, stood a few feet away from his bicycle, which had either fallen or been snatched from him. Around him, at a safe distance, six or seven younger children, wearing their Sabbath hats and long jackets, looked angrily at the owner of the bicycle, who was daring them to come closer. Across the street a young man had noticed the commotion and was approaching the group. He was dressed like the younger boys, but kept his jacket around his shoulders, the sleeves flapping by his side.

"Get away from here," he said as he came to the boy with the bicycle, who stood his ground and retorted only with a sharp and ugly Arabic curse. The young man came closer, and repeated grimly, "I asked you to get away from here quickly." The boy hesitated, then, looking around at the group, spat his curse at them again, picked up his bicycle, and rode away. The passers-by resumed their Sabbath stroll.

As I turned the corner of Meah Shearim in the heart of the Orthodox quarter, I took the *yarmelke* out of my pocket and put it on my head. Suddenly I heard the loud sound of a motorcycle. All stopped in their paths, and turned around to see what was happening.

Down the hill rode a tanned young man, his shirt open at the collar, smiling gleefully at the calls of *"Shabbos! Shabbos!"* ringing out about him. In the seat behind him was a girl, obviously disturbed at her boy friend's bravado. The motorcycle traveled swiftly and was out of range before the stones which had been picked up by passers-by could be thrown.

These scenes were an appropriate prelude to my meeting with Zvi Yehudah Kook, for it was to this problem—the religious schisms of Israel—that his father had dedicated most of his life and thought.

Zvi Yehudah Kook lived on the first door of a small building. When I knocked at the door, the landlady answered and told me that Rabbi Kook was still at the Yeshiva. She showed me into his room, which was refreshingly cool, the hot summer sun having been kept out of it by closed shutters. As the woman turned to leave, I asked whether the Rabbi lived here alone. "Yes," she replied, "since his wife died he lives here alone." She added, "His wife was a wonderful person, and they were very, very happy together. Unfortunately they had no children. He has been living here with my husband and myself many years." At the door she stopped again. "He is really a Tsaddik . . . a saintly person . . . kind and humble. He'll be in soon. Do make yourself comfortable."

On one side of the room there were shelves with books and manuscripts, and on the opposite wall was a full-length photograph of Rabbi Abraham Isaac Kook. It was not difficult to associate this picture of the bearded Orthodox rabbi in fur hat with some of the stories told of Rav Kook.

A comrade of his youth recalls that once on Tisha B'Av, while reading the Lamentations of Jeremiah, young Abraham Isaac Kook's tears had dropped so profusely that his friend couldn't help saying, "Look, I too love Israel, and bewail its destruction . . . but why do you seem to feel it all so much more deeply?"

"You don't understand," the young man had replied, "you are not a Kohen—a priest—as I am." Kook never forgot that as a descendant of the priests he possessed special responsibilities for maintaining holiness in the land of Israel.

In those days he was known among his fellow students and teachers as the "squint-eyed genius," because of the peculiar set of his eyes. I looked more closely at the large, dark eyes in the photograph, for those who knew him in his lifetime always

164

remarked about their glow and their quality of seeming to look into distances: "Expanses . . . my soul craves expanses."

When Zvi Yehudah Kook entered, he took my hand and greeted me warmly by my first name. Then, urging me to sit down, he hurried into the kitchen, returning in a moment with two cups of water and a bowl of grapes. After offering me the grapes he sat down at the table beside me, and quietly moved his lips in a benediction before drinking from his cup of water.

"Well, how shall we begin?" he said. "Shall we read from my father's writings?" He motioned to the shelves. "You know, most of his writings are still unpublished."

I began to suggest a question, but he interrupted, and placing his hand on mine said, "You know, if you will be more comfortable, you don't have to wear the *yarmelke* here."

The invitation to remove my *yarmelke* seemed strange coming from an Orthodox rabbi, who not only wore a skullcap himself, but whose fringed undergarment peeked through his shirt in complete fulfillment of the biblical commandment, "And thou shalt look upon them." Smiling a bit at my surprise, Rabbi Kook explained, "You see, I don't want any *mechitza*—any artificial boundaries—between us. I want us to be really close, and I want you to feel natural, and it seems to me you are not really accustomed to wearing a *yarmelke*." I muttered something about being quite comfortable in one, and even wearing it in my own home on occasion. But Rabbi Kook patted my hand reassuringly. "It's all right. We will get to know each other better, and you won't feel so strained."

Flustered, yet encouraged by his warm, personal tone, I decided suddenly to put aside the general questions about religion in Israel, and raise the more intimate ones. I found difficulty in conveying my thought to Rabbi Kook. What I wanted to know about his father was . . . had he really succeeded in feeling in his own life that harmony and peace of soul and mind which he claimed could exist along with that "restlessness which arises from the never-ceasing expansion of the soul?" And had he really reconciled the fleshly with the spiritual? And what of the other conflicts which must have existed in the actual life of one who, as Chief Rabbi, was so deeply involved in the petty details

165

and political wranglings of community life? Were these not burdensome to a spirit which yearned for "boundless heights?" And what about his personal life? So often the family life of a community leader is impoverished because of his outside activities. How was it in their home? I was somewhat abashed at the boldness of my own questions, and Zvi Yehudah Kook also seemed surprised at the turn of the interview, but his eyes retained their good humor.

"We have so little time that we should really talk about his teachings, and some of your questions can best be answered if we understand my father's way of thinking."

He hesitated, then decided to answer. "As to my personal memories of him . . . of course, he was always overburdened with the needs of the community. Everything came to him. A call from the High Commissioner asking his intervention in keeping the Jews from blowing the *shofar* at the Wailing Wall, or someone asking for help in getting a visa. And everything he liked to do personally. Even when he was sick the last months of his life, I can remember his running through the streets to the consulate to arrange some papers for somebody . . . the water bottles, which he carried to relieve his pain, flapping about his body as he hurried. He always wanted to do things with his own hands."

He pointed to the shelves filled with manuscripts. "He even refused help in the simple copying from other books required for his legal writing. He called it his 'black work.' If others could build roads and sweep streets, then he wanted to do some 'black work.' Still, despite all his activities, he tried his best to save time for study with me. And in the home I can only remember his face gentle and good toward everybody and on all occasions."

He glanced at the picture of his father. In the photograph there was a serene half-smile about Rav Kook's lips, but the dark eyes seemed more sad than smiling. Rav Kook had spoken much of the joy to be found in holiness, but he had also written so eloquently about that "melancholy pressing on his heart, saddening and embittering his life without conscious explanation." He had tried to explain it. It was the result, he wrote, of the

166

"struggle of the soul, caged in its physical bonds and reaching out for a life of freedom . . . a life finer, clearer, and brighter . . . yet failing to attain it . . . and this struggle is the cause of the melancholy of the soul."

"And since this is its source," he wrote, "why, then, one should take advantage of this mood of the soul, lift pearls out of murky depths, and distill from this melancholy exquisite emotions. For, after all, in whatever manner and wherever a man's soul makes itself evident, there is evidence of the beginning of deliverance; the light of salvation pushing to reveal itself from behind the blackness."

Had Rav Kook really succeeded in feeling the "light of salvation pushing to reveal itself from behind the blackness?" Such matters only a very close friend—or a son—could reveal, and I tried to explain again to Zvi Yehudah Kook what I was after. He listened to me closely, his eyes still twinkling a bit, and nodded his head encouragingly. When I had finished, he placed his hand on mine and said, "Yes, there were conflicts. But he was always able to lift his soul above them."

I must have looked a bit unhappy at his answer, for he added as if eager to please, "But of course there were a few times that I can recall when he was provoked and did lose his composure . . . but those were very few."

He went to the bookcase and leafed through the pages of a book he had edited, containing his father's many letters. "Look," he said, "maybe I can show you something interesting," and he turned to a letter written to somebody who had evidently accused Rav Kook of shirking his "obligation" in not reviewing a book which had been sent him. Rav Kook had answered him, and Zvi Yehudah Kook read a sentence aloud from the letter. "I am obligated to no man, but only to God alone." He looked to see if this satisfied me, explaining, "Of course he was not quite right. He was a community servant, and was obligated to man." He continued to turn the leaves of the book as if looking for some further revelation of his father's weaker moments, and finally found a letter written to himself. He read it aloud. In this letter Rav Kook complained to his son about the multitude of petty community tasks which robbed him of time for study and for other important matters. But even this bit of "wickedness" was dulled by the observation in the same letter that "after all, one cannot know how great in importance are even the seemingly small things."

"This was his way," Zvi Yehudah Kook explained, "to see always the great principle and possibility, even in the smallest detail, and the detail in the principle. As for the conflict between his poetic talents and his interest in legal detail, you may have heard how he once put it: 'Even as there are laws of poetry, so there is a poetry in law.'

"Actually, there were times when my father did act and speak with irritation, but mostly it was calculated sharpness, to achieve a certain end, as when he ignored a government official—you must have heard about that."

I confessed that I hadn't, and he told me how, one day in 1929, a British government official had ordered the small Jewish community of Hebron to surrender its arms and how, a few days later, they had been attacked by Arabs, and most of the community killed. Shortly thereafter, the government official and the Chief Rabbi had attended the same function. The official extended his hand as the Chief Rabbi passed him on the platform, but Rav Kook ignored him, explaining later that he could not touch the hand which, in the phrase of Isaiah, was "stretched forth but covered with blood."

"But as to the uncalculated moments of irritation or sharpness," Zvi Yehudah concluded, "they were very few."

"Even when he was being attacked by people of his own Orthodox community?" I pressed.

"Yes, even then. He was able, always, to achieve an elevation of the soul. To 'lift the soul'—this was the technique he always used in approaching all the problems of life. To go 'up to the roots,' to 'see things from above.' This was always his ability, and the secret of his strength."

Quite discouraged by now at this picture of unalloyed saintliness, I was about to ask just how "going up to the roots" could help solve the very concrete and sharp-edged religious and political problems of modern Israel, but the hour was late, and I decided to save this question for another meeting.

The next few days I spent away from Jerusalem, visiting in the immigration camps and outlying settlements. The Cabalistic advice to "go up to the roots" seemed more and more inadequate to the realistic problems which were threatening the very survival of the new state. As dangerous as the Arab threats and the export-import imbalance, was the political, cultural, and religious fragmentation of the little country; the distrust and antagonism between Israel Number 1 and Israel Number 2, as they half facetiously called themselves; the complaint of "veteran settlers" that the dreamland of Herzl and Achad Haam was becoming but another trivial Levantine state; the lack of communication and understanding between Western and Oriental Jew, and between the various groups of Oriental Jews themselves; the continuing and sharpening religious strife between the Orthodox and non-Orthodox communities over the problems of religion and state. All pointed up Israel's pressing need for some inner quality of nationhood that could rise above present fragmentation. This was the problem I had hoped to hear something about from the son of Rav Kook. After all, it was to this problem of bringing the "diverse" together that Rav Kook had devoted most of his life and thought.

Rav Kook did not become the Chief Rabbi of Palestine until 1921. But long before then, as the Rabbi of Jaffa, he had become a figure beloved by "religious" and "freethinkers" alike. The Orthodox liked to tell of their rabbi whose prayer was so intense that once, before the evening service, he was seen to leave the synagogue suddenly and engage the gardener outside in conversation about trivial matters. He explained later that the fervor of his heart was at that moment too intense for containment in the words of the prayer book. In order to cool his ardor, he had chatted a while with the gardener.

The nonreligious like to remind the Orthodox of how their beloved Chief Rabbi had suffered calumny and persecution from extremists in his own camp. There were, indeed, religious fanatics who had accused the pious rabbi of heterodoxy. In 1909, while in Jaffa, Rav Kook found himself in the midst of a trying controversy with Orthodox colleagues, both in and outside of Israel. With the settlement of Jews in Israel, a law that had once

169

been but discussion material for the Yeshiva suddenly became a real problem. According to biblical proscription, land owned by Jews in Israel must lie fallow every seventh year, the *shmitta* year. This year arrived in the Jewish calendar, and with it the problem. Rav Kook did not sidestep the difficulty of reconciling life with Torah. He found some rabbinic authorities who agreed that in the "hour of urgent necessity" it was permissible to work the land by a legal fiction—that is, by a fictitious selling of the land to a non-Jew for the year. Kook decided to follow these authorities. It was apparent to him that if the *shmitta* were enforced, there would be no future possibility of receiving investment capital for Palestine. The newly planted settlement would be unable to survive. He ruled, therefore, that the *shmitta* year could be circumvented. His decision was attacked by a number of leading rabbis, but Rav Kook stood his ground.

Not that Rav Kook ever surrendered one jot or tittle of the law. Rather, he claimed, Orthodoxy was not revealing its fullest dimensions to the world. In a letter to a critic he outlined his attitude. "We have abandoned the soul of Torah. Orthodoxy is occupied with negative quarreling, and concerns itself with vain delusions which are destroyed by the realities of life. Nor should we take comfort in the thought that the atheistic elements of our population will likely be the first to meet destruction. Such trouble is not 'half comfort' but double trouble. The proper way is open before us. *All* the Torah, with *all* its spiritual connotations should be known to us. If only a portion of our talented people, who know Torah and are blessed with good minds, would volunteer to try to reveal the pure ideas of our faith, to clarify our theology, the meaning of our Prophets, the depths of our divine spirit . . . our great ideas and clear thoughts so worthy of being the life foundations of many peoples . . . we could then begin that great heavenly work of clearing the contaminated spirit from off the earth, and of making a beginning of the establishment of the Kingdom of God.

"But some, because of darkness of heart, and smallness of faith, and others, because of pride and lack of information, still think that the smaller type of Torah, narrow and dry, which did not have the power to resist the depredations of other cultures

170

and antagonistic spiritual forces, will still, today, be our source of healing. Do not accuse me, my dear friend, and I hope no man will accuse me, of smallness of love, God forbid, for the practical aspects of Torah, or of lack of enthusiasm in study and expansion of this practical Torah. . . . But at a time like this, when the possibility of the destruction of the higher Torah is at hand . . . when someone does come along and say that our help can be found in the *soul* of Torah . . . the critics complain and object: 'What do you want . . . mysticism, ethics, science, philosophy, sermonics, poetry . . . didn't all of these things once deceive us?'

"Complaints like this are enough to choke the voice of God within us crying 'Seek me and ye shall live.' . . ."

And Rav Kook concluded his letter with a postscript. "As regards that rumor you mentioned . . . I have not seen the book, but in no way is there any place for strife between lovers of truth like ourselves."

Of course, the majority of Israel's citizens today do not see the religious difficulties of the land in terms of Torah, whether limited or expanded. Many were upset by the decision of the coalition government to place intimate matters of marriage and divorce completely in the hands of the Orthodox rabbinate, in return for a promise on the part of some members of the religious bloc to vote for the national conscription bill. They are embittered and frustrated by what they feel is a lack of leadership and courage on the part of the official rabbis.

I was determined, in my next visit to Rabbi Kook, not to let him escape a discussion of these concrete problems with advice about "going up to the roots" or "lifting the soul."

The next time I went to see him I began our discussion with a story, probably apocryphal, about an American who had visited a so-called "freethinking" kibbutz and engaged a member of the settlement in a conversation about religious matters. After some preliminaries, the American rabbi had come out and asked the settler, "But aren't you at all religious?" The settler looked at him in surprise, and said, "Of course not." The visitor had pressed further. "But don't you have any belief in God, or any convictions about the possibility of a spiritual contact between

171

man and the mystery of life?" The kibbutznik appeared surprised, for he had been expressing strong positive convictions on these very questions. "Why, of course I believe in God . . . but what has God got to do with religion?"

Zvi Yehudah Kook smiled at the story. "Sometimes I think," he said, "that what we need in Israel is more belief for the believers and more freedom for the freethinkers. The Orthodox, the believers, need more faith in the power of a God who evidently has a place in His pattern for all types of Jews, and they must stop worrying about whether their own type of holiness is being copied by others, and have faith that their God, who has preserved Israel and brought the people again to its land, has His designs and purposes. As for the freethinkers, they should be more free in their thought, free enough to break through the little political and economic formulas by which they define their lives and the world, to press beyond the limitations of ideological catchwords and glimpse the mysteries and vistas which are not encompassed by small definitions. Our difficulty is that in both camps we have smallness of mind and littleness of heart. Yes, more belief for the believers, and more freedom of thought for the freethinkers, and above all, love, a bit more love." He had been talking with a half-smile, but now he became serious.

"Our Orthodox Jews say that they observe the commandments. And they do carefully observe the commandment to hate those who desecrate the law. But there is a commandment greater than all of these: the commandment to love. To love one's neighbor, even if he doesn't agree with you, and this, the greatest of all commandments, they neglect."

He paused as if wondering whether to continue the thought. "Of course, our world does not always recognize the full meaning of love. People associate love with sentimental feelings alone. But love includes much more. The act of love should bring all levels of the human being into play, his intuitions, his emotions, and his logic and mind as well. You know that in the Cabala the attribute of 'lovingkindness' is identified with *chochma*— wisdom. Love really is a *chochma,* a total wisdom. And like any other wisdom it requires study and analysis and thought, and

172

it cannot be left to depend on a bit of emotion or sentiment alone.

"You asked what my father would have said at this time about the religious controversies in our country. He believed in the oneness of all Israel, and in the holiness of all its parts. And he always urged one section of the people to recognize the spark of holiness which exists even on the other side. The nonreligious must realize, even if they don't agree, that the Orthodox are upholding a heritage and values which do possess holiness, and for this they must be treated with respect and consideration. And the Orthodox must remember that all of Israel, even nonreligious Israel, has sparks of holiness, and must not be treated with contempt or read out of the Jewish people. They must remember that although their own religious institutions are holy, our religion declares that the institutions of the Jewish state, by virtue of the fact that they are instruments of a Jewish land and a Jewish people, also possess a certain sanctity, and must not be slandered. It is in this spirit of seeing 'from the roots,' from above, the oneness of Israel, that all discussions should be held and all decisions made."

He spoke rapidly and with an eager intensity. When he finally released his grip on my hand, it was almost time for the evening prayers. "But we should spend more time on my father's basic teachings," he said. "Have you read *The Lights of Repentance*? This book really contains his fundamental ideas. He not only recommended it to others, but would set aside periods of time to study it himself every year before the High Holy Days."

Then, looking at the sun beginning to set outside, he rose and put on his neat black coat. As we went out together, I asked him if he could sum up himself the major characteristics of his father's thought. We walked along, and he considered the question.

"Well," he said slowly, "I think that the secret of my father's thought was his power of 'inclusion,' of being able always to see what seemed to be isolated events and fragments of reality as included within a larger whole. He was able to see not only the branches but also the roots and the tree as a whole."

Abraham Isaac Kook, though involved all his life with the

"dry and practical" areas of Jewish law, was attracted from the depths of his soul to the Cabala, the Jewish mystical writings. He was himself a mystic and tried again and again to convey in rhapsodic outpourings of prose and poetry the intuitive flashes of harmony and joy which he personally experienced. But he realized that the knowledge of the mystic could be conveyed to others only by the use of visual imagery, and he often presented his ideas in that Cabalistic terminology of "the tree and the root" to which his son so often referred.

Man's visible life, his thoughts, deeds, and physical appearance, are likened to the trunk and branches of a tree. It is, so to speak, an upside-down tree whose visible exterior is on earth, but whose invisible roots come from heaven. In terms of this image, the concepts of good and evil, wisdom and sin, receive their meaning.

It is necessary for the branch or leaf of a tree to maintain its connection with the root. Should it sever or even narrow its channels to that root source, it would be emptied of life-giving content and ultimately wither and die. Sin is such an act of "cutting off" or narrowing of communication between branch and root, between part and whole, and its result is pain and destruction. To avoid such destruction, individuals must realize themselves to be not independent entities, but branches connected to a larger totality—a people or a nation—through which connection they can best draw from the root source of life. And these larger social groupings, too, should feel themselves to be branches on the tree of humanity.

Sometimes when the "connections" are broken or warped, more then self-destruction takes place. The power which is in the root runs amuck, as if the force coming from the heart of the universe, which should have been used to bring together man and God, neighbor and neighbor, nation and nation, as if all this energy, unable to flow into proper channels, runs wild and moves the individual parts to unreasonable acts of destruction upon others as well as themselves.

It is the purpose of the Torah to see that such "cutting" of connections does not take place. The purpose of the commandments or *mitzvot* of the Torah is to give us a pattern of thought

174

and action which can widen, rather than narrow, the channels of communication between individual and group, and between man and his root source of life. The goal of the Torah, and, indeed, of religion, is therefore to achieve a greater and more abundant flow of life for man and his world from the Source of Life.

Since, then, the good deed or mitzvah is a source of fuller life, and since sin is essentially an emptying of life content, it requires only "wisdom" to bring us to the right path—the wisdom which perceives that all the seemingly separate parts of creation are bound together in unity, that all men and nations share an ultimate identity of fate and well-being, and no fragment of the whole—no party, no ideology, no single incident or fact—should be seen in isolation, but always "lifted to the roots" and comprehended within its larger meaning. To the degree that one achieves such wisdom or *chochma,* one develops one's capacity for faith and love: faith is really the understanding that all isolated events in time and space are necessary and ultimately good when seen from the total perspective, and love—that is, respect and consideration and feeling for the other—comes when we are conscious of our basic identification with that other.

In the book *The Lights of Repentance,* and in other writings of Rav Kook, these thoughts are poetically phrased and infused by the spirit of a man who, in his own personality and life, seems to have achieved the wisdom and power often to "ascend to the roots."

But there was one afternoon when the shaded room and Rabbi Kook's gentle voice were not enough to lift us above the violent tensions of life. It was the day that I came upon a demonstration of Orthodox women, several hundred in number, before the Knesset. Crowding up to the doors of the Knesset, the women insisted on interrupting the session to protest the national conscription bill which, they shouted, would separate pious daughters from their families, their faith, and their chastity. The organized demonstration soon degenerated into bedlam. The hats of the distraught guards were flung from their heads by the women, and the streets resounded with screams of "Nazi!" "Murderer!" "Shoot us! Why don't you shoot us?"

The crowd which had gathered on the sidewalks looked on

175

with mixed emotions of amusement and disgust. But one little man moved into the midst of the women and shouted, "Nazis, you say! If they were Nazis they would take guns and mow you down like this"—and he held his arms in front of him in imitation of a machine gun. "What right have you got here? Why didn't you bring *it* with you?" His voice rose even above the shrieking of the women. "Why didn't you bring your white flag with you?"

It was obvious that the man was articulating the bitterness of many others who were grimly watching the demonstration. In their minds were angry memories of the war period: the edict exempting all rabbinical students from war service; the young men who came bearing certificates of their Orthodoxy from bearded uncles or cousins, but who lost their faith as soon as the war was over. Watching from the street were fathers and mothers whose children had been killed or crippled by a war whose "holiness" was not sufficient, in the eyes of the rabbis, to distract Yeshiva students from their studies. Now their children were again guarding the borders, policing the streets, running electric plants and hospitals on the Sabbath, and doing those tasks which the Orthodox considered a "desecration of the Name," but the benefits of which they did not refuse.

The man continued shouting about the white flag until the police managed to push the women back from the entrance. When a space had been cleared, an Orthodox member of the Knesset came out and stood quietly looking over the scene. The cigar in his hand seemed to fit, rather than contrast, with his well-fed and well-clad body and his luxurious black beard. Despite the Orthodox cut of his clothes there was something about him more redolent of back-room political caucuses than of the Chambers of Torah. After calmly watching the progress of the demonstration with obvious satisfaction he slowly turned and walked back to the Knesset. The demonstration went on until the fire trucks turned their hoses on the women. Then they quickly re-formed their ranks and marched to the house of the Chief Rabbi to continue their protest.

I had come upon the scene on my way to Rabbi Kook's. I described the affair to him, evidently conveying the bitterness I

176

had shared with the onlookers at the behavior of the women and the bearded representative of the Knesset, who had probably arranged the demonstration; for even as I spoke, I saw the distress in Rabbi Kook's face. But I was wrong to identify him with those demonstrators. He was alone, and so, too, must his father have been. An Orthodox Jew, alienated from the "free-thinkers" who made so light of what was sacred to him, but alienated also from the Orthodox community, whose spirit has been so largely absorbed into small-visioned legalism and politics, leaving little over for the many in Israel who thirst for spirit and religiosity. Perhaps no person is more alone in Israel today than the genuine religious traditionalist, who desires the "full Torah of heart and soul."

Rabbi Kook bent his head and said quietly, "Yes, we do have smallness of mind and heart. We know so well the laws of milk and meat, but the laws of community life, of respect for the institutions and instruments of the community . . . these laws we have forgotten." He placed his hand on mine. "My father, whose memory is a blessing, used to be criticized because he extended his hand to nonreligious kibbutzniks. They told him that one who desecrated the Torah was not worthy of his friendship, but he would say to them, 'Better that I should risk the sin of "causeless love" than that of "causeless hate." ' "

His voice became stronger, and he looked directly at me. "It is true that things are bad with us now, and they will yet grow worse. There is corruption in the land, and a lowering of morale. There is hatred between groups and an ugliness of behavior all about. This is the last chapter of two thousand years of exile and degradation, and all the economic, political, and religious sub-jugation, yes, all the words and all the blows that have ever been dealt us, now their wounds are showing."

He spoke rapidly, and his eyes were bright. "These are the difficulties, yes. But these are also the very proof and sign of the great moment now unfolding itself here. Israel is like a laboratory in which is taking place the greatest synthesis and climax of our history. Peoples who have been separated from each other by two thousand years, different in language, color of skin, tastes in food, are suddenly being molded together into oneness. And

177

even as in the laboratory when there is a synthesis of diverse elements, it is accomplished by noise, so here, too, we have our boiling and fury and storm. But all of this—it is the very proof of this great and unique moment of the ingathering and of the re-creation of the Jewish Tree of Life." His voice was quiet, but tense with effort as if he was trying to lift us both "to the upper roots."

But the ugliness of the demonstration I had just witnessed persisted in my mind. Wasn't there, I asked him, a danger in this advice always to "lift above?" Didn't it tend to make too distant the very real and immediate problems of right and wrong? Could not one "lift" oneself away from the responsibility of taking definite sides in the issues of the day?

He leaned forward, eager for me to understand. "But specific decisions and strategy can be even better clarified from the upper roots. One must make specific judgments, but they should be made from the viewpoint, not of the individual section or political party, but from the level where the whole is seen. The detail is not less important or less clear because you see it as part of the whole. On the contrary, it is more important precisely because it manifests the whole. My father was able to make decisions on a very practical and logical level."

Feeling that the point was not yet clear, he went on. "Look . . . in this room there are light and dark objects. If we let the outside light in, then the gradations of light and dark here will change. What seems light now may, in contrast to the light outside, be dark, but the objects we saw before—they are not more blurred, but are made clearer by letting in the brighter light from outside."

I persisted, thinking still how easy it was to be philosophical in his shaded room. "If we are always trying to see our concrete problems from a higher light, revealing the faultiness of our own judgments, then perhaps our struggles and distinctions of good and evil aren't worth the effort."

He was silent as if forming his thought, and then spoke slowly. "It may be, indeed, that there are different levels of truth in the universe. What is light in this room now may certainly be dark as compared to the brilliant sunlight outside. Even our distinctions

178

between good and evil, or life and death, may be inadequate from a point of view which encompasses more than our limited approach to reality. But why couldn't our universe, by design, have different standards of truth operating on different levels? And we must work only on our level, and with the limited world and vision given to us."

We were again in the "hidden" world of "lights and trees," so different from the concrete world of violence that had manifested itself in Jerusalem that morning. But perhaps Rav Kook was right in claiming that our activities in the "revealed world" would be clearer and wiser if they were influenced by wisdom and light of the hidden world. Perhaps that vague atmosphere termed "causeless love," and the vision of a historic destiny, inclusive of all the diverse political and religious groupings of the Jewish people—perhaps these seemingly abstract ideas and moods were needed to achieve both wiser and more practical judgments even on matters like the national conscription bill. Perhaps, as the Cabala claims, our troubles do derive from "separations"—from separation of man from man, of flesh from spirit, of the outer life of activity from the inner life of ideas, or of the practical decisions of everyday life from the invisible mood of "causeless love."

When the time came for me to leave Jerusalem and Zvi Yehudah Kook, I brought along a movie camera. All partings, the sages say, are like a sixtieth part of death, and I hoped my films would somewhat minimize this fraction. Our talks together had come to mean much in a very personal way, for his eagerness "not to allow any boundaries" had taken our relationship beyond the formal.

He looked at the movie apparatus on my shoulder as I entered the room, but said nothing. I told him I was leaving that afternoon, and we spoke for a while about Jews coming to and leaving the Holy Land. His father, of course, had firmly believed that all Jews should return to the land of their historic birth, and I asked him if he also felt that way. He chose his words delicately, conscious of the fact that I was leaving.

"There is, I think, a special connection between this land and Jews. They do fit each other. After all, this is the cradle.

179

Here the Jewish soul was created. I really think," he smiled gently, "that even the light, the climate, the shape of the hills, particularly fit the soul of the Jew and bring the highest out of it."

"But," I said, "what about the five million Jews in America? Don't you think they also have a special destiny and role in Jewish history?"

"Of course, of course," he said quickly. "But though you live in a wonderful and free country, isn't there, Jewishly, a type of 'slavery?' Not, of course, of the body, but a twisting of mind and spirit, no matter how slight. For instance, when you try to think through problems about the Jewish people or Jewish ideas, don't you even subconsciously strive for conclusions which make your relationship with non-Jews more comfortable? Don't you avoid certain conclusions, even if they be true? But you certainly have important work there," he added, as if unwilling to push the point. "Tell me about your own work."

I tried to describe the work of a rabbi in the United States. He was particularly interested in the description of services in a liberal synagogue. He asked what prayers the Reform group omitted or changed, and nodded his head encouragingly as I answered.

"But I see," he interrupted me gently, "that you haven't taken off your own *yarmelke*. I am afraid I haven't been able to remove entirely the *mechitza*—the boundary between us. I am really sorry." His eyes were smiling, but I was still at a loss for an answer, and mumbled the talmudic injunction about "respecting the sensitivity of others." For the first time I saw a flicker of irritation pass over his face. "No, no, that is exactly what I do not want, for you to be something not natural to yourself out of deference to me. Why should we have to think that we must always stamp our image upon others?"

He spoke with deep feeling, and then, dropping the subject abruptly, rose from the table and went to the shelves on which his father's manuscripts were stacked. "We should really spend our little time studying a bit." He looked through some manuscripts. "My father, blessed be his memory, didn't organize his writings. He always envied those who had a talent for putting

180

their creativity in order, but still he felt that such creativity was secondary. Primary creativity is like the lightning flash."

He brought a few manuscripts to the table. "He wrote and wrote. He would take up his pen whenever he had a moment, and everything—poems, legal observations, philosophy, commentaries on the prayers—he wrote swiftly, and would rarely rewrite or cross out." He showed me a page of manuscript in the fine handwriting of his father, and read aloud, "There are times when I feel low and worthless, but then I think of the divine soul within me, and I am raised. . . ."

Rabbi Kook's eyes twinkled. "You see, he even wrote personal confessions."

I interrupted to ask if he himself had not written something we could read this last hour. He seemed surprised, but pleased, and took down a magazine from the bookshelf. It contained one of his own pieces and we began to read it together. It was finely written, and the ideas were stimulating and well worked out.

I could not resist the question which had been with me ever since meeting the son of Abraham Isaac Kook. So often the children of great men break from their father's path in order to assert their own talents. Did Zvi Yehudah Kook not feel any resentment at being known as "the son of Rav Kook?" His eyes lit up in amusement. "I would really be satisfied to consider myself a continuation of my father. Of course," he smiled playfully, "his style, some say, was a bit too poetic and vague, and I try to make my writings clearer. But he is the source, I am only the continuation." Then he became serious. "The truth is that Ha-Rav was one of the truly gigantic personalities of all generations. There are great minds who specialize in this or that talent, but only rarely does someone rise above and synthesize them all. Rav Kook had such a primary-source mind. It drew from an elemental creative power which expressed its genius on different levels and through diverse talents."

The time had come for parting, and Zvi Yehudah Kook took my arm and accompanied me through the door and onto the sidewalk. Hesitatingly I stopped and asked him if he would mind being photographed. He patted my arm and said, "But it isn't necessary."

"Well," I persisted awkwardly, "just to remember everything better."

He grasped my hand. "We will remember each other in better ways."

Zvi Yehudah was right, and the memories I have of later visits with this gentle rabbi are better than the picture I was never able to snap. These visits always were accompanied by a warm handclasp and a word of Torah from his late father, usually something about the importance of the land of Israel, and a reminder that all that happened in this land must be understood by "ascending to the roots" and seeing it from the perspective of the whole. But the last time I knocked at the door of his little room there was no answer. When I inquired at the Yeshiva, Rabbi Levine, the secretary, told me that Zvi Yehudah was hardly ever at home these days. He was usually at the printer trying to complete work on two of his father's books, one on Jewish Law and the other on Jewish legends. He wanted them to be published for the anniversary of his nephew's death. Levine sighed and asked if I had heard of the tragedy which struck the family the summer before. The twenty-one-year-old son of Rabbi Kook's sister—his name was also Abraham Isaac and he had shown promise of following in the footsteps of his famed grandfather—had been drowned while bathing near Tel Aviv. Rabbi Levine warned me not to speak about the tragedy to the family—they still burst into uncontrollable tears. But I would be able to meet Zvi Yehudah later at the synagogue.

I did see Zvi Yehudah again, a few days later, but this time there was no chance to talk. It was the night of Tisha B'Av—the fast day which in Jewish tradition commemorates the fall of the first two Temples, and which has also become a symbol of Jewish national tragedy in a general sense. Outside of Orthodox circles few Israelis still mark Tisha B'Av, the Ninth of Av. Neither are they very sorry about the destruction of the Temples, nor in agreement with the main thesis of the day's prayers, namely that the great tragedies in Jewish life are brought about by the sins of the Jewish people. Even among religious Jews,

182

traditional wailing and weeping on this day has become weaker. Some rabbis have even suggested that the fast be annulled now that a Jewish state has again arisen. But in the Yeshiva of Rav Kook, the benches were overturned and men and boys sat on the floor in positions of mourning. The room was dark and they held candles over little books which contained the lamentations of Jeremiah along with some of the saddest prayers in Jewish tradition. In the semidarkness it was hard to recognize anyone, and the individual voices were subdued under the heartbreaking melody to which the cantor was chanting the verses from Jeremiah. Only after some minutes had passed did I hear the suppressed sound of sobs coming from the corner of the room.

It was Zvi Yehudah, his little figure in black bent over the book, crying. It is hard to see a man crying, and I had never seen Zvi Yehudah even sad. Always there had been the warm twinkle in his eye and the comforting word about the future. After all, why should a person who has faith in a good and merciful God cry very much? The great second-century rabbi Akiva, Abraham Isaac Kook had once pointed out in one of his commentaries on the prayer book, had shocked his fellow rabbis by laughing when he saw a fox walking among the ruins of the destroyed Temple. Later, while visiting in Rome, he had again surprised his colleagues when he had laughed joyously at the sight of Roman grandeur and might. The reason, suggested Rav Kook, was because the Divine wisdom in his wondrous heart assured him, "through almost living imagery, that Rome and all its idols would pass away, and the light of Zion would shine forever. In this certain knowledge of the future his pure heart was so filled with love and delight that scarcely any place was left in it for a sigh about the horrible present, which he recognized to be as but a light cloud on the face of the shining sun in the heavens."

That was the greatness of Rabbi Akiva, pointed out Kook, the same greatness which enabled him when the Romans were stripping his skin with iron combs, to cry out, "Blessed am I, that I can now fulfill the commandment to love God with all my soul—by giving Him my soul."

Perhaps this indeed is the example of a man of faith, and the reward of all who can truly ascend to the roots. If so, then it is good that the tradition allows at least one day for even the ascenders to remain for a moment in the branches below. At least on one day they can cry, like Zvi Yehudah was crying that night, for the sufferings of his people, for the loss of his nephew, for all those who remain caught in the world of the branches.

CHAPTER X

The New Yishuv: Conversations in Dagania

"I recall from the teaching of the sages: Whoever walks by the way and interrupts his study to remark, How fine is that tree, how fine is that field—forfeits his life!

But I assert that then alone will Judah and Israel be saved, when another teaching is given unto us, namely: Whoever walks by the way and sees a fine tree and a fine field and a fine sky and leaves them to think on other thoughts—that man is like one who forfeits his life!

Give us back our fine trees and fine fields! Give us back the Universe. . . ."

—*Berdichevski*

A. D. Gordon, Religion of Labour

"Here, you know, was the cradle of it all," Mottke Hadash said, when he saw me looking at the anniversary program of Kibbutz Kinneret on the bulletin board of the dining room at Ohelo, the hostel on the shores of Lake Kinneret dedicated to the memory of Berel Katzenelson, one of the ideological leaders of Labour Zionism. Mottke was in charge of the hostel and also a member of the kibbutz, which had arranged the program in commemoration of its forty-eighth anniversary as a collective settlement, and he seemed to feel the need for explaining why the program booklet was so elaborately printed.

"You might say that this valley was the spiritual birthplace of modern Israel. Here was born the idea of the kibbutz, the communal settlement of the halutz—the pioneer—redeeming the land by the sweat of his own brow. Ben Gurion, Ben Zvi, Berel

185

—in fact, many of the present and past leaders of the country—worked here when they came to Israel in 1904–05 with the famous Second Aliyah."

"How about A. D. Gordon?" I asked, noting that the program contained no quotation from Gordon's writings, though some of the others were represented. "Of course, Gordon," Mottke added. "He also worked in the Kibbutz Kinneret as well as in Dagania where he is buried. He really belonged to no particular settlement, but he has become associated with Dagania, and is buried there."

But it was Gordon in whom I was most interested, I told Mottke, as we walked toward the office of the hostel. Wasn't Gordon the clerk who at the age of forty-eight became a farmer in Palestine, the prophet of the Second Aliyah's "religion of labor?"

Mottke sat down behind a large, glass-covered executive desk and offered me a comfortable upholstered chair. He switched on two little white plaster fans, turning one in my direction and the other so that a breeze fell on his heavily sweating shoulders.

"You might say that Gordon's ideals were in the air at that time. They were shared by most of the workers who came here. But in many ways, those who founded the Labour movement didn't follow Gordon. He disagreed, for example, with people like Ben Gurion or Katzenelson. Nor was he a socialist, and he was very unhappy when the present Mapai Party, Israel's majority party, was formed. But of course even though people didn't agree with him they all respected him."

Mottke hadn't known Gordon himself, but there were people in Kibbutz Dagania a few minutes away who did know him. Mottke promised to make arrangements for me to see them.

"But times have changed, and ideals too. When we came here there were only barren hills and a few Arab tents. Now," he waved his hands in the direction of the green fields and settlements all about us, "we have only ten thousand dunams in this part of the Jordan valley, that is about five hundred acres, yet we supply almost ten per cent of the country's food." Mottke moved the fans again so that the breeze would blow upon us more comfortably. I wondered how the rather weary, mild-mannered grandfather sitting hunched over the desk before me had looked when he came here forty years ago. One of the workers at Ohelo had told me that in his youth Mottke was the first champion of a swimming contest across the Kinneret. He was also famous for having disappeared one year from the kibbutz without saying a word to anybody. When he came back a year later they found that he had gone to live with the Bedouins. Now Mottke Hadash had seven grandchildren and his two sons were farmers in pioneer settlements near the Dead Sea and in the Negev.

Later that afternoon I sat on a bench in Ohelo's lovely garden, and looked at the program pamphlet which Mottke had given me. It included some excerpts from the writings of the pioneers who had come to the Kinneret valley fifty years ago. I could not have chosen a more appropriate physical setting for what I was reading. Below was the sea of Galilee, shaped like a rounded harp—*kinneret* in Hebrew—its deep blue flecked by miniature white waves. On the other side of the lake was the curved ridge of the Gilead Mountains, called "the Horse" by the Romans because of its shape. This was the scenery which had confronted the young men and women who had come here, and even the most hard-headed of them were inspired by it to poetic words. A page in the pamphlet contains some lines written to his parents by a young man with a stubborn chin, who was then called David Green.

"About an hour and a half from Tiberias on the southern end of Lake Kinneret, on the top of a small hill stands a small farm. Over against us are the hard proud hills of Gilead. Their soil is filled with wrinkles and furrows, as if time had sealed into them the ageless secrets of long ago memories. And on their summit rests the spirit of the ancient hero Jethro the Giladi. Time is so short and there is so much work—the work burns." Evidently the young man who was later to call himself Ben Gurion was even in those days attracted to the military heroes of the Jewish saga. Like all those who had come with the Second Aliyah, the future Prime Minister of Israel believed that "a homeland is not given or received as a gift; not acquired by privilege or political contracts; not bought with gold or held by force. No,

187

it is created by the sweat of the brow. The true right to a country, as to anything else, springs not from political or military authority, but from work."

This had been the thought which fifty years ago had brought a group of twelve young men and women to the banks of the Kinneret. There on a small hill they found "a black house without windows or holes in the wall, and beyond, mountains strewn with black rocks. Between the house and the mountains are black goat-skin tents. Nobody greeted us, nobody gave us the blessing of peace. Nobody asked why or from where we came. We unloaded the wagon and began to clean the filth which had filled the house almost to the roof. We had to prepare a security position before the night. . . ." So wrote the leader of Kibbutz Kinneret which was established near Dagania a year later.

Another page of the pamphlet quoted the dark-eyed poetess Rachel. Before her death, after only a few years of life on the shores of her beloved Kinneret, she had written the poems which are now popular folk songs in Israel.

"As the dawn rose we began to work," were the words quoted in the pamphlet, ". . . blistered feet, sunburned scratched faces, keen and burning. The air was filled with the ring of our songs, our talk and our laughter. Our hoes lift and fall without pause. For a short moment you stop, and wipe the sweat off your brow with the edge of the kaffiyeh [the Arab-style head scarf] and look lovingly at the lake—how blue, blue beyond expression, bearing peace and healing for the soul. How good it is to walk in the path along the lake until we come to the Wall of Tiberius with its round towers. So old is Tiberias that it hardly seems to me to be a city, but more like a painting out of an old history book. These skies saw the pale face of the preacher from Nazareth, heard the teachings of the Rabbis. . . ."

Gordon came a year or two later. He joined the young people, most of them half his age, in the fields, working at their side with an intensity and mystic ecstasy which even they in their youthful romanticism could scarcely comprehend. His thin, gaunt body would sway as he wielded his hoe or pick in a quick, almost trance-like rhythm. In the evenings the "Old Man" would join the young people in the circle dance, the hora, a dance which was more like an expression of a mystic rite than of light joy. They would dance sometime in happiness, more often in a kind of entranced despair, until they fell in exhaustion, and Gordon would be the last to stop. Then in the early mornings while his comrades still slept, Gordon would write his letters and essays. Often the topic he chose dealt with some practical matter of the day—politics, or labor. But suddenly his prose would lift up into a flow of words as if the pen in his hand were whipped by a power beyond his control.

"Then in that day, son of Man, you shall raise your eyes, you shall raise your eyes upwards and you shall see the land and the creation and all which is in it. You shall see the heaven and all its hosts and all the worlds which are in them, without end and beyond understanding—and behold, all of them shall be close to your soul, and behold, all of them shall bear unto you a blessing. Then shall you attain the eternity which is in the moment. Then shall you know how great is your richness, how great is the blessing which life bears for you. Then you shall know and say in your heart: how impoverished and how poor is life taken from others, the rule over others, the light taken from others! And on that day you shall love all that exist, you shall love man and you shall love yourself, for your heart shall be full of love. And you shall have faith in yourself and faith in man. You shall believe in all that requires belief—you shall be completely filled with life."

He wrote soaring words about the joy and cosmic meaning of labor, and about life which would annul the distinction between goals and means. This was his constant theme—the mistake of dividing life into moments of preparation and of "life."

"For, if there is no life in the preparation for life, there is also no life. . . . Life is only a continuously extending ladder of goals, and we will never do more than climb toward goals. Hence we must find life in the 'climbing,' in the 'preparation'—for there will be nothing else."

Ambitious words. How had they survived the test of reality during these fifty years? For that matter, how much of what was said today about those days and about Gordon had been reality?

189

People need saints, and the pioneers at that time needed someone who by his life could testify that their dreams were valuable
—that man could sense cosmic mystery in ordinary "black labor";
that a person could utterly recreate himself, turn even his pain
and suffering into instruments which would enlarge his capacity
for life. Had Gordon really done this? Was he such a saint?
This, too, was what I wanted to ask the people in Dagania who
had actually known Gordon. In a few years it would be too
late.

Near the bench where I was sitting, a gray-haired gardener
was bent over a flower bed. He was an excellent worker, Mottke
had told me, though when he had come from Iraq five years
ago he had known nothing about gardening. Now he was doing
the kind of work which Gordon had recommended. I wondered
how he would react to the division of labor and life which was
expressed in the little pamphlet I held in my hand. I asked him
how he liked his work.

He straightened his back. "I am fifty-three," he said, pointing
to his gray beard and hair. "Grown old fast, eh? But what can
I do? I have five children."

But did he like his work? The old man shrugged. "Not bad,
the people here are nice, but the tiredness is great. What can
you do—we want to send our son to school so that he can get
an education and not be a dirt-worker like his father." The old
man sighed. "In the sweat of thy brow shalt thou labor," he
said, and returned to his weeding.

In the Arabic world from which the Iraqi gardener had come
nobody endowed hard physical work with the quality of moral
virtue. This was one of the problems in modern Israel. The
Jewish peddler in the ghetto at Casablanca might have been
starving, but he had one consolation, his status was at least one
level above that of the fellah, the peasant laborer in the fields.
When he came to Israel and heard words from the officials of
the Jewish agency about the glory of physical labor, he was
likely to regard his lecturer with a cynical grin, seeing this as a
device of the Ashkenazim—the European Jews—who wanted to
make the Eastern Jew a fellah. For the Oriental immigrants,
and they were the largest part of recent immigrations into Israel,

190

Gordon's "religion of labor" was quite meaningless. The halutzim —the pioneers who came from Russia and Poland to the shores of the Kinneret fifty years ago—had come out of a culture which produced men like Tolstoi, who put on peasant shirts and went to work in the fields because they had convictions about the religious and moral values of physical labor. They had come here with a daring idea—that the commandment to earn one's bread by the sweat of the brow was not a curse. They wanted to annul the distinction which the Cabalists made between the "taste of the shell" and the "taste of the fruit." Was it really possible to so transmute the prosaic tasks of man's life, even backbreaking physical labor, so that it became exalted and meaningful? This, too, was one of the questions I wanted to ask the people in Dagania. Were they even making the attempt these days to carry out ideals like these? How much of Gordon's teaching was still alive and meaningful in the land which had enshrined him as a saint of the "religion of labor?"

I already had received one authoritative opinion. Before coming to Kinneret I had visited S. H. Bergmann, Professor of Philosophy at the Hebrew University, who had edited four volumes of A. D. Gordon's letters and essays. I questioned him about what had happened to Gordon's ideas.

"Mata—dead," the white-haired professor had replied softly, lowering his eyes for a moment to the desk.

"That which Gordon feared most in our society—hypnosis— has taken over," he said. This was Bergmann's analysis of Gordon's central demand—that man resist being hypnotized by empty phrases, slogans, and formulas which come from without rather than from his own work and thoughts. It is a form of hypnosis, claimed Gordon, which enables others' judgments and feelings, institutions and political parties, to enslave our judgments and feelings and to have power over us because we are empty within and have lost contact with the source of our own creative life.

"These ideas are meaningless to us today." Bergmann shook his head. "I know—I have spoken to young people about A. D. Gordon. No, our goals now are material accomplishments, technical efficiency—that which Gordon did not want."

191

"*Mata*—dead.*" The professor bent his head again.

Was this what Mottke had meant when he said that times had changed and ideals too?

The next morning the irrigation pipes and sprinklers were already fighting their battle with the hot sun as I walked from Ohelo along the lake road to Kibbutz Dagania. The fields on both sides of the road were very green. Near the bottom of the small hills around the lake were the silvery fishing ponds maintained by the prosperous kibbutzim of the Kinneret Valley. From the road I could see the lovely houses with balconies, trees, and gardens in which the early pioneers now lived. Much had changed, as Mottke had said, but in one respect conditions were the same. Only a few yards away from the settlements were people who disliked them heartily, would destroy them if they could. The Jordan border is not more than a five- or ten-minute walk from the fields of Dagania. Near the main gate of the kibbutz was a cement pillbox heavily chipped by bullet pockmarks. A few yards farther on was Dagania "B" formerly a part of the original kibbutz, but later split from it. Near the entrance to Dagania "B" stood the Syrian tank which had been stopped there in 1948 by a Molotov cocktail. Had this tank not been stopped—it was leading a Syrian column of tanks—Dagania and the other settlements in the area would have been destroyed in the early days of the War for Independence.

In Dagania itself the lawns are still criss-crossed by trenches. I passed a young girl dressed in the customary kibbutz uniform —blue bloomer pants and white blouse. She directed me toward Bet Gordon—the ornithological Museum named after the Poet of Labor, as he is sometimes called. Here, on the second floor, I found Palmoni, the Director whom Mottke had suggested I see. He was bald, with thick spectacles and rather tired eyes. I interrupted him discussing a dew chart with a young lady, but he politely agreed to chat for a few minutes. We walked through some rooms with exhibits of wild-animal life to his office. Palmoni sat behind his desk wiping his glasses and waited for my questions about Gordon.

He had not known Gordon personally, Palmoni told me. Furthermore he was a scientist, not a philosopher. There were others in the kibbutz who could tell me more about Gordon, because they had known him. But, more important than what even they could tell me, suggested Palmoni, were Gordon's writings, which I could read in the room above that was called the Gordon Corner. Still, the museum director would try to answer my questions.

I began by telling Palmoni about Bergmann's opinion of what had happened to Gordon's ideas.

Palmoni narrowed his eyes and answered slowly as if trying hard to be objective.

"It seems to me that in the past three years the ears have become more attentive to what Gordon had to say. There is a search for values here, values beyond Zionism and politics, and a growing recognition that it might be found in Gordon—in his profound linkage of man, nation, world, and cosmos. To be sure," Palmoni nodded, "you will often hear native Israelis use the word *Gordonist* in a mocking tone, describing somebody who has an overdeveloped sense of duty. But cynicism is a tribute paid to an ideal, though it may be an admission that the ideal cannot be achieved. At any rate, in the past few years there has been a reaction to nihilism. How long can you live with *nihil?*"

Despite his disavowal it soon became obvious that Palmoni was thoroughly acquainted with Gordon's ideas and the most intimate details of his life. He disagreed with those who claimed Gordon as a kind of Jewish Tolstoi.

"Of course, everyone in that age had read Nietzsche, Schopenhauer and Tolstoi, and the latter's ideas are close to Gordon. But if you squeeze Tolstoi, you find in him a spirit essentially alien to Judaism. Tolstoi didn't really like or understand Judaism. Gordon's thought, though original, comes out of a completely Jewish framework of ideas and feelings. At the same time it can be of great meaning to non-Jewish people. I have received letters from a Burmese visitor to whom I gave a book about Gordon, and he cannot begin to thank me enough for having acquainted him with the man and his thought. Of course, Gordon looked upon his writing as but an incidental expression of his total living. He would write at his small desk, between the hours of three and five in the morning. That was the only special privilege he asked—a table, pen, ink and paper, and a light to write by.

193

Otherwise, he shared everything with his comrades. He said his writing was a way of clarifying and gathering his thoughts as if they were sheaves that had grown in the fields of life activity during the day, and could in this way be harvested and neatly tied together. But more than his ideas and his writing," Palmoni said, "was the influence of his personality. He was always happy and inwardly rich."

"Was he really?" I asked. "How authentic was the legendary picture of Gordon? Was he able to find light and life in his own sorrows; was he really able to make out of what for most people was life's 'preparatory moments,' the essence of life?"

Palmoni shrugged. "I would suggest that you look over Gordon's letters for a more intimate insight into his soul. I can tell you only a few things that personally impressed me in the stories told about him by his comrades. He did have tragedies in his life, great tragedies. He lost five children in Europe, and his last remaining son refused to join him in Palestine. This parting must have hurt him deeply, though Gordon never spoke about it. Somebody has recorded a moment in Gordon's life when he received news of his son's death. The son had been more religious than his father and had refused to follow him to Palestine, going instead to a Yeshiva. Several years later Gordon was working here in the settlement, and during lunch somebody brought him a letter. I think it was his daughter who told the story. The letter contained the information that his son had died. She told how a look of profound sadness and absorption came over her father's face as he read the letter. He stopped eating and went to his room, where he lay on his bed for half an hour. He spoke to no one. When the bell rang for work, he took his hoe and went out into the fields again, still speaking to no one. He believed in silent mourning. Yes, he had tragedies in his life. Even the fact that his daughter Yael, who lived here in Dagania, was unmarried must have oppressed him. He tried always to break somewhat the bond between them, to wean his daughter away, but failed.

"It seems," Palmoni hesitated in trying to sum up the essence of Gordon's influence, "that he had a kind of magic personality. There was something magnetic about his bearing, his blue eyes, the way he looked directly at everybody. But again, I recommend that you read his own writings and maybe something by one of his biographers, Tzemach. I can take you, if you like, to the Gordon Corner."

I followed Palmoni up the stairs again to a small, rather bare room. Hung on one wall of the room was one of the few pictures which Gordon had reluctantly allowed to be taken of himself. It showed a thin, ascetic face with high cheekbones, and a long straggly beard. Even in the picture his light eyes appeared remarkably keen and pure. Another picture showed him in the working clothes which he always wore—a Russian-style sacklike shirt which buttoned down the middle and shapeless pants encased in high rubber boots. Framed on another wall was a page of manuscript from one of his essays. Gordon always wrote on the same type of paper, in a careful square script. Palmoni drew a curtain in the room enclosing a rickety green table and chair which Gordon used for his writing. Alongside it was the wooden chest in which he kept his manuscripts. There was also a very small faded army-style knapsack which Gordon used to take on the hikes which he loved so much.

I spent the rest of the afternoon in the Gordon Corner, reading some of his writings.

The problem to which Gordon frequently addressed himself in these writings was the relationship between the individual, the nation, and the family of nations—a typical problem of nineteenth-century nationalism.

"Every person," wrote Gordon, "belongs by natural grouping to an organic 'family of men,' a nation—just as all nations are part of the family of nations. There is no such creature as 'man' in the world. There are Russians, Germans, Englishmen, and so on. And to the degree that the Jew destroys the natural Jewish foundation in his soul, he substitutes therefore an unnatural national foundation. In other words, he becomes an unnatural Russian, German, and so on. You cannot in rebuttal cite the fact that there are assimilated Jews of great ability, for who knows how much such men would have gained in depth of soul, in originality, had they developed their Jewish foundation instead of having destroyed it?" The national entity, like the individual,

195

claimed Gordon, could be moral or immoral. Therefore he proposed the concept of a "man-nation"—that is, a national entity which would take upon itself the same high level of morality which is asked by Judaism of the individual. This was the kind of nation which should be regenerated in the land of Israel. "Not because we are better, but because we have purchased the right to reveal such a light through our suffering. . . ." There ought to be no conflict between humanism, nationalism, and individualism. Of course, the prophets, Gordon points out, "were all three at the same time."

"The nation may be likened to a funnel: at its wide receiving end, endless existence is poured in, while through its concentrated, restricted end, the funnel empties its contents into the soul of man. The nation therefore is the force which creates the spirit of man. It is the link which unites the life of the individual to the life of mankind and to the world at large." But a people, thought Gordon, could best make contact with "cosmic life" if it were rooted in its natural geographic habitat. The natural habitat of the Jews is Palestine. But Jews had to do more than reroot themselves in their ancient land. They had to transform their character as a people. They had to cease being a "half-people, a semi-nationality" and become whole again and healthy, which for Gordon meant that they must return to nature. This return must not be a "knowing about," but a living with nature. Specifically, Jews had to become again manual laborers and do physical work, preferably on the land and in agriculture. "Only when a man works with his hands on the land are the barriers between him and the deep cosmic forces of the universe removed. Like air to the bird, like water to the fish is the environment of nature to man. To the degree that he removes himself from it, his life force, his most basic feelings and relationships dwindle in vitality."

Important as ideas like these were to the pioneers of the Second Aliyah, they were not original with Gordon. They were, as Mottke said, "in the air" at that time. What impressed the admirer of A. D. Gordon was his personal "concretization" of these ideas. He was the living example of a thesis terribly important to those who talked of becoming farmers in Palestine. This was the proposition as Tzemach, one of his biographers, phrased it: "that instead of adapting the desires of the soul to the framework of life in which people happen to find themselves, they can change the framework to fit the desires of the soul." That it could be done Gordon proved by leaving the clerical work he had been doing in Russia for twenty-seven years, giving up a secure financial position—Gordon was related to the wealthy family of Baron Ginsberg and worked on one of their estates—and in the end becoming a manual laborer in Palestine. Others were leaving eastern Europe for Palestine in those days also. But they were young men and women. Their lives were before them. Gordon was forty-eight. He had a wife and two surviving children with no source of support—a framework of life not easy to break for a man of conscience, and Gordon loved his family. But he gave what little money he had saved to his family and left for Palestine. Two years later he sent for his wife and daughter. In Palestine, Gordon immediately began working on the most difficult jobs available—laying roads, or digging irrigation ditches around the orange trees. He worked in various places, mostly in Galilee, sharing both the hard labor and the disillusionments which the early pioneers encountered in those days. They met not only malaria, danger, and hard work, but Jewish employers who preferred cheap Arab labor to the Jewish intellectuals who had never wielded a hoe before coming to Palestine. Many of them gave up and left. Some committed suicide. The reality of life in Palestine shattered the dreams which the young people had brought with them, including the almost religious faith in the holiness of physical labor. For those who remained, Gordon was the rock upon which their despair and doubt could rest—the living proof that their ideas were not a chimera.

Tzemach asks the question which most biographers do not attempt to answer. How and at what point in his life did Gordon the clerk or even Gordon the pioneer suddenly become Gordon the legend, the spiritual teacher of the Second Aliyah?

"One night," theorizes Tzemach, "one of those nights when he could not sleep and wandered around the vineyards or the dark alleys of Petach Tikvah . . . he suddenly realized that there really were no farmers or farm settlements in Israel and there

197

was really no Jewish community there. He must have suddenly seen this truth and felt the despair in this moment of recognition." It is at this moment of ultimate despair that everything was suddenly clarified for him. One thing had to be obtained, then everything that didn't exist up until that time would begin to exist—settlements and farmers and Zion itself. What was that thing which would make possible what was now lacking? Precisely that which was lacking—namely, physical labor. Gordon's basic idea, says Tzemach, is the complete identification of the love of Zion with physical labor. They are not two spheres, one of which influences or is influenced by the other. These two phenomena are really one—this is the essence of Gordon's thought. All that came after this were simply details of elaboration. He never could understand after this personal revelation why other people did not do as he did—behold, it was all so clear and so evident.

How did this sudden change come about? Tzemach says, "It was the fruit of despair—Gordon did not become changed before his searching eyes rested upon the terrible congealed emptiness. He didn't come to it until something essential—perhaps the one foundation in his life—crumbled beneath his legs."

Tzemach does not use the terminology of "second birth" and "conversion" to describe what he is trying to say happened to Gordon. But he does seem to be describing just this kind of phenomenon, and Gordon himself speaks in his letters of the feeling of "having been born again."

In fact, Gordon's writings do have an apocalyptic mood and vision akin to the ecstatic vision of the prophets in the Old Testament and of some of the writings in the New Testament.

This apocalyptic religious tendency in Gordon's nature is not the part of his thought and life which impresses his more secularly minded comrades. That it is, however, at the center of Gordon's life and experience, becomes clear when we read a passage which can also be found in Tzemach's anthology—Gordon's last words as recorded by his daughter Yael.

Yael and others tell how one winter Gordon began to feel pain in his digestive system. He went to a local doctor in Safed, and the illness was diagnosed as cancer. Dagania, his kibbutz, sent him to Europe for treatment. The doctor in Vienna, who was much impressed by Gordon and insisted on taking his picture— one of the few pictures of him now in existence—revealed to him his fatal illness. Gordon decided to return to Israel and to die there. During the last few months of his life he remained very alert, writing letters to friends and interesting himself in every aspect of national and local life. When he spoke about death he spoke about it as a natural phenomenon. There were other times though, his daughter Yael relates, when he would remain quiet and nobody knew what he was thinking. On the last days of his life, she writes, "he expressed the following thoughts:

"There would come a day when man would penetrate deeply into those areas of his soul which had hitherto remained sealed. . . . In generations to come great and mighty secrets of science and technology would be revealed. There would be as well a process of inner revelation within man which would parallel this progress in science and technology. Man would reveal hidden and mighty forces within himself which would enrich mankind and bring him to new levels of culture and soul. In this sense, he compared all mankind to individual man who in the dawn of his life began to turn his mind away from his inner private world and to recognize the outer world about him. Only in the years of understanding, after he has gained some knowledge of the external reality about him, does he begin to turn his mind again to his soul, to his inner world. "With great excitement my father described the exalted future of man when he would begin to find and dig up that which was hidden in his soul—how the hidden light would burst out, light up and perfect the relations of man until he reached the level of a new sky and a new earth. . . ."

I confess that that afternoon at the Gordon Corner in Dagania as I read some of his writings, I felt my plans to "de-mythologize" him ebbing away. A. D. Gordon was one of the saints of the world.

But there remained a large question. Was there anything of the new man, and new sky and earth which Gordon dreamed about, present along the banks of the Kinneret, where Gordon had worked and lived? Mottke had arranged an appointment for me the next day with Yaacov Berkowitz, who had lived with Gordon.

What Has Happened to the Dream?

Yaacov Berkowitz was a ruddy-faced man with white hair and a small mustache and mild, very blue, eyes. His wife, who has written many children's stories under the name of Miriam Singer, was a dark-haired, vigorous little lady. With a warm smile she told me that Edmund Wilson had visited her some years ago. "Perhaps you read about me in his book."

Miriam Singer was very proud of the little two-and-a-half-room apartment in which she lived with her husband. They had a beautiful picture window opening up on the hills of Gilead, tastefully arranged furniture, bookcases, and a radio.

"Yes, it's not luxurious, but very adequate and comfortable for us."

Miriam kept urging her husband, Yaacov, to tell me something about Gordon, but Yaacov seemed to have little to say.

"There is nothing to tell which hasn't been written. After all, when Gordon wasn't working, he was usually sunk in his own thoughts, or riding alone. You have to understand," he said to me almost apologetically, "that in those days there was little time after work."

"But there are some personal impressions you can give him," Miriam broke in eagerly. "Like his eyes—they were very, very blue, like Kafka's eyes." Kafka she added, had been their friend in Prague, which was her original home. Again, bashfully, Miriam took down a book from her library and showed me a personal inscription to her from Kafka. As if trying to make up for her husband's reluctance to talk, she went on to tell me how "girls in those early days lived in a room not far from the boys. At three o'clock in the morning she would hear Gordon walking up and down in his heavy boots, collecting his thoughts before sitting down to write. Once during the night she had peeped in and seen the green light of his lamp suffusing the room as he sat

200

hunched over a square piece of paper, writing. "And there was another incident that I can tell you about personally, even though it may be in the category of tale-telling.

"Once our Zionist youth movement in Prague invited both Martin Buber and A. D. Gordon to speak to us. I remember clearly how Buber spoke—with elegance and eloquence. Then Gordon got up, very plainly dressed, and waited quietly for a while, until he felt the words coming to him. Then he offered his thoughts. Buber," Miriam smiled, "stayed at the best hotel and later presented us with a handsome bill. Gordon stayed in some awful hole in another part of town and walked from there to the meeting. He never sent us a bill. You have no idea how we were impressed by this and by him."

Again Miriam looked at her husband, and this time Yaacov obliged by an anecdote. "I do remember once when he was attacked by an Arab and severely hurt. What bothered him then was not the hurt, nor a desire for revenge, but the degradation to man involved in such an affair. This made him sad, that man could do such a thing to man. It was the way that he always thought of things. Our youth would react differently—they would strike back if struck."

I visited Yaacov and Miriam at their apartment on several afternoons, and frequently the conversation turned on the subject of the youth. Miriam felt that they were "not the same, that something is missing in their lives which we once felt." The Israeli younger generation was "too closed in. They read very little, and when they do talk to each other they talk only about crops and farm problems."

Yaacov differed with his wife.

"That doesn't mean that they are lacking in culture—by culture I mean the relationship of man to man. They don't have to speak of this to themselves. Believe me," Yaacov's voice grew stronger, "this youth is just as idealistic—they are ready to offer themselves completely for the defense of their homeland."

"Ah, that isn't what I mean, Yaacov." Miriam shook her head.

One day Miriam arranged a meeting for me in her apartment with two members of the "young" generation. One of them was

201

already in his thirties, and had a son of sixteen. He was a good-looking, ruddy-faced blond, with strong hands which he moved as slowly as he spoke. He was, I found out later, the son of Palmoni, the director of the Museum, and he was also in charge of one of Dagania's most important agricultural products, the banana crop. The young man who came with him was in his early twenties. He kept his eyes lowered and spoke in a monotonous voice, making his answers as brief as possible.

Did the younger people, I asked them, think much of Gordon's idea of a man-nation or his "religion-of-labor" ideas?

The two young farmers looked at each other. "We don't indulge in this kind of talk," the younger one said. "Most of us don't feel a need for that sort of thing. We have enough satisfaction in our work and in the fulfillment of our national duties."

"This youth is ready to sacrifice itself," Yaacov burst into our conversation, "completely for their homeland, like Hannah and her seven sons."

"But Hannah's sacrifice was for a religious ideal," I said to Yaacov.

"They have their ideals," Yaacov maintained, "their country —and they will offer themselves up readily for it."

"As for religion," the younger Israeli said with a smile, "we have the problem of the religious, not religious problems."

He laughed at his own analysis of the situation.

"He means that he finds the activities of the religious parties in Israel quite disgusting," Miriam added in explanation. She seemed concerned at the lack of depth in the conversation she had arranged.

"To be religious," Palmoni's son said, speaking obviously because it was expected rather than because he was interested in the subject, "means to believe in God and in a personal providence. If one doesn't believe in God, then why does one need religion and prayer?"

Yaacov nodded in agreement and Miriam shook her head in disagreement.

I remained with Yaacov and Miriam after the young men had left and Miriam's feelings burst out explosively.

"No, they are not the same as us—and I don't agree with them or with my husband on the subject of religion."

Dagania, Miriam told me, was a freethinking kibbutz, everyone was free to follow their own religious convictions. But this freedom did not work out so well in the educational process, she felt. Miriam told me of an argument which had arisen among a gathering of teachers once with regard to teaching the Bible and answering children's questions about God. A teacher had told about an incident which had arisen in her class when a child in the settlement had died. The children had asked questions about death and life and she had finally brought in the concept of God. The next day a child came back to say, "My father says that God did not make us, but that we come from monkeys." There had ensued an argument which ran for several days, each child bringing into the discussion the attitude given him by his own home. The controversy had finally ended when one bright young girl suggested that "even if man comes from a monkey, God creates the monkeys."

Miriam's point of view was that whether or not there was a God, teachers ought not to deliberately destroy a child's belief in Him. "After all, they do not destroy children's belief in giants or fairies or in any other inhabitant of the imaginative world which people agree belongs in a child's universe. However, here in Dagania we are a bit more traditional than other kibbutzim." Miriam and Yaacov invited me to attend their Sabbath, which this week was to be followed by a special holiday celebration. "One of the holidays we have created and revived here, Tu B'Av. You know that's the day when the Talmud says the boys and girls went out into the vineyard to dance with each other."

"'There were no days so happy in Israel as the days of Yom Kippur and Tu B'Av,'" Yaacov quoted from the Talmud.

"You mustn't expect too much of this kind of creative holiday," Miriam warned me, again disagreeing with her husband.

Before the Tu B'Av celebration I visited the nearby Kibbutz Kinneret and chatted for an hour with another man who had known Gordon. Miriam had told me about Aaron Shidlovsky.

"We call him a young Turk," she said. "He has eccentric ideas which nobody wants to follow but everybody respects him.

For example, when we had a shortage of electricity, he insisted on using only a fifteen-watt bulb in his room. Also, when the older settlers got new apartments, he refused to move into the newer section, but remained in the older one, on principle. His wife disagrees with him too, on these things." Miriam laughed, looking at her husband.

"You should see the way he runs up and down the telephone pole, even though he is over sixty," Miriam added. "He is really worth visiting. He too knew Gordon. It is worthwhile talking to him."

Aaron Shidlovsky was bald, with strong face and jaws, direct blue eyes, and a careful, measured manner of speech. We talked on the grass lawn outside of the house, one of the poorer dwellings in the kibbutz, from which he had refused to move on principle. His eight-year-old granddaughter danced on the lawn around us, coming up every once in a while to tug at his sleeve and interrupt our conversation.

Like Yaacov, Aaron insisted that there was nothing that he could add to what had already been said about Gordon by others or written by Gordon himself.

"He was a man who lived out his ideals. He knew that it was inevitable that any organization brought together for achieving a goal ultimately became a goal in itself," Shidlovsky said softly but with bitterness. "This is evidently what has happened.

"Several years ago I attended a meeting of the Vatikin, the old settlers, and listened to their speeches. I wondered if they ever had known what I had thought they knew, or whether they were always bluffing. They spoke about accomplishments—by accomplishments they meant a new dining room, tractors, two-room apartments. Are these the accomplishments we started out to achieve? Wasn't it rather a new society, a new type of human being? Where is that accomplishment?"

I pressed Shidlovsky to tell me something more about Gordon. Had he really found the happiness which he spoke about?

"Happiness?" Shidlovsky lifted his head and looked upward toward the sky. "Gordon wasn't happy—that happiness and joy he expressed through song and dance was more like sadness, more like an expression of despair than happiness. When he

204

danced he would close his eyes like the Hasidim in their religious dances. All our dances in those days were an expression of our awful despair, not our happiness. I never joined in them."

"Why is it forbidden to dance?" his little granddaughter, who had been listening, asked saucily. "Please don't interrupt," Aaron answered her with a smile.

"Was Gordon then religious?"

"Of course he was religious," Shidlovsky said. "He said prayers on the Sabbath and the holidays—perhaps not always, but very often."

What specifically were Shidlovsky's objections to the present life in the kibbutz, I asked.

He shook his head bitterly. "Objections—we speak too much about our rights, too little about our obligations. We have no 'right' to land, to better buildings—we have only obligation."

"To whom are we obligated?" I asked. Shidlovsky remained silent a moment, and I expanded my question. "Doesn't the word *obligation* presuppose a 'something' to which we are duty bound? A religious Jew, for example, would say that he was obligated to God."

"We are obligated to our own inner self, I would say—I don't distinguish between outside and inside, it's all one."

"So you are disappointed at what has taken place here in the kibbutz and in the country?"

"Yes, for the most part," Shidlovsky answered quietly. "Still, if I had to do it over again, even if I knew the result in advance, I would do it."

"Why?" I asked.

"The early kibbutz settlement was primarily for individuals. I found my place in it that way. Today it is very often the opposite type that is attracted. Besides, I still believe in physical work—believe it makes life better.

"As far as what has happened to the movements and the organizations—I suppose it is in the nature of a movement to operate this way. So it has been and so perhaps it will always be." The basic mistake, thought Shidlovsky, when he reflected on it, was that the collective settlement was not meant to be a mass movement. It was really meant for small groups who wanted to

205

assume a special way of life—a life which assumed obligations rather than talked about rights.

"Perhaps in a hundred years there will be a reaction and again some small groups will try to do what we tried. After all, we are not obligated to succeed, only to try. 'The task is not for you to finish,'" Shidlovsky said, quoting the Talmud, "'but neither are you free to desist from it.'" As for the relationship of Israeli youth to Gordon and his ideas, "things grow only in relationship to external pressures. The pressures here, the need for security, the constant threat of attack have produced a type of youth which cannot be interested in Gordon," Shidlovsky said flatly. "But perhaps in a hundred years there will again be small groups," he repeated.

The "New Jew" in Process of Formation

The next afternoon I told Miriam and Yaacov about my conversation with Shidlovsky. We sat on the balcony of their apartment. Yaacov had been reading *Macbeth* in Hebrew and the play may have put him in a wondering mood, for instead of defending the kibbutz against Shidlovsky's charges, he seemed troubled.

"It is a difficult problem that we have here in the kibbutz. In many ways kibbutz life was easier when Gordon was alive than now. Of course we had here, when we came, only rocks, barren rocks and malaria. We ate tomatoes three times a day. But the problems of communal life, of property were easier. Then the children came, and they had their own needs and ambitions. And there were the problems of immigration; the needs of the state and all became more complicated. Even before the Second World War many of the kibbutzim found that their own manpower was not enough to handle the intensified agricultural projects which they wanted to add to their farms and which the state said they had to create. Furthermore, we have special seasons when we need large numbers of additional workers. So we began to hire help to work on the kibbutz." Yaacov nodded his head unhappily.

Miriam objected to Yaacov's line of thinking. "It's not so

206

simple a problem as hired labor. True, it's good for us, and without their help we wouldn't be able to expand our farms, but it's also good for them. Where else would thousands of immigrants be able to find work? Where else would they learn trades and become adjusted to life here? In this respect Ben Gurion was perfectly right when he called on kibbutzim to hire the new immigrant labor as a national duty."

Yaacov shook his head impatiently. "You are not right, Miriam."

"Ah," Miriam argued, "exploitation you call it. It is the laborers who are exploiting the kibbutzim. They receive here more than they give."

Yaacov shook his head again. "We have done something which is a contradiction of our principles—we have stepped away from the truth. Look, I have been reading since your coming," Yaacov nodded to me, "some of Gordon's writings. Wait a moment." He went into the house and brought back a yellow volume. "Listen," he said and began reading.

"We always seek easy and simple ways to fool ourselves. We want to find excuses and blame things upon the 'iron rule of historic necessity' or say that historic needs force us to seek compromises. Or we say that when we achieve our final goal we will then have better things. But if we in our lives will not to the degree possible be completely 'holy' we may be sure that the future toward which we direct our souls and for which we are living will also be completely nonholy."

Miriam was quiet for a moment after Yaacov finished. "Oh, it's hard. They accuse us of being selfish, of not wanting to open ourselves to the needs of the land, if we don't hire help, and don't increase productivity. Then if we do hire, we become unprincipled. Just last year we had a discussion. The army asked that one of our children become permanently attached to the Air Force. Many in other settlements would have said no— there are plenty in the city who can become fliers. If our children leave the farm, who will work here? We are old now. One person got up at the meeting and said 'If we don't have security, we don't have the farm either,' and all of us voted to let him go."

"You are not right." Yaacov shook his head again. "No matter how we try to justify ourselves, there is a breaking of principles."

It was time to go to the dining room, Miriam said. The Sabbath meal had begun and immediately afterward was the Tu B'Av celebration.

Still talking, Yaacov followed us to the door.

"Of course it isn't easy. Work on the soil in itself is not a solution—even Gordon knew that. It requires *hakara* (understanding)—constant self-education, a conscious effort to maintain the essence of life which is the relationship between persons." Yaacov continued talking as if reluctant to let me go, but Miriam pulled me away.

The tables in Dagania's dining room were covered that night with white tablecloths. Everyone had changed from working clothes into freshly laundered, though informal, garments. Most of the men wore white shirts and many of the women had put on dresses instead of the customary slacks or bloomer pants. Miriam asked me if I had seen the new dining hall at Dagania "B". It had air-conditioning, and fine imported furniture from Denmark—a real show place. "I don't agree with this type of luxury," Miriam said. The Sabbath meal was ample, with choices of chicken or vegetarian meals for everybody, along with soup, the customary green salad, and the thick juice squeezed out of assorted fruits. Proudly Miriam pointed to the back of the room where a seven-branched electric candelabra was lit. This Sabbath there were to be no songs or program, perhaps because of the scheduled Tu B'Av celebration. After the meal the older people went their various ways, some to sleep in their rooms, others like Yaacov to read the papers in the library. Miriam was eager to return to her room in order to hear a news broadcast. I stood around the dining room waiting for her and Yaacov to return. Except for the tall date trees, the square outside the dining hall could have been a night scene in any small-town main street. The little children played games among themselves, the teen-agers grouped together in small bunches or leaned against the trees, watching their friends go by. About nine o'clock the young people started moving toward the lake, where the celebration was to take place. Yaacov and Miriam returned and we walked out of the settlement, across the Jordan bridge, and up some stone steps which led by a hill that in Canaanite days had been called Bet Yerech. As we passed some of the excavations glistening in the moonlight, Miriam called out to a straight-backed young man walking ahead of us.

"What period of history is this from, Yoni?"

"From the period of the Patriarchs," Yoni called back.

"You see," Miriam proudly said, "archaeology is a religion with these young people. They are utterly fascinated with it."

She herself was interested in archaeology, and the Kinneret Valley is rich ground for archaeologists. Near the lake are settlements dating back to all layers of Palestinian history. The large mound of earth which we were passing had at one time been a Canaanite temple. Archaeologists had uncovered nine large circles whose purpose was not clear but which seemed to have something to do with religious rites, for several stones were marked with the number nine and male and female fertility symbols. The number nine may have had a connection with moon worship—the name Bet Yerech means House of the Moon. The Tu B'Av celebration was going to take place directly below the wall of what once had been a Canaanite fortification overlooking Lake Kinneret. A few yards beyond the fortification were the remains of a Roman bath, complete with heating ovens and a pipe water system, and alongside of that a fifth- or sixth-century Byzantine church with its typical three circular apses. There were also synagogues dating from the early centuries of this era when the main Jewish settlement in Palestine had been in Tiberias and along this lake.

We sat down on the ground amid the teen-agers who had begun singing. After a while a mustached youngster stood up and asked for silence. An accordionist and one of the girls in charge of the program announced to the group what songs they were going to play and invited them to sing along. The youngsters joined in the singing but without too much spirit. Only when they came to one of the less melodious rhythmical "clapping" songs did they show some animation. The main program of the evening began with a Bible reading.

The reader, Miriam whispered to me, was the young lad whom the kibbutz had given to the army. He was followed by six girls with long dresses embroidered in Yemenite style, who placed some mats in the moonlight and offered a delicate and graceful dance. They represented the daughters of Shiloh, in a dance they had composed, and were accompanied by a drum and a soft melody sung by a trio of three girls' voices.

This was the end of the program. The master of ceremonies stood up and announced that there were ample refreshments for everybody a few yards away. There would also be swimming and "other sports," everybody tittered, "according to the spirit of co-operation which prevails this evening among the girls."

"Well, that's it," Yaacov told me as we turned to leave. "I told you not to expect too much."

I kept Yaacov's warning in mind later when I tried to sum up my impression of Tu B'Av at Dagania and of the "new Israeli" that now lives and works in the valley where Gordon and his comrades dreamed their dreams. But one particular impression of the evening troubled me even more than the obvious artificiality and spiritlessness of the new holiday. It was the feeling that there was no natural connection between these young people and the Canaanite fortifications which looked down upon them, despite all of Ben Gurion's talk about a leap backward through time. These young sabras loved the land in which they had been born and were willing, as Yaacov said, to offer their lives up for it, but were they rooted in it? The melodies of songs that they sang came from Yemen and Russia, not Israel. The decorations on the dancers' gowns were from a Mid-Eastern Arabic culture. Nor were these sabras and their re-created new holiday rooted even in the tradition of their own fathers. They were free from the yoke of the past—but such freedom is not always pleasant or good, suggests Yishar Smilensky, a member of the Knesset as well as a writer.

"Many of the people sitting in this hall," Smilensky said one day to a conference of fellow writers in Tel Aviv, "have a lineage they can trace back many generations. But those of us who were born in Israel go back only one generation. Before our parents, there was the dark. History begins with Father. Perhaps there was something Father knew and loved, but all we know about is the negation of the Diaspora. . . . So we swash-

210

buckle around our island in history bold as a soldier. But growing on thin soil leaves its marks. There is no denying that
beginning a new society has its fascinations . . . but there is
also something lean about it, just scratch and you come to bare
rock . . . for there is a hard rock bed between ourselves and
the period before Father's immigration to Israel. No wonder
we're so expert in world literature: from Iceland to China, we
know all the literary movements, major and minor, the way we
know American jazz. But we have to admit our own roots are
shallow.

"Look, to be free of the yoke of the past, to have all open,
all permitted, is a great and inspiring thing, no doubt. On the
other hand, it is a condition without mercy, lacking shade, dried
out, bereft of contact with moisture.

"We have lost the power given to plants to break through
rocks with their roots though we know how to dynamite the
rocks and mountains."

Smilensky, who signs his novels and stories Yishar, continued
in a mood of self-reflection to which the old-timers paid close
attention, because Yishar is himself a sabra, broad-shouldered,
tousle-haired, with white shirt open at the collar.

"Whatever the reason, we aren't writing for the most part
about the phenomenon of Israel, in all its breadth, depth, and
limitation—perhaps because we really are not here, not at home;
perhaps it's because this is not really our place, our environment,
ourselves. . . .

"Finally, we have no idea of what the individual is like in
Israel, for there is a new type of individual being born and
growing up in this country, a type that is not quite formed yet,
that has not come out of the mold."

Yishar's feeling is often shared by the visitor to Israel. Even
the sabra Hebrew seems to be without modulation, as if the
language has not yet had time to pattern its tones. And the
sabra, too, seems at times like an unfinished product—"primal
matter," not yet stylized by the shaping forces of deeply rooted
life patterns. But as Yaacov said, one should not expect too
much. It is, after all, little more than fifty years that have passed

211

since Gordon and his comrades came here, dreaming of a new heaven and earth and a new kind of man.

One should not expect too much. Yet, there must be hours, nights like Tu B'Av when the old-timers walk alone near the quiet pine grove where A. D. Gordon is buried and hear again in their minds the warm, half-joking greeting of the "Old one": *"Nu poritz"*—how's it going, big shot? What would they say on such a night if looking into Gordon's keen, truth-seeking blue eyes, they tried to make "accounting of the soul?"

It would be no use trying to fool their old comrade. They might be able to impress tourists with the air-conditioned dining room of Dagania "B", and its acoustic tile ceiling and its modern furniture above which in large Hebrew letters is one of Gordon's favorite biblical quotations:

"And the commandment which I give you this day is not far from you, but close to you in your heart, in your mouth. . . ."

But they know, these old-timers, that it was not the commandment to build gorgeous dining rooms or comfortable two-story apartment dwellings or even rich farms which moved Gordon's life. He was satisfied with his "living room" on the mat in front of his small shack. The commandment which Gordon strove to fulfill had to do with something more difficult: the "interior" achievements of life—a new kind of human being whose life was so inwardly rich, whose relations with other human beings were so vital and full of feeling that houses, possessions, radios, and other "achievements" of this sort became quite unimportant. And the old-timers know now that Gordon was right—organizational and economic arrangements are not in themselves effective in creating a new man.

As to the "new dimensions of soul" which Gordon hoped would come out of the return to nature and to clean physical labor, where are they? Do the farmers in Dagania today and their children understand what Gordon meant when he said, "If you do not grasp for much, you do not grasp anything?"

The fact is that these young people, who had not read Gordon but claimed that they lived his theories, hardly knew about the life experience which was at the center of Gordon's life. The gaunt-cheeked, bearded man who danced with sadness on his

212

face and pulled weeds with ecstasy in his eyes, was a religious mystic. He knew from personal experience that a man could be reborn and that even the trivial moment could be invested with high cosmic meaning. He knew that man through his free will could utterly transform his own life and cultivate a *hakara,* an inner consciousness, which could transmute even sorrow into an instrument for broadening the current of life. But this type of mystic experience, central in Gordon's life, had not been transmitted to others in Dagania. Lacking were what the Hasidim of Meah Shearim would call the "vessels" of such transmission. The old religious vessels had been thrown away, and the new ones, like Tu B'Av, were empty of emotional content and historic depth.

The fact is that talk about cosmic experiences and a new heaven and earth would not interest the new generation of farmers in Dagania. The young people sitting along the moonlit banks of the Kinneret under the Canaanite fortress were like young people in other country villages of the world. In some ways they were more mature, for they had been raised in a condition of constant crisis and taught from an early age to assume responsibilities to their community and people. But basically, they were husky, clean-limbed youngsters, decent in speech and ideals, not very different from good youth anywhere in the world.

Granted then that there is no "new heaven and earth" in the valley of the Kinneret. "Is it then a small thing that has happened here?" Yishar had asked toward the end of the aforementioned speech. This is a new "world where many flags have been raised and many and good banners fallen and dragged through the mud. All the pretty formulas and great and wonderful beliefs which were articles of faith yesterday, have been stripped of their glory, even for those who are still alive. Go out and see what has happened to ideals like humanism, socialism, even Zionism," says Yishar. "But if we look for something to lift the spirit, where, nevertheless, can we find it better than through a glance at what has happened in Israel these forty years.

For is it a small thing that has happened here?—the renewal of a people's fate and faith, of its land and of its human material."

Entries can be made on both sides of the ledger. Gordon believed in the creative power of man's will—the power of this will to successfully bring about the seemingly absurd. What happened in Israel can prove him both right and wrong. To have said fifty years ago, when Palestine was a neglected, almost nameless barren land under Turkish sovereignty, that a young group of Jewish farmers would be singing Hebrew songs along the banks of the Kinneret was as absurd a dream as one could entertain. What brought it about? Russian pogroms, Hitler, or the will of human beings? Israel can be proof for either thesis. No land has seen great historical forces make more of a mockery of the idea that man can control his destiny. And no land has been able in the past and is able today to offer more proof of the power of an individual's will to change "the framework of life so that it adjusts to the soul rather than the soul to it." Perhaps this is always the choice we have in looking at our inner and outer world. "There is enough design in the universe to make atheism look silly; there is enough heartlessness in the universe to make religion heartbreak house," says Henry Slonimsky. The same type of choice exists for anyone who makes an accounting of soul among the kibbutzim of the Jordan Valley. We can see here what happens to all great ideals—how they grow old and tired with their bearers; how organization and instruments made to achieve an ideal become themselves the ideal. Or, one can look at the green fields of Dagania, at the faces of the young people, and wonder if Gordon's faith was really without fruit. In the meantime, even as we make up our balance sheet, we must note how Yishar, sabra that he is, impatient therefore with the sentimentality and phraseology that sabras contemptuously label "Zioniut-Zionism," concludes his talk to his fellow writers. "Of all that has been written during the past fifty years, most worthy of being taken into account and being thought about again is not a work by a professional writer. It was written "by a Jew not young and not a writer; a worker who lived not today but forty years ago; on the shores of the Jordan and the Kinneret. And in the evenings by the light of a wick he wrote what he wrote—'that the real foundation of all spiritual labor is the actual work of our hands . . . that such work not in an economic, but

in a moral sense is the basis of truth for all spiritual building.'
I don't know," says Yishar, "but it seems to me that the proclamation which came from Gordon and was born on this land is a profound and deeply rooted truth which still waits for a generation to realize it. It is a truth to which previous generations listened and which generations to come will yet hear."

CHAPTER XI

Ben Gurion and the Bible

"A Good Man Lives by His Faith"

Despite the occasional glance of respect toward the man who wrote by the light of a wick on the banks of the Kinneret, it is not A. D. Gordon but one of his fellow workers who is looked upon, and who indeed looks upon himself, as the mirror of modern Israel's true values. If so, then these values are somewhat different from those of the bearded mystical poet of labor whose aversion to force was so great that the only weapon he would carry, even on guard duty, was a whistle. Ben Gurion, when he worked in the Kinneret Valley with Gordon, looked upon himself as a conquistador even in those days. His battle then was with malaria, swamps, hunger. But the wiry little worker with the stubborn chin was attracted to the military image— Jepthah, the soldier of Gilead, Joshua ben Nun, the conqueror of the promised land. And the name he later adopted, "Son of a Lion," was the name of a valiant fighter in the days of the Bar Kochba revolt against Rome. The key to Ben Gurion's violent break with his old colleague, Lavon, during the "affair" which broke up the government in 1961, was the latter's sneering allegations about the Israeli army. But it is easy, and fallacious, to oversimplify the character of Israel's Prime Minister by emphasizing his attraction to military heroes. For it was not Gordon, but young Ben Gurion who wrote lines like the following soon after arriving in Palestine in 1917.

"Beautiful are the days in our Land, days flushed with light and full of luster, rich in vistas of sea and hill. . . . But infinitely more splendid are the nights: nights deep with secrets and wrapt in mystery.

The drops of burning gold, twinkling in the soft blue dome of the sky, the dim-lit purity of moonlit nights, the lucid crystal of the transparent mountain air—all is steeped in yearning, in half-felt longings, secret undertones. You are moved by urgings not of this world. . . ."

Ben Gurion is, in fact, a complex personality of richly developed and varied interests. His interests in Yoga, Indian thought, Spinoza, Greek literature, and the Bible, though well publicized, are in fact based on genuine enthusiasm and knowledge. Sentiment and realism, poetry and practicality, and other potentially warring antitheses dwell together in a personality which seems more simple than it really is because it is totally committed to a single guiding life idea—the thought that a man should try to realize in life deeds the ideals he professes, or in the words of his favorite biblical phrase, "A good man lives by his faith"—with the emphasis on the word *lives*.

It was this idea, in addition to political circumstances of the moment, that impelled him some years ago to resign from the government and move to a Negev kibbutz. Sdeh Boker, the kibbutz to which Ben Gurion still retreats on weekends and between governments, had the virtue not only of being in the wilderness—and the "Old Man" likes to think of himself as a "man of the wilderness"—but its young boys and girls were unaffiliated with any political party, a fact that falls in with the Prime Minister's dislike of his country's present fragmented party system.

In 1955, while Ben Gurion was in retirement at Sdeh Boker, I visited him and heard his thoughts about religion in Israel. Transportation arrangements to the Negev were difficult then. It was before the Sinai campaign and the Egyptian Fedayeen were active. Luckily I was offered a ride with Paula Ben Gurion, who was returning from Tel Aviv to Sdeh Boker for the Sabbath. It was an interesting ride though a bit uncomfortable at first. Chaim, the driver, came into the lobby to say that Paula was waiting impatiently in the car. I ran out quickly.

"*Shalom,*" I said, opening the front door and gingerly pushing aside the tommy gun lying across the seat.

218

"Shalom," Paula Ben Gurion replied. "Are you a rabbi? I hate rabbis, they are all hypocrites."

I had heard that Mrs. Ben Gurion was not famous for her diplomacy, and anyway I knew she was half joking—but still, it was only half a joke.

"Well," I said, punning weakly, "I'm a *rav m'tukan*" (*m'tukan* in Hebrew meaning both "reform" and "adjusted").

"They are just as bad." But by now I was inside the car, where I could see the broad, good-natured lines of her face, and felt more at ease. We drove a few blocks farther to pick up another passenger, a friend of Ben Gurion's, which precipitated a momentary social crisis. "I brought a young girl from my kibbutz along," said the friend to Paula, stooping down to the car window.

"What, you brought a friend?" Paula groaned. "How will we take her—where is the room? You should have asked if we had room. The car is filled with luggage."

"Well, if there's no room it's all right," the man said in embarrassment, for the girl was standing near him. "I told her that there might not be room."

Paula uttered a few more loud sighs and finally said, *"Nu—* let's move over." But by this time the young girl, who had overheard the conversation—it was not hard to overhear Paula—was gone. The friend wanted to leave without her, assuring us that she had other places to go, but Paula would not have it. "Go find her," she told Chaim imperiously. He spent the next few minutes searching for the girl, and finally found her.

Once we had all settled back and were well on our way, Paula began to regale us with her recent adventures in Tel Aviv. She had been to see the American production of *Porgy and Bess* that week. "The American ambassador invited me as his personal guest. So much fuss. I even dressed up and wore my ermine wrap. This is the second time I have ever worn it. A rich American gave it to me several years ago, but when do I have a chance to wear such things?" She continued to tell us about *Porgy and Bess* as the car sped along a highway flanked by eucalyptus trees. These trees had been Ben Gurion's idea; they grew fast

219

and could shield troop movements from enemy observation as well as afford a pleasant shade to the road.

When we came to Beersheba, the streets were already empty in anticipation of the Sabbath. Only one restaurant was still open, and we ordered some tea while Chaim made arrangements at the police station for the military escort which was to accompany us in the next lap of the journey through the Negev to Sdeh Boker.

Paula lost no time in asking the waiter why the cups weren't clean, but he evidently knew who she was and took it all good-naturedly.

The road from Beersheba runs through barren land, and we passed one of the oil derricks then under construction whose progress the whole country was eagerly watching. Paula kept assuring me that "it is not too late—we may still run into some shooting." After an hour of traveling we saw the thirty-odd wooden shacks, surrounded by a barbed-wire fence, which had been the home of the former Prime Minister and his wife for over eighteen months. At the gate our military escort turned around and we drove into the settlement alone. The guard, who was standing some yards away, waved us by. Paula was incensed. "What idiocy not to look and see who is in the car." Chaim protested that the guard recognized our car, but Paula was still angry. "How can they know from a distance? They have to realize that Ben Gurion is here and not be so sloppy. Well, how do you like my garden?" she said, interrupting the outburst and waving to the empty expanse all around.

We drove up to one of the wooden cottages and Ben Gurion came out to greet us. He was wearing khaki pants and a heavy white sweater which he later told us was made from the wool of the settlement's sheep. The "Old Man," as the young people like to call him, appeared to be in good health, and after greeting us briefly, went with his wife into their cottage. My two companions on the trip and I strolled over to some wooden stalls and watched two boys and a girl feeding the few hundred sheep and goats that are Sdeh Boker's chief occupation.

The man who was visiting Ben Gurion with me had once been a shepherd on a kibbutz, and he watched the evening feeding of

220

the animals with interest. When one of the boys called out, "Bakbuki—here, bottle-baby," and placed a nursing bottle into an eagerly upturned mouth, I asked him why. He explained that in cases where the mother had no milk to give its offspring, bottle-feeding was necessary. I decided not to ask whether it was a lamb or a kid that was being fed—I was too ashamed to confess I couldn't tell the difference. We watched quietly while the three young kibbutzniks went efficiently about their work.

Darkness had fallen. It was Sabbath now, and some stars began to twinkle in the night sky. They were the stars, I couldn't help thinking, that Abraham must have seen in the Negev when he heard a voice saying, "Look now toward heaven, and count the stars, if thou be able to count them. . . ." It is hard not to slip back and forth in time like this in Israel. The "baas" of the lambs and goats, the barbed-wire fence about, the guns and ammunition hung along the inside of the sheep stall—it all seemed almost too much like what it was supposed to be.

A bell rang and we walked toward the dining room. As we approached we could hear singing, and I was surprised to recognize a traditional Sabbath hymn. But this seemed to be all there was of tradition. There were no candles in the room. The young people sitting at the rows of wooden tables were dressed in clean khaki clothes, some wearing white woolen sweaters. Most of them were members of Nachal—boys and girls in army units who worked on the land as part of their military training. They ranged in age from seventeen to the early twenties. I sat between Mrs. Ben Gurion and her husband, who, apart from a few sharp comments on people who insisted on calling themselves Zionists and were yet unwilling to come to Israel, did not say much during the meal. He seemed to enjoy the few potatoes, vegetables, and the small piece of meat served in honor of the Sabbath. I found the meat almost impossible to chew. But one of the boys pointed out that in this kibbutz they at least enjoyed hot meals on the Sabbath—a luxury not permitted in the army, whose messes were operated under strictly Orthodox supervision.

After we finished the meal B.G. invited me to his house and we walked over to his small cottage. Paula insisted on showing me through each of the three rooms and appealed to me to admire her chintz curtains and colorful rugs. Ben Gurion's study was filled with books in Hebrew, English, Spanish, Greek, and other languages. He sat behind a modern blond wood desk on which piles of books, magazines, and papers were neatly arranged. He was not at all officious, but I had the feeling that he had neither the talent nor the inclination for chit-chat. We spoke about liberal Judaism in Israel. Quite a number of rabbis, he told me, had come to him with this same question. "I told them, and I tell you," his voice rose oratorically, "we need to have liberal Judaism in Israel. The state needs it for the sake of religious freedom and freedom of conscience. Come and set up a liberal synagogue. Let the youth here see something else besides *them*. Ach," his voice dropped, "I tell you, I know them. Most of them don't have God in their hearts." His wife came into the room carrying a broken flour sifter and asked if we could fix it. I reached for it, but B.G. was ahead of me; he seized the sifter and started to bang it against the desk, declining any assistance from me. "Not with strength and not with might," he said, as his face grew red with exertion, "but with common sense." After a few minutes of effort there was a click, and with a grunt of satisfaction he returned the utensil to his wife. We resumed our conversation.

I asked him if he would associate himself officially with a liberal religious movement. He shook his head. "No, my way has always been to ask of anyone else only that which I am prepared to do myself. And I am not a synagogue Jew. During the last High Holy Days I did go to services, to be together with the soldiers there, and I read the prayers carefully—some of them are magnificent but some absolutely horrible. But I can understand," he went on, "how other people might need religion. I have a daughter-in-law, an English girl who was originally Christian. Now she lights candles every Friday night. She feels the need to express her Judaism this way. But as for me and my son, her husband—to live here and to fight and work for the land is enough for us." He mused for a moment, then added, "I am sure Moses believed God spoke to him, and perhaps there is a God, but I just can't believe God really spoke to him. However, these views of mine have nothing to do with the principle of freedom of religion here. You know, we faced this question at the beginning of the state. There was a problem of phraseology in the Declaration of Independence. Rabbi Maimon had insisted that the first proclamation of the Jewish state must mention God; he wanted to include the phrase 'Rock and Redeemer of Israel.' A good Marxist Mapamnik, who happens to be the son of a rabbi, insisted that God was not responsible for the coming into being of the state and wanted no credit given Him. I finally suggested that they compromise and use only the words 'Rock of Israel' which each group might interpret according to its own philosophy. So it was."

We talked a while longer and I asked him what there would be left to link the Jewries of America and Israel together if in the end the Yishuv could offer only the alternatives of Ben Gurion's nationalism or a rigid Orthodoxy. He frowned. "It is *the* problem." Then, hesitating a moment, he continued, "Hebrew—Hebrew must be our connection." It was an answer I had heard before, but I had the feeling that B.G. was not really convinced by it. Perhaps somewhere in his mind he had already settled for there being no connection—and no Jewry outside of Israel with which to connect.

We got on to Maimonides. Israel had just begun celebrating the 750th anniversary of his death. B.G. said of him, "Oh, a great mind. You know, the Rambam could easily, as he said, have proven that the world was not created *ex nihilo* according to the Bible." He was referring to the medieval dispute over the Aristotelian and Jewish concepts of creation. He reached over to the little Bible on the corner of his desk. "There is actually one element, you know, which is not created, according to the Bible." He started reading from the first chapter of Genesis. "Water," he pointed out, "is not mentioned as having been created; this passage could be interpreted as saying that it existed before the creation."

Suddenly he looked at his watch. "Oh, oh, I almost forgot. You will have to excuse me, but I must make my readings." We said *"Shalom."* He reached into his desk for a flashlight and hurried outside—to measure the dewfall and temperature, which was one of his duties in the kibbutz.

223

I left the little house and walked across the field to the room where I was to spend the night. One of the members of the kibbutz had gone to the city for a few days; I was to sleep in his bed. There were two young boys sitting on the other bed when I came in. They greeted me and watched me unpack my bag. There was a knock on the door, and two other boys sauntered in. I reached into my bag for some cognac, which may or may not have been helping my week-old cold, and asked the boys if they would join me. They hesitated. Then one of them rather bashfully accepted, poured a little into a cup, and, to my surprise, put his hand upon his head and offered a blessing. He drank, and passed the cup along to the lad standing near him, who awkwardly went through the same ritual. It suddenly dawned on me that they must have heard I was a rabbi and had taken my invitation as a suggestion that we make kiddush together on the Sabbath. The cup went the rounds, and everyone blessed it. I asked one of the boys, a tall serious-faced lad from Tel Aviv, if he preferred the kibbutz to the city. "It's all right," was the reply. I asked him whether he had come because he felt it was his duty, and he shrugged his shoulders. The boy sitting near him spoke for him. "Of course that's why he came. He just doesn't want to say. Somebody has to come here."

Outside a bell rang and the boys told me that a special Sabbath program had been prepared for the evening. We went outside and walked toward the darkened dining room. Inside I saw that the electric lights had been switched off, and in their place three candles were burning on a table in the far corner of the room. Behind this table sat two girls and three boys with some books open before them. As my eyes became accustomed to the candlelight, I could see the others sitting on benches along the walls. They were singing a mournful song about the Negev, about the dew and blood with which it had been sprinkled. They finished and there was a moment of silence. Then one of the girls whose blond hair and spectacles glinted softly in the candlelight announced in a low husky Hebrew that this Sabbath eve was dedicated to the memory of the "thirty-five." She was referring to the thirty-five Hebrew University students who had been killed by Arabs at the beginning of the war when they

224

tried to bring help to a kibbutz near Hebron. There was another pause after this, and from the other end of the table a boy with Yemenite features, large dark eyes, and curly black hair began to read *"L'Dovid,"* a Psalm of David. "Blessed be the Lord my Rock, Who skills my hands for battle, my fingers for war. . . . Deliver me out of many waters, from the hand of strangers. . . ." Then a shot was heard outside. Coming at that moment it seemed almost too appropriate. Several of the young soldiers left the room immediately. Everyone waited and listened, but there was silence. The young soldier finished his reading. Then a girl read a poem about the thirty-five.

Again there was a pause, and then another song. Somebody called out that they ought to have some dancing and everybody laughed—the proportion of boys to girls was about five to one—and they went on singing. There was a final song, evidently their favorite—they sang it over at least a dozen times: "When Ben Gurion puts on *tefillin,* and Sdeh Boker keeps the Sabbath, and Moshe Sharett takes up ballet, then will the Messiah come."

A sturdy blond boy stood up and offered to organize some games. They played blindman's buff and the room rang with laughter. The games were still going on when I left the room and walked out into the night. It was impossible to turn in and I walked over toward the barbed-wire fence. My thoughts spun round—so young, these boys and girls, yet exposed at any moment to the very tragedies of the psalm they had read.

I walked back to the little room in which I was to spend the night. My young roommate had thoughtfully left a light burning for me. I noticed copies of *Moby Dick* and *War and Peace,* in English, among his things, along with some agricultural manuals and a few Hebrew books. And on top of the bookcase stood two hand grenades, apparently for decoration. The evening's events kept me awake. There was something in them deeply relevant, I felt, to the questions whose answers I was seeking in Israel—but what?

I remembered how when I came to Israel, the papers had been filled with accounts of the fighting around the clubhouse built by the Histadrut near the Orthodox Meah Shearim quarter of Jerusalem. The Orthodox claimed the building was a deliberate provocation, an attempt to demoralize their youth, while the Histadrut stood on its rights. A commission, appointed to find a way of ending the ugly fights that occurred almost daily, proposed building a wall around the clubhouse to shut the two groups out of each other's sight. But a wall already existed, not only between the extremist Neturai Karta and the Histadrut, but between all that was associated with religion—rabbis, synagogues, and prayer books—and the rest of Israel, in which latter category was that very Yemenite boy who had read a Psalm of David in the Negev. For were you to suggest that there was something of religion in the life of this boy working in the Negev and reading from the Psalms, the Orthodox would protest, "But he carries a gun on the Sabbath and eats no kosher food"; and what is more, the boy would agree with them. What have the daily problems of a soldier in the Negev to do with prayer and God and religion? No, the religious problem was not the ugly fracas around the clubhouse, nor adjustments in ritual, nor even the laws establishing religious control over marriage and divorce. The problem was this towering wall, accepted by both the religious and the secular camps in Israel, between the ideals and values of the average Israeli and the spiritual and religious matrix from which they had once sprung. And joined with this was what Ben Gurion called *the* problem of Jewish history: the growing split between an Israeli community which feels no need for religion and the Jewish community in the West which seems destined to conceive of its Jewish identification more and more in exclusively religious terms. What would be the effect on Jewish life in America of an Israel that would proclaim to Jews and all the world that the Jewish religion was irrelevant and outmoded? For wasn't this the meaning of what was going on in Israel? How long could the bustle of organization and the large membership lists of synagogues in America disguise the knowledge that at the center of it all was a religion that was not meeting one of its greatest tests?

There was no bell the next morning, for it was Sabbath, but the Negev sun awakened me early enough to see B.G. again out measuring the dewfall. After breakfast B.G. and I, with Chaim at the wheel, rode out to a nearby canyon. We stood for a while

226

following the play of color that faded away into the far blue hills of Transjordan. On the way back we paused at a little mound of stones marking the spot where five boys had been killed last year. B.G. noticed me staring about at the barren hills. "Depressing, eh?" he asked with a smile.

Ben Gurion has since returned to head the government. He remains attached to Sdeh Boker, visiting there whenever possible and threatening to live there permanently whenever such threats would appear to have political value. His repeated appeals for volunteers to populate the Negev remain largely ignored these days. But the Old Man does not desist from them, even over-doing it on some occasions, in the opinion of his comrades. Such an occasion may have been a celebration held on the lawn of Kibbutz Kinneret when a group of old-timers came together to honor Yanai Avihu, who had just published a book.

The book was a fascinating account of a mission which Yanai and Ben Zvi, a member of Kibbutz Kinneret who had since died, had undertaken. They were to purchase and smuggle out of Iraq a particular type of date tree which that country refused to export. The book reads like a mystery thriller, replete with intrigues and near misses which would have struck even a Holly-wood script writer as too corny. Somehow, though they could hardly speak Arabic, the two Israelis had managed to transport several hundred thousand date saplings to the port of embarkation. Then the ship which was to receive them failed to arrive. Days of delay stretched into weeks and months while the trees lay in the port attracting attention they could not afford. What was worse, the hot summer sun began to wither and kill the precious saplings. All seemed lost until Yanai was struck by a fantastic idea. Why not lease some ground and replant the sap-lings till the ship arrived? The desperate scheme had worked, and now thousands of Iraqi date trees were blossoming in Negev desert areas.

"It was worthwhile, Yanai," one of the old-timers said at the celebration, and the words touched a chord which moved memo-ries. "Yes, it was worthwhile," the old-timers said to themselves as they sat that evening around long, white-clothed tables piled high with bowls of fruit from the Kinneret Valley, which fifty

227

years ago had been a barren malarial waste. The electric lights strung between the rows of tall palms, the black and silver play of the moon on the lake below, the music of the children's choir and their flutes, impelled Nathan Alterman, one of the land's popular poets, to mutter out loud several times, "It is a Temple, a veritable Temple."

Many eyes were moist that evening as the few survivors of the Second Aliyah recalled "the days that were." Even Ben Gurion was in an unusually relaxed and reflective mood. From time to time he would banteringly interrupt the speeches of his old comrades—"Send a hundred youngsters to the Negev, as well as date saplings"—while his wife, Paula, shushed him and chuckled. A poet rose to say that the scene before him that evening was like an enchanted palace. Ben Gurion gave the last speech of the evening. His voice at first trembled.

"I see palm trees, fruitful land, children, and only yesterday when I came here fifty-two years younger, there was nothing but barrenness."

Suddenly the Old Man's tone grew sharp and he turned to the poet. "There are things higher than literature—spirit, vision, and the daring to change the very foundations of creation."

The Old Man banged his fist on the table. "Not with literature was this enchanted palace created. It is not to the Jews of the Diaspora that my heart goes out this evening." He turned now to a previous speaker who had bewailed the fate of the destroyed Jewish communities abroad. "No, my heart goes out this evening to those portions of our cradle land which have no sign of a tree, no mark of green; that thirst for crazily creative people—and those people are here, and in Affikim, and Dagania; and it is forbidden for them to remain here. You must go and create enchanted palaces in the dry Negev. . . . If you go, thousands will stream after you from the Diaspora, and from Tel Aviv and Haifa, where they play cards at night."

There were some that evening who thought that the Prime Minister might have for once foregone his usual finger-shaking and permitted the old-timers their hour of sentiment. But Ben Gurion is not a man to lose sight of his goal. If anything, the years have made the Old Man's chin firmer, his belief that

228

Israel's future is linked with the desert more intense. And all explanations and excuses are turned away with a quote like "a good man lives by his faith" or some similar thought taken from the Bible which is always in the Prime Minister's pocket or hand.

The Transformazia of the Bible

Ben Gurion's passionate interest in the Bible occasionally evokes criticism as well as admiration. Not long ago it even provoked a censure motion in the Israeli Knesset. It was the religious parties who moved the censure when they heard that the Prime Minister had publicly stated his belief that the number of families who left Egypt with Moses was closer to six hundred than to the six-hundred-thousand figure assumed in the traditional translation. The censure motion failed, and the Old Man went right ahead publicly displaying his remarkable knowledge of biblical sources and history. But there are times when even the non-Orthodox have somewhat ambivalent reactions to Ben Gurion's biblical enthusiasm. The first World Bible Quiz that was held in the summer of 1958 was such a time.

The whole country seemed then to be lifted on a wave of national self-congratulation. Israelis are still proud of the fact that while American marines were landing in Lebanon and the Russians were threatening war in the Middle East, Radio Kol Israel canceled its news broadcasts so that the country could pay undivided attention to a Bible quiz. "Where else," was the rhetorical question on everybody's lips, "would you see the population of a country go wild about a Bible contest? Where else would the President of a state (one of the questions in the preceding National Bible Contest had been submitted by President Ben Zvi) and the Prime Minister, and intellectuals, and farmers and children, stay up until two o'clock in the morning because of a Bible quiz?"

With bated breath the nation waited for the representatives of thirteen countries to meet in an international confrontation which to many Israelis seemed as significant, on its level, as the debate then going on at the same time in the United Nations.

"Only," a paper pointed out, "this is one contest Israelis cannot afford to lose."

I was not among the twenty-two hundred people who crowded into the stadium of the Hebrew University at Jerusalem the night of the contest, in August 1958. But I had managed to find a radio, which I shared with two Israeli children. The announcer gave a vivid description of the scene, which was witnessed by Israel's own highest dignitaries, by the foreign diplomatic corps, and by other important guests. They beheld a brilliantly lighted, elevated platform, with a lower stage for the contestants and an upper level for the chief judge of the contest and his colleagues. Below, to one side, were tables for the consultants, translators, and other functionaries. Against the dark background of the sky, lighted by powerful spotlights, rose twelve colorful banners representing the tribes of Israel. Above was the overarching canopy of a cloudless Jerusalem night jeweled with a slim crescent moon and bright masses of stars.

The World Bible Quiz opened with a flourish of trumpets and the appearance on the platform of the tall, kindly figure of Israel's President, Ben Zvi. The Nasi said a few words about the symbolic significance of an event dealing with Torah, on the hills of Jerusalem. Then the Kol Israel Choral Group sang, "I shall lift up mine eyes unto the hills . . ." and modulated from the religious mood of this psalm into the hora-tempo "And from Zion shall go forth the Law." The massed banners of the tribes under the Jerusalem sky, the trumpets announcing the President of the state, and the two song moods, bridging two thousand years of history—the scene seemed to signify the miracle of the past ten years.

The contest got under way when the President introduced Justice Cheshin of the Supreme Court, elected Quiz Master. In a voice that could not have been less solemn than the High Priest's in the ancient Temple, he called the contest to order. He bade the other judges "ascend" the platform, intoning the name of each while the audience responded with appropriate applause. He then called on the consultants, the contestants, and the translators also to ascend. The applause rose to a crescendo when Amos Chacham, the Israeli national champion, took his place.

One of my listening companions at our radio, a nine-year-old boy, joined excitedly in the applause.

"Is Bible one of your favorite subjects?" I asked him.

"Tk," he clicked his teeth Arab-style. "It's boring." But this obviously had nothing to do with his enthusiasm for Israel's new national hero, Amos Chacham, whose name and life story were by now known to almost every adult and child in the land. Everyone knew, for example, that Chacham had had to borrow a shirt for his first appearance in the national contest. The Israeli champion was a thirty-one-year-old bachelor who lived alone in a barely furnished room, and worked as a clerk in a Jerusalem institution for the blind. He had never finished secondary school, and, outside of his work, had only two enjoyments—the study of mathematics at home and the reading of the Torah in a local synagogue. As a baby he had fallen from his crib and received a spinal injury which had partially paralyzed his face and body and impaired the quality of his speech.

The new national hero had confessed to reporters after winning the contest that he had not been altogether surprised, though he had been mistaken in calculating which of his competitors was "most dangerous." He had chided the press for taking up too much of his time—he could not, he said, properly prepare for the contest in which he would have to represent his country. Amos Chacham was quite serious about his mission, but he had little cause for worry.

The gap in points between him and the foreign contestants was embarrassing. Chacham (the name means "wise") replied with ease to questions such as, "Where do we find things mentioned in threes and fours, or in sixes and sevens?" He not only gave the correct place and quotations, but supplemented his reply with masses of extra detail which evoked gasps of admiration from the audience. Justice Cheshin forgot his neutrality and complimented the Israeli champion, while the radio announcer pointed out that "this is an example of the keen analytic brain of Amos Chacham at work." Several times the white-haired Ben Gurion, sitting in the front row, could be seen literally jumping out of his seat, Bible in hand, when Amos succeeded in answering a particularly difficult question. Despite his lead, however,

231

it was observed that the Israeli champion carefully kept his own score in a little black book which he grasped in his hands all evening.

The weary rounds of questions, translations, and retranslations went on until the early morning, and finally put my little companions to sleep. They were not up to hear the occasional diverting moments of the contest, as when Sara Rabinowitz, the elderly Mexican champion, who told reporters when she arrived that she believed in the New Testament, suffered some traumatic regression and asked that the question put to her be translated into Yiddish. The panel of judges refused on the ground that the eight official languages of the contest had previously been established, and Yiddish was not among them.

In the early hours of the morning Amos Chacham was proclaimed *Aluf Ha-Tanach*—Champion of the Bible, and led in triumphant procession to a Jerusalem hotel where a crowd of several thousand had waited up to greet him. The champion stood on a balcony, at three o'clock in the morning. "Just like the Day of Independence," he said, as he waved awkwardly to his admirers below.

Following the contest, the press burst into another round of enthusiastic editorial comment. The newspaper *Herut,* of the right-wing Revisionist party, suggested that the real value of the contest might be the pricking of the world's conscience into realizing that Abraham had been promised both sides of the Jordan by the Bible. Other papers pointed out the international public-relations value of the quiz. But the main thought expressed everywhere was that the Bible contest had been a revelation not only to the world but to the Israelis themselves of how alive the Bible was in modern Israel. If the world wanted to see an example of the values that still prevailed in the land of the Bible, let it gaze on the type of person who becomes a national hero there—"Champion of the Bible, Amos Chacham."

A day or two after the contest, in among the enthusiastic editorials, appeared a letter complimenting the organizers of the contest and Amos Chacham, but asking mildly whether the title "Champion of the Bible" might not better be reserved for something other than the winner of a quiz contest?

Other voices were troubled about what this "historic event" indicated as to the meaning of the Bible for the modern Israeli. Some were concerned about the mingling of biblical psalms and Madison Avenue quiz techniques, fearing it was typical of that confusion of the holy and the secular which characterizes so much of Israeli life. They still remembered the newspaper photographs of a bearded army chaplain in a jeep on his way to the Sinai campaign, with a submachine gun on one arm and a Torah on the other. Others asked whether it was right to treat the Bible as if it were some national asset like oil, to be utilized as a tool for public relations? And there were still others who shared the compunction of the writer of the letter who was troubled by the title "Champion of the Bible." Could or should one's understanding of the Bible be tested as one tests the ability to acquire facts about automobiles or geography? Isn't the kind of understanding called for by the Bible itself related to life, to character and deeds, rather than to memory responses?

The significance of the World Bible Quiz was still a subject of discussion at the opening of the Seventh Annual Bible Congress in Jerusalem the next year. More than a thousand people had gathered to discuss thirty-four papers on the Books of Jeremiah and Ezekiel. In the center of the long speakers' table on the platform sat the Prime Minister, and he seemed more interested in turning the pages of his little black Bible than in listening to the opening formalities. The background light shining through the famous but thinning tangle of his white hair gave it a diaphanous, halo-like effect. But there was nothing angelic about the Prime Minister's chin-jutting style of delivery when he rose to speak.

"Only here in the land of its birth," said Ben Gurion, "can the Bible be understood properly." Then to make sure that those with whom he disagreed would get his point, the Prime Minister went on to say that the rabbis who had labored to interpret the Bible outside of Israel, during two thousand years of post-biblical history, might have served some other purpose by their tortuous explanations, but they had perverted the original meaning of the Book of Books. The audience understood that Ben Gurion was jousting with two views—the Orthodox religious,

233

and those of his own party who accused him of "Bibliolatry."

The Prime Minister made no mention of the Bible quiz, which he had at the time proclaimed to be "a historic event." Others on the platform, however, alluded to it with glowing nostalgia. In contrast, there was an apologetic tone in the rather cryptic statement of Justice Cheshin to the effect that he understood perfectly the necessity of not confusing "the boundaries between the holy and the profane." A bit weakly, the Judge insisted that despite criticism the Bible contest had been of value.

Whatever differences of opinion the Bible quiz continues to evoke, it has by now slipped into the framework of a larger discussion of unabating intensity in Israel—the meaning of the Bible in that land today.

Like most subjects in Israel, this one cannot be discussed very long without reference to the political-ideological blocs into which the nation is divided. All groups—whether committed to the full Orthodoxy of the religious parties, the antireligious view of Mapam, or the noncommittal religious neutrality of the majority Mapai grouping—begin with seeming agreement: the Bible is and must remain the cornerstone of Jewish education and culture. Not even the most avid church-state separationist would dare suggest that the government radio eliminate its daily Bible readings, or change the program time signal imitating a traditional biblical chant. The schools of the secular socialist parties are at one with the religious school system in allotting the Bible a core position in the curriculum. Study of Tanach is given five hours per week in the latter system, and four hours in the former. Thus there is no disagreement among the political groups about the importance of the Bible's role in modern Israeli culture; it is only with regard to "understanding" of the Bible that they differ sharply.

Here, the least ambiguous response is that of the Orthodox, who say that a proper understanding of the Bible (as Chief Rabbi Unterman of Tel Aviv quickly replied to Ben Gurion after his speech at the Bible Congress) must involve the post-biblical interpretations of the rabbis. And the qualification for a "Bible champion" should certainly include a commitment to the Sinaitic revelation and to the hundreds of commandments listed

234

in the Bible or implied in its text, as taught by the post-biblical rabbinic authorities. This is the "understanding" of the Bible given to the children in Israel's Orthodox religious schools, which comprise about thirty-five per cent of the total educational system.

As proof that such an approach to the Bible can be exciting even in modern Israel, Orthodox educators point to a teacher like Nehama Leibowitz. For many years she has been conducting her own weekly Bible quiz. She draws up questionnaires on the meaning of sentences in the "portion of the week." Most of her questions involve a reading of the Bible in the light of rabbinic commentators like the eleventh-century Rashi or the twelfth-century Maimonides. This questionnaire, which she personally corrects, is eagerly read and answered not only by religious Jews, but by hundreds of freethinkers who still remember their old-country religious training. In classroom at night, or in her own dimly lighted, book-filled house, Nehama Leibowitz teaches both young and old to read the Bible through what she calls the "problem" approach. From out of her long, angular face Nehama's dark eyes glitter with excitement as her "learners" raise their hands to line up with one rabbinic authority against another in the interpretation of a text. Under her prodding, students fulfill the midrashic suggestion that the Bible be studied as "a rock" upon which the mind acts as an intellectual hammer, "bringing forth a variety of sparks," all of them exposing a different aspect of the truth. Miss Leibowitz does not disguise her contempt for those who would claim to understand the Bible without its historic rabbinic interpretation.

Also Orthodox, but in a softer, more mystical mood, is the biblical understanding advocated by Rabbi Zvi Yehudah Kook, son of the former Chief Rabbi of Israel. I saw Zvi Yehudah Kook a few days after the World Bible Quiz. He had been asked, he told me, to be a judge in the contest, but had declined, and in a press interview the day before he had offered his reasons. Zvi Yehudah did not seem disturbed that the papers had neglected to print his remarks. He exonerated the reporters, who, he said "might not have understood"—and they well might not. Zvi Yehudah speaks with a rush of words that include a heavy sprinkling of rabbinic and Cabalistic terms. In his quiet office, with the portrait of his famous father looking down, he stated his view for me. His brown eyes twinkled.

"Not that one should deny the positive value of such an affair —the quiz. There are all kinds of sports—football, baseball— and this kind of sport is better than most. Yes, there are good sides as well as bad sides."

"And what is the bad side?" I asked. It is always hard for him to say something negative about Israel.

"Well, the bad side is a *transformazia*—a falsification of the essential nature of the Torah—our Bible. For example," he explained, "a World Bible Quiz in which representatives of various religions display their understanding of the Bible implies that every religion can have its authentic view of the Torah. This is not the way our fathers looked at the Torah," he said. "Not that there has been any lack of saintly non-Jews, worthy of the world to come. But there have also been scholars who cut off the Bible from the living Jewish people about them, and saw no contradiction between praising the biblical Israelites while persecuting flesh-and-blood Jews around them.

"Actually," said Zvi Yehudah, "the Torah is but an expression of the historic Jewish soul concentrated into a specific form. Jewish history and Torah and the Jewish people are but different aspects of the same living organic reality." To imply that one can understand the Torah while cutting it away from its special connection with the living Jewish people is a falsification, according to him.

It is also a falsification to imply that the Torah can be understood "cut off" from the interpretations and meanings that have grown organically out of it during the last two thousand years of its historic life. "This," said Zvi Yehudah, "is the smallness of vision affecting many, including Ben Gurion."

"And there is another 'cutting off,'" the Rabbi went on, "more serious. We hear the phrase 'people of the Book' so often that we think it comes from Jewish sources. Actually, it is a Moslem-coined phrase. From the Jewish point of view we are not a 'people of the Book' but a 'people of God.' The Book is just one of the instruments that connects us with a Higher Source. It is but a partial revelation of this Higher Source. This too is

236

a 'cutting off,' a form of idolatry—a substitution of the part for the whole, of knowledge of a Book, for submission to the will of God."

"And what did the reporters say to all this?" I asked him.

The rabbi's eyes crinkled again in a smile. "One of the reporters asked me if the quiz and the image shown to the world of a Prime Minister jumping out of his seat in the excitement of the contest was not good from the political and public-relations point of view. But this is the great error of Ben Gurion and Achad Haam—the use of the Bible as a means of serving man or the state rather than the study of the Bible for its own sake or as a revelation of God's will."

Zvi Yehudah sighed. "As a leader of the state, Ben Gurion has all my respect. But in matters of Torah and spirit . . ." The rabbi shook his head.

Ben Gurion and Achad Haam—discussion of the Bible in Israel frequently centers about these two names. The ideology of Achad Haam has become the special target of the attack against the understanding of the Bible as taught in most of the nonreligious schools.

Asher Ginzberg, the Russian-born essayist who wrote under the pen name of "One of the people"—Achad Haam, influenced the Zionist circles in Eastern Europe which produced Ben Gurion, Chaim Weizmann, and most of Israel's present leadership. It was he who best expressed the "solution" sought by the nonreligious nationalist elements of that generation. Basically, they had the problem of reconciling loyalty to the heritage of their people with nineteenth-century ideas of nationalism and evolution. They wished to remain committed to their people's God-saturated cultural and literary tradition, though no longer sharing their fathers' faith in a living God. They liked to think of themselves as the generation that stood "at the crossroads"— the title of one of Achad Haam's famous essays. But it was not necessary, suggested Achad Haam, to choose one or the other of the crossroads. It was possible to combine reverence for the old literature with modern thinking, biblical criticism, and science. For example, he said, it was not important for those who wanted to be "scientific" about the Bible to believe that Moses ever existed. It was enough to realize that the Bible image of the great prophet was "true" in that it revealed the true spiritual ideals of the Jewish people. "And the ideal is created in the spirit of our people and the creator creates in its own image. And images like these, in which the spirit of the people embodies its inner yearnings, continually form themselves unconsciously and without deliberate intent."

Achad Haam's thesis was that the Jewish people possessed a national ego, a "will to live" capable of creating not only prophets like Moses, but an image of the Creator of the World. In this sense even a nonreligious Zionist might call the God of Israel his God, since it is an expression of his people's national ego. It was, of course, a semantic blur, but of pragmatic value in the early Zionist days, when it enabled all shades of religious opinion to join in the common goal of establishing a Jewish homeland in Palestine.

This is the *transformazia* which, Zvi Yehudah Kook mildly complains, cuts off the Jewish nation and its Bible from a living God. But not so gentle is the criticism leveled against this type of theology by the sharp-penned literary critic Baruch Kurzweil. "The teaching of Achad Haam to this day works as a force in the destruction of whatever remnants of religious faith are still left in the hearts of our youth," says Kurzweil, who doesn't hesitate to attack the sacrosanct figure of Achad Haam himself, calling him a mediocre thinker, who put together an unprofound hash of "nineteenth-century positivist pragmatist evolutionary ideas—a combination of Hume, Spencer, J. S. Mill, Darwin, and Welhausen." Achad Haam was personally a man of high ethical sensitivity, admits Kurzweil, but the "blurring" of the transcendental God of Israel with the "Rock of Israel" which expresses the "will to live" of a nation, is the first step in an ethical desensitization inevitably leading to incidents like Kibya and Kafr Kassem. It is not enough for Ben Gurion to rise in the Knesset and express horror at the killing of innocent Arabs in Kafr Kassem. He should realize that this is the consequence of a philosophy which substitutes the ego of a people for the transcendental God of Israel who in the past was the Judge of that ego.

238

Needless to say, Kurzweil's religious criticism of an understanding of the Bible which eliminates God makes slight impression on the educators of the leftist-oriented Mapam party. In the high schools and elementary schools under their influence, children learn to reconcile the biblical text with Marxism as interpreted by Boruchov. The prophets are seen "not only as religious fighters but really as national workers, communal servants of the people. Only the style of the prophetic language was religious . . . they speak in the name of God only because no other form of expression was known to the ancient Hebrew." As for the chapters on creation, another of their educators says bluntly, "The stories about the creation of the world implant in the young child a feeling of dependence upon some upper power . . . they sow in the heart of the little child religious seeds of fear and subservience, weakening the hands of man. . . . All this is completely opposed to our world view and educational approach. . . ."

But most Israeli schools and educators incline neither to the criticism of Kurzweil nor to the dogmatic secularist certainties of Mapam. In what is called "the majority trend" of the public-school system, teachers are free to express their own religious feelings and whatever doubts they have about the official approaches. These days a not infrequent complaint is heard, as reported in an article by a teacher in the Galilee: "Even nine- and ten-year-old children are capable of understanding the obvious contradiction—if there is no God and the Bible is only legend, what reason is there for devoting four lessons a week to the subject? . . . How can a pupil develop respect for the Bible when he is told—either directly or through clear hints— that it is based upon a lie?"

The complaining teacher concludes, "Whether we believe that God exists in his own right or that the people create its God—it is an unquestionable fact that the people have survived both in their own land and in the Diaspora by virtue of its collective engrossment with the idea of the God of Israel." The self-contradictory logic in this last statement reflects the problem of many Israeli teachers who are troubled by the difficulty of teaching the Bible without a "real" God—the *k'ilu,* the "as if" approach, as some call it in Israel. But they are unable to accept the criticism and conclusions of someone like Kurzweil. Most of them are not so sure that a people cannot maintain, as Kurzweil thinks, a strong pattern of moral standards without a belief in a transcendent God, or conversely, that a belief in such a God insures moral standards. Committed themselves to the historic approach to the Bible identified with Achad Haam, they cannot join in the criticism of Ben Gurion on this point; some of them, however, do quarrel with their leader's so-called "bibliolatry."

"The distant past," wrote Ben Gurion in one of his frequent ideological epistles on the subject, "is closer to us than the recent past of the last two thousand years. . . . Our father Abraham, his sons and grandsons; Moses and Aaron, King David—all they did and said is closer to us than the utterances of Rav Ashi, Alfasi, Maimonides, and the rest. . . ."

It is this tendency to make light not only of the rabbinic interpretations of the Bible but of the spiritual productivity of the past two thousand years that impel some members of Mapai to accuse their leader of bibliolatry. The Prime Minister, they warn, is encouraging the already advanced tendency of the native-born Israeli to belittle the spiritual productivity of the Diaspora. It would be much better, suggest the critics, if he joined in a campaign for something sadly missing in the education of the native Israeli, something that has been called "Jewish consciousness."

By now the widely publicized phrase "Jewish consciousness" evokes some self-conscious smiles even on the part of the program's proponents. No one is quite sure what it means exactly, and what the "new look" in Jewish education is supposed to accomplish. Public explanations hint of something now missing in Israeli education which the old-timers received in their Diaspora background.[1]

[1] Apart from its historic importance and influence on world opinion, the Eichmann Trial was supposed to have had a positive influence on the "Jewish consciousness" of Israeli youth and their sense of kinship with Diaspora Jewry. In some ways, however, the revelations of the trial appear to have further alienated the younger generation from their Diaspora

The committee engaged in developing the Jewish-consciousness program in the schools defines its goals as a respect for "tradition and Jewish holidays," and for "the spiritual creativity of the last two millennia of Jewish history." But all along, Israeli educators have been teaching Jewish holidays and traditions, and post-biblical literature and history. Most of them are left wondering what this Jewish consciousness is supposed to add, except a little more folklore. Their wonderment is increased by assurances on the part of Jewish-consciousness advocates that the new program will have nothing to do with religion—an announcement forestalling the obvious suggestion that this is the something now missing which was the basic ingredient of Jewish education in the past. In any case, with respect to the Bible, the program of Jewish consciousness as finally released to the press promised to make no change in "the historic approach," that is, the theologically noncommittal understanding of the Bible.

According to the elaborately publicized final announcements, the Prime Minister was in accord with a program for increased Jewish consciousness. But it was also clear that Ben Gurion defined the vague term simply as "a sense of unity with the Diaspora." The Old Man has not changed his belief that "though there may be precious jewels in post-biblical literature, they are buried in accumulations of legalistic debates, quibbles, and mystical speculations which mean little to most people in our generation." The fact is, says Ben Gurion, that ". . . we who have come to settle in the Jewish state have taken a leap in time which makes us feel closer to David, Uzziah, and Joshua bin Nun than to the *shtetl* in Cracow or the nineteenth-century ideologists of Warsaw."

This is Ben Gurion's main point—that for the Israeli speaking Hebrew in the land of his fathers, biblical references, whose pristine meaning has been blurred or allegorized, suddenly "leap through time." This is what happened, for example, in 1948, to

past. "Why didn't they fight back?" was the typical question asked by the young Israeli whose sense of horror at the Nazi atrocities was matched by his shame and bewilderment at what appeared as the "sheep-like" acquiescence of most European Jews to their fate.

241

a passage in Isaiah when the Prime Minister quoted it, while five Arab states began marching against reborn Israel:

Wherefore art thou red in thy apparel, and thy garment like him that treadeth in the wine vat? I have trodden the wine press alone and of the people there was none with me. . . . For the day of vengeance was in my heart, and my day of redemption was come; and I looked and there was none to help; and I wandered, and there was none to uphold; therefore my own arm brought salvation to me, and my fury, it upheld me.

Eliezer Sukenik translating the then newly discovered Dead Sea Scrolls while his famous archaeologist son, Yigael Yadin, was in the field commanding the Israeli forces, described the same experience. "Shells and mortars pierced the air of Jerusalem day and night . . . little by little we unrolled the first fragments of the scrolls, and as we listened to faraway echoes of an early period in the life of our people in this land, there were moments when the boundaries of time seemed blurred, as if the ancient scrolls were telling not of long ago events, but were pages of our own lives."

It is this identity of historic predicament along with language and land that makes Ben Gurion insist that "The youth of Israel now looks at the Jewish people through the spectacles of the Jewish state and the Bible. . . ."

Certainly circumstances of environment and faith profoundly influence one's reading of the Bible. The pious Orthodox Jew reading the story of David's adultery was bound to discover in the text a hint that Uriah contracted a "conditional divorce" with his wife, thereby saving the impetuous King from breaking the Ten Commandments. The Jew who visualized King David as a holier and more observant version of his own rabbi found it almost impossible to picture the lusty brigand and impetuous lover who appears in the Bible story to less pious eyes. Similarly, the words of Joshua—"Be strong and courageous"—spoken to the Israelites while they were battling their enemies, were interpreted by the powerless Jew in the Diaspora as a summons to be "strong as a lion" in fulfilling the 613 commandments of the

242

Law, or storming the gates of heaven with prayer. It would hardly have occurred to the pious Jew who shrank from a firm handshake on the grounds that physical strength belonged to "them"—the children of Esau—that Joshua's words could have the meaning they had during the Sinai campaign when whispered by a company commander to his troops at the moment of battle.

As the travel posters say, the Bible does "come to life" in the land of Israel. But whether it is read by the native Israeli through the same "spectacles" used by Ben Gurion is quite another question. With all his talk about the spectacles of the Diaspora Jew, the Prime Minister seems to forget that he himself learned to read the Bible through the spectacles of "an ideology created in the Warsaw of sixty years ago." The fact is that through Ben Gurion's spectacles the Isaiah who cried out "Holy, holy, holy" becomes a modern-day statesman and political analyst and Joshua bin Nun, the "servant of the Lord," becomes a soldier-communal leader closely resembling the Prime Minister. In the same way, the "prophetic vision and Messianic ideal," so often quoted by the Israeli leader, are through his reading deprived of their other-worldly dimensions and compressed into a Messianism very much like the Mapai political program for Israel and the world. "He politicizes the Bible," is Martin Buber's complaint about Ben Gurion's reading. Ben Gurion's "leap of time" brings together a religious and secular age, and results in a blurring of terms and a Biblical interpretation as far removed from the original as the reading of rabbis like Zvi Yehudah Kook. It might even be argued that the latter is somewhat closer to the original than Ben Gurion, for at least he shares the belief in a living God, which is certainly at the center of the Bible.

In summary, it might be said that most people in Israel, including those who complain about Diaspora spectacles, find that the Bible's "coming to life" produces an uncomfortable blurring of terms and feelings. There is that mingling of the "holy and profane," the ideal and the real, which troubles pilgrims to the Holy Land, or the critics of the World Bible Quiz. Perhaps it is a necessary phase of any "coming to life," not only of the Bible but of any spiritual or intellectual ideal.

One who thought most profoundly about this question was the

late Abraham Isaac Kook. As he watched the polarization of the Israeli community into religious and secularist camps, he could sympathize with the reluctance of some Orthodox Jews to use Hebrew for calling dogs, reading cartoons, or winning contests of any kind; the "holy tongue" cannot be used for "ordinary" matters without losing some of its sanctity. But he asked, too, Can a heavenly Zion become earthly without the entrance of mundane sights and odors? Isaiah's dream about "making the desert to bloom," in its reality must lose something of its spiritual aura. The smell of sweat and the lack of toilet facilities in the Negev are not pleasant, but it is only to the accompaniment of such odors that the prophet's dream is realized.

The revival of a people, too, may be accompanied by some unpleasant phenomena. For, said the Chief Rabbi, the Jews during two thousand years of Diaspora existence had also in a sense been "disembodied." Indeed, they had almost perished from "overspiritualization." Power and muscles, elemental physical courage and stamina—the "gross" qualities were assigned to the "others," the non-Jewish world. It was, of course, a matter of historic necessity. Cut off from their land, forced to surrender even the power of self-defense to Gentile rulers, Jews made a virtue of necessity, and looked for their life challenges in a narrower world. The result was a separation of the holy and the profane, with an amazing cultivation of the former. But now the Jews had to regain their "animal qualities," become "thick" vessels—even like their biblical forebears—so that they might contain similar "great spiritual charges." To be sure, in the process of thickening, a people may temporarily swing from an excess of holiness to an excess of earthliness. It was natural for the new Israeli proudly to call himself "sabra," after the tough prickly-pear fruit of the land, and to honor the lad *k'eisen*— "like iron"—while scornfully labeling those who are squeamish about handling a rifle *artistim*—"artists."

In this process of thickening, said Rav Kook, there might even be a growth of "God-denial." But this was—part of the dialectic by which the spirit enters into and transmutes the world. "And in the end," promised Rav Kook, "the profane will be swallowed up by the holy, and transmuted—then the holy will reign with a power and strength it did not have before." Thus Rav Kook evidently resolved his own ambivalences of feeling, and it may point the way for some others still.

But if in Israel the "new" Jew is as impatient with "involuted" explanations as people say, he is not likely to be convinced by the Cabalistic dialectics of Rav Kook. Neither will he be content with Ben Gurion's attempt to identify a hypostatized national ego called the "Rock of Israel" with the living God of the Bible. For this "direct" sabra, the "coming to life" of the Bible may mean a confrontation not only with biblical allusions suddenly becoming concrete, but with a question to which he will demand an unambivalent and equally concrete answer. Namely, is the religious experience which the Bible offers as the central reality in the life of Abraham, Isaac, and Jacob, and in the life of Joshua bin Nun too, still central to the life of any man—to the life of the sabra, as well?

Eventually, then all discussions about the Bible and religion in Israel lead to speculation about the native-born Israeli and his yearning for "something."

CHAPTER XII

The Israeli Yearning for "Something"

> "I regard religion as mankind's supreme and most important concern, but I think the word "God," as currently employed, about the emptiest, hollowest and most repetitious word in the language. Saying you believe in God is about the most gratuitous utterance one can make. Belief in God is an inference from one's action and life; if we show love and depth we are rooted in the Divine, whatever we say. We can even say we are freethinkers and atheists (like Shelley and Debs) and still be rooted in God. Or we can invoke God until we are blue in the face, but if we go off in our actual life on a totally different basis, what good is the assertion? . . .
>
> —*Henry Slonimsky*

One unexpected result of the establishment of a Jewish state has been the realization of a vacuum in the spiritual life of its residents. "Something," the Israelis agree, vanished in 1948 at the moment when the Zionist dream was consummated. As might be expected, there is no shortage of either diagnoses or prescriptions for this "condition of spirit," as Israelis call it. Orthodox Jewish leaders suggest a return to "Torah-true" Judaism. Christian missionaries lift their eyes speculatively, and offer their wares. Ben Gurion insists that pioneer work in the Negev is the answer. There are also a few in Israel—and many more outside the country—who think that a form of non-Orthodox religious expression is necessary. Such is the opinion of General Dori, the President of the Haifa Technion.

247

"I will explain to you exactly how I feel about the possibilities of modern religion," the still dynamic though elderly and ailing organizer of the pre-Israeli-army Haganah said one evening at his home. "I came to Israel as a very young boy and like the others received a good education in the Bible, but no religion. Nor was I ever interested in religion. Nor am I fanatically interested now. But with the coming of the state, certain things have happened. Until then we had our work to do, and it completely occupied us. The task of each moment was meaningful enough to fulfill our lives. We established our state. There is much yet to be built, but everybody knows now that this is it, this is life in the Jewish state, and lo and behold it leaves something unfulfilled and unsatisfied. It is evident there are problems in life that cannot be solved by great events or politics. I don't say that religion can solve them either, but they are problems that religion at least deals with. And if there were here on Mount Carmel a synagogue with prayer services arranged aesthetically, and with religious ideas interpreted in a way that could be meaningful to my life and times, I would certainly be interested in going. The world of the Orthodox synagogue—it's just a foreign world to me. We have nothing in common."

Another Haifa resident, an American who left a kibbutz in the Galilee partly because he too found something lacking there, has a similar analysis.

"We found out, living in a kibbutz, that not all problems are solved by communal living. The girl who can't find a husband and sits in a room alone at night, or the parents who lose a child—they need solace. Is that not part of what religion deals with—the blows and puzzles of life?"

He also described the semantic problem involved in any Israeli discussion of religion.

"I didn't know that you were *Aduk*—'Orthodox,'" a member of the kibbutz who had come from Lithuania commented upon entering the American's room and seeing the Ten Commandments hung on the wall. The American had found it almost impossible to explain to his fellow kibbutz member that one could be religious and still not Orthodox. Still, there were definite signs of some yearning for religion in the kibbutz, he felt. "When

248

I came to my settlement in 1947, only three people had registered for fasting on Yom Kippur. Five years later half the kibbutz was fasting. Why?"

He described the Bar Mitzvah ceremony which had been instituted at his kibbutz. A boy or girl, when they reached the age of thirteen, prepared a paper on a portion of the Bible and delivered it before the kibbutz on a Sabbath eve. Thirteen mitzvot—commandments—were also involved in the ceremony. These commandments had, of course, nothing to do with religion. They consisted of tests in which the boy proved himself —as, for example, working a full day in a certain branch of agriculture, or spending a day by himself in the city. One year, the story goes, one of the commandments was to shoot rats that were overrunning the settlement that year. "But," asks this American, "why did they have to have a Bar Mitzvah ceremony at the age of thirteen? The time of entrance to the political parties is sixteen." No, something deeper was involved here— a sense of spiritual frustration. Look, he said, at the bitter political contention that had split one of the oldest kibbutzim in Israel—Ein Charod. Ostensibly it was a difference over an East- or West-oriented foreign policy. But can political differences account for the violent hatreds which flared up between families and friends who had worked together for so many years? The American felt that the antagonisms there were really rooted in an ever-growing feeling of emptiness.

This young man now belongs to a synagogue in Haifa which, without proclaiming itself un-Orthodox, does try to offer a more modern expression of religion. Men and women sit together—a practice not allowed in Orthodox synagogues. There is decorum and an attempt to "adjust" the prayer book and to offer a more meaningful religious service. In Jerusalem, another group goes further in its attempts to revise the service, and even breaks the Orthodox ban of instrumental music on the Sabbath by permitting an organ.

A journalist, Ben-Horin, leads this small congregation in their attempt to concoct an Israeli form of liberal religious Judaism. For a while in Tel Aviv a similarly oriented group conducted liberal religious services, but their attempts ran into organizational difficulties and fell apart. Recently, another "reform" congregation was started in Nazareth. The small number of Israelis at present interested in this non-Orthodox expression of liberal Judaism say they could do better if they had proper leadership, organization, and finances. They point out that the hundreds of Orthodox congregations and their rabbis are sub- sidized by the government, and backed up by a network of government-supported religious schools as well as the religious political parties in the country, the latter holding at one time some sixteen per cent of the seats in the Knesset. But so far, there is little to indicate that better organization or increased budgets would substantially alter the general indifference which these attempts at a modern expression of synagogue Judaism encounter among most Israelis.

"No," says Rabbi Philip, who now heads an Orthodox syna- gogue in Jerusalem but was at one time a liberal rabbi in Germany, "those visitors to Israel who call for a type of Reform Judaism in Israel don't understand that people who are interested in praying in the synagogue are not interested in launching any crusade for changes in the prayers. While those who are interested in attacking present-day religious life are really not interested in praying in a synagogue." Rabbi Philip, a round-faced, middle- aged man who has after many years finally won from the Chief Rabbinate official recognition as a rabbi, is not eager to crusade for liberal religion. Besides, he thinks that if any changes come about in the future, they will come from liberal elements in the Orthodox kibbutz movement.

There are, as a matter of fact, many who look to Orthodox young people in the religious kibbutzim or to a youth movement like B'nai Akiva, as the possible source of a spiritual renewal in Israeli religious life. The young people in these religious kibbutzim do not use their religion as an excuse for avoiding army duty. Their attempts to combine citizenship and productive farm labor with religious commitments earn them the respect of all elements in the Israeli community. Nor can it be denied that there is some strain between these Orthodox farmers and the official religious leadership ensconced in the synagogues and Yeshivas of Jerusalem.

250

"I have worked hard," the late Chief Rabbi Herzog wrote in an article illustrating the success of Israel's religious leadership in trying to meet the problems of an Orthodox farmer's religious life, "to solve the problem of milking cows on the Sabbath, with the help of technicians. . . . I have finally reached a solution whereby it can be done by a machine operated and set by an automatic clock before the Sabbath."

There are changes of this sort within the Orthodox Jewish life of these settlements. An individual who uses an electric razor instead of the more approved sulphur depilatories to remove the hair of his beard, is less likely these days to meet communal disapproval. Biblical prohibitions against sowing two kinds of grain in the same furrow, or grafting different kinds of plants are sometimes by-passed with only a slight nod to the rabbinic research teams which are trying to modernize religion within the bounds of Orthodox Law. But, says an Orthodox scholar, Dr. I. Leibowitz, these kinds of changes will never meet the needs of people trying earnestly to combine their traditional faith with the demands of life in a modern Jewish land.

There is no more vigorous critic of Israel's present rabbinic leadership than Leibowitz, a wry-tongued professor of chemistry at the Hebrew University, with a talent for polemics that gives the current rabbinical authorities no peace. Some of his essays on religious problems in his land are quite an antidote to the "peace of mind," "the family that prays together, stays together," kind of religion. He objects strenuously to any attempt "to sell religion" on the basis of health, psychology, or even ethics. In Judaism "there is a complete contradiction between the worship of the God of the Torah and the worship of the God in the heart or conscience, which is really the worship of man. . . ."

"The purpose of the Sabbath," he writes, "is not to take care of the recreational needs of the working man. For this purpose we have the Histadrut. . . . There is no purpose to the Sabbath except holiness—to impose upon one-seventh of the life of man a special way of living which does not stem from his own nature, inclinations, and needs, but from his decision to subject himself to the Kingdom of Heaven—a way of life different from the natural way of life." It is from this almost austere Orthodoxy that

251

Dr. Leibowtiz lashes out at the present rabbinic leadership in Israel. He points out that those who protest against Jews working on the Sabbath do not hesitate to drink the water of Tel Aviv brought to them by Jews working on the Sabbath; that they take full advantage of the security provided by the non-Orthodox youth who guard the borders on the Sabbath. The truth is, he claims, that the leaders of Orthodox Jewry do not really want to undertake the responsibility of applying the laws of tradition to the new conditions of the Jewish state. They prefer to maintain the illusion that Jews are still a society living under the protection of a non-Jewish government, and thus maintain the laws which were adopted only for the Exile.

More recently, Dr. Leibowitz has further shocked rabbinic authorities by advocating an American-style separation of church and state in his country, and suggesting that civil marriage be allowed by the government. The latter suggestion, usually advanced by freethinking elements in the land, is bitterly resented by the Orthodox authorities. It would cause, they say, an irreconcilable split in the Jewish community. For according to Orthodox Jewish law, the offspring of a Jewish marriage who does not live by traditional religious law is liable to be religiously "illegitimate." A religious Jew would find it impossible to marry the issue of such a marriage. They grant that many Jews are not religious, but at least they all have been married properly according to religious law, so that their children may be presumed to be religiously legitimate. Dr. Leibowitz, as usual, takes a startlingly opposite view but bases it also on Jewish Orthodox law. He claims that the offspring of a civil marriage (which in his eyes is not really a marriage) would be less objectionable in terms of Jewish religious law than the children of a proper religious marriage in a family where the parents do not observe the religious laws of family purity.[1]

The scholarly attacks of authorities like Dr. Leibowitz, the

[1] Among such laws is the requirement that the woman visit a ritual bath after menstruation, and refrain from intercourse until seven days after the menstrual period. A child conceived in circumstances which break this law would be considered religiously "defective" in some Orthodox circles.

criticisms of their own leadership by the Orthodox youth movements and religious communal settlements, the constant talk about a renewal of Jewish spirit and law are all evidence of ferment within the broad domains of Jewish religious Orthodoxy in Israel today. But those who look upon these differences within the Orthodox camp as the beginnings of an Israeli variety of Reform or liberal Judaism, are likely to be disappointed. The members of B'nai Akiva, the Orthodox kibbutzim, Dr. Leibowitz, and the most Orthodox rabbis still agree that what God wrote, man dare not change—except by the procedure ordained in the divinely inspired writings. When presented with the prospect of a religious Judaism which is not committed to a belief in the divine inspiration of the 613 commandments of the Torah, as these commandments are interpreted and expanded by the Orthodox sages, they would agree with the Lubavitcher rebbe, one of Orthodox Jewry's present-day leaders, that "all an unorthodox religious Judaism can do is to deprive people of their conscience. Today, though the secular may fight religion, at least they know what it is. They know that religion means the full observance of the Torah. Knowing this, if they some day become *Baaleh t'shuvah*—returners—they will at least know to what to return. Liberal or conservative religion is worse than no religion at all, because it sanctifies the errors of the people."

Thus, the semantic identification of the word *dati*—religion—with complete Orthodoxy, which distresses many in Israel, is precisely what the Orthodox wish to maintain.

Either the Real Thing—or Nothing

In the meantime all arguments about definition of religion, changes in Jewish religious law, Orthodox versus liberal synagogues, remain a very peripheral concern of most Israelis.

"Our problem," says a teacher interested in these matters, "is not whether we should change the form of a particular prayer. Our problem is that prayer itself is not even a problem."

The name of the man who makes this observation is Dmiel— a vigorous, white-haired teacher with a theatrical manner and

253

eloquent flow of speech. He was recommended to me not only as important because of his own influence and ideas, but because he was supposedly typical of Israel's dominant intellectual element, the generation of the old Russian-Zionist immigration of 1904–05. I met him one afternoon at his home in Ramat Gan, a suburb of Tel Aviv. Over the traditional glass of tea he told me enthusiastically about his own religious experiments. He had been meeting with some fifteen families for a number of years. Their approach was practical. "Words like *religion* or *faith*," he explained, "must be avoided because the Israeli identifies them with concepts that they are not ready to accept." His group was trying to arrange a sort of modern Shulhan Aruk—a new code of laws. They had already decided to light candles on Sabbath eve, although many of the group refused to offer a blessing over them. They had also decided to refrain from cooking during the Sabbath day, and lately they had been gathering in the morning to read the Torah together. "As for prayer—well, we're just beginning our discussion on what to do on Yom Kippur, and so we will have to face that question." Dmiel indicated that he himself would like to see the group participate in prayer services. Despite the warm reception he gave me, Dmiel was somewhat suspicious of the interest of Reform Jewish organizations in Israeli religious matters.

"Reform to many of us," he explained, "is still associated with assimilation and anti-Zionism."

One Friday evening I went to the Dmiels' for supper; his seventeen-year-old son joined us. He was wearing a thin blue shirt, open wide at the collar as if to proclaim that, though it was winter, he needed no undershirt. The young lad placed a knapsack in the corner of the room and then came to the table, where he sat silently, smiling slightly while his father put on a battered hat and recited the kiddush. I asked the boy if young people he knew were at all interested in the subjects his father and I were discussing. "They're too abstract for us," he said with a good-natured grin. A short while later he excused himself from the table, picked up the small knapsack, said *"Shalom,"* and went out.

"He is going on an overnight hike," his father explained; and

254

then as if further explanation were needed, added, "That's our sabra. They are a generation educated for outer deeds more than inner thoughts."

Following our supper, Dmiel accompanied me to a nearby village, where we shared an experience perhaps more revelatory of Israel's religious reality than discussions about a new prayer book or revised religious codes of laws.

The meeting which we attended had been arranged in an effort to sample some opinions on the subject of liberal Judaism among the "grass roots." A friend at Ramat Hadar, a settlement specializing in chicken farming, not far from Tel Aviv, had managed to call some people together. Since some of those who were willing to come to the meeting had nevertheless felt that it would not be proper to discuss a subject like liberal Judaism in a community building which some of the older men used for services on the Sabbath, we met in the schoolhouse. It was chilly, and we sat in our overcoats. Some twenty-five people had listened to my carefully prepared talk. Then a Yugoslav Jew who had helped to arrange the meeting opened the discussion. He felt the need, he said, for a communal type of religious expression that he could offer his child. "I've tried to go to synagogue a number of times," he said, "but never yet have I heard a word there that goes to my heart, or bears upon my own life." One young teacher, who seemed to have followed my talk sympathetically, confessed that he felt he was raising a "generation of Karaites who knew the Bible but little else of the spirit of Jewish life as it had been developed after the biblical period."

At that point somebody standing in back of the room asked for the floor and cleared his throat. I was told that he was a former member of the Marxist Mapam, and now a teacher at Ramat Hadar. He launched into a vehement defense of the character of Israeli youth, objecting to the "constant maligning" of it that was going on in Israel. If I wanted to see true religion, he suggested, then I ought to go to the Negev and see the youth working and fighting there. To be willing to work on the land and to offer one's life to the freedom of the state—that was ethics and religion in the highest sense.

255

I tried to warm up the discussion by contrasting the last speaker's words with the ideas of Dr. Leibowitz, but few had apparently heard of him. I read them a passage from one of his essays. "We must ask ourselves whence comes this youth, that sees nothing wrong in carrying out a terrible act of retaliation [the Kibya attack]. It is all the result of using the religious category of 'holiness' for values which are social, national, and political—a type of usage which is frequent among us—the use of the category of the absolute—that which is beyond any human revaluation or reckoning—applied to secular matters . . . the use of the Bible and the prayer book as sanctions for values which really spring from the human conscience and feeling. . . . If the nation and its welfare and the state and its defense are 'holy,' then even Kibya is possible and permissible. This is the terrible punishment that results from the transgression of the commandment, Thou shalt not take the name of Thy God in vain."

The only reaction to this passage was the comment of an elderly man, who in a mixture of German and Hebrew said, "These are interesting matters and perhaps when we have straightened out some of our economic and military problems, we will be able to think about them more seriously." The Yugoslav again tried to help. "If we can find so much time and energy for politics, we should find time for this as well."

In the back of the room Dmiel stood up and told everybody that he too had been a farmer, and had come to Israel with the Second Aliyah in 1905. He was uninterested in debating definitions of faith, but he wanted to meet with people who were eager to find more spiritual content in life. Was anybody interested?

One or two hesitatingly raised their hands. It was obvious that the discussion was ended.

Afterward some people present told me that there had not been more discussion because most of those present had not understood my Hebrew. Although they had lived in Israel for over twenty years, they could participate in discussions of this sort only if there was a German translation. The farmers in Ramat Hadar could speak a market-place Hebrew, read a newspaper, but to read a book in Hebrew, or to participate in an

256

intellectual discussion on an unusual subject, was still a strain—this after twenty years.

"One language means one heart" is a slogan that can be read at times in buses or in the streets. There is no question but that Hebrew is the language of Israel, and its revival is one of the cultural miracles of history. But the miracle is still in process. A sizable proportion of the country still cannot comfortably read a book in Hebrew, and even native-born Israelis must speak a language which is rather thin and unsubtle compared to the tongues that have been naturally developing over the generations. Certainly language affects not only the powers of communication but thought processes as well. Of course, the difficulty of language communication in modern Israel is only one of the problems which push subjects of the kind we tried to discuss at Ramat Hadar into the background of life. There are more vital priorities of interest. There is the border, never more than a few miles or a few yards away. There is the problem of the merging of over seventy disparate cultural and ethnic blocs into one land and people, and the tension of adjustment in a land where nearly half of the population is newly arrived. These take precedence over some inchoate yearning for "something," which may or may not be related to religious concerns.

Basically, this is the answer to those who wonder why there is such lack of religious interest among non-Orthodox Jews in the Holy Land today. Israelis are probably religious and irreligious in the same proportion as can be found in any Western land. The present conditions of life in Israel, however, make it difficult to find time or energy for anything except the absolutely vital and necessary. A "hothouse" religion which may flourish in suburban America, where people have time, energy, and money for nonessentials, is a kind of luxury religiosity that cannot find roots in a land which only has time for the absolutely necessary. Nor will Israelis affiliate with synagogues for reasons which motivate such affiliation in the West—for social or business reasons, or for their children's Jewish education. The topics taught in American-Jewish religious schools—history, Hebrew, Jewish literature and holidays, etc.—are all part of public-school education in Israel. There is then only one basic reason which might

257

move an Israeli to affiliate with religious institutions—a genuine faith in God and a need for prayer. This is the disadvantage, but also the advantage, of Jewish religious life in the Holy Land. It will be vital and real—as real as the problem of border security, as vital as the exhausting heat of the Israeli sun—or it will not be at all, as far as most Israelis are concerned.

"The Real Thing"

That religion in the Holy Land is at present not this kind of a vital force, but that it must and can become such, is the conviction of a small but influential group that calls itself Amana. The founder and guiding force of the group is Joseph Bentwich, a professor of education at the Hebrew University in Jerusalem and a member of a distinguished English Zionist family. There is something ascetic in Bentwich's lean appearance, and in his disdain for organized religious activities, especially those supported by budgets from abroad. In turn, Bentwich is accused by those trying to establish liberal synagogues in Israel of substituting interminable discussions for practical organizational efforts.

White-haired S. H. Bergmann, professor of philosophy at the Hebrew University, is a frequent speaker at Amana. In his lectures Bergmann often tries to reconcile his philosophically trained mind with his own interest in the mystical psychological insights of Hasidism. In his late seventies Bergmann is still a fervent "searcher," praying in an Orthodox synagogue one day, and praising the religiosity of a Catholic thinker the next. Despite his years of active concern with religion in Israel, when asked about a concrete program, Bergmann shakes his head in puzzlement.

"Perhaps some books or pamphlets, explaining in an elementary way what Judaism is," he suggests doubtfully.

Bergmann is one of the small but distinguished group who in previous years supported the program of Ichud, the party which, in the years before the establishment of the state, advocated a bi-national state in Palestine. Many of the members of Ichud were united not only by a common political program, but also by their concern for spirituality, or the lack of it, in daily Israeli life. Among them was the late Judah Magnes, founding president of

258

the Hebrew University, Martin Buber, Gershom Scholem, and Ernst Simon. The last is still one of the land's most active and popular lecturers on religious themes. Simon's warm personality and courageous sincerity have endeared him to Israelis despite their dislike of his politics. But with the passage of years Simon has become more traditional and perhaps for that reason less interested in a group as uncommitted to the commandments of the Jewish tradition—as are most of the members of Amana.

It was at a meeting of Amana that I met what struck me as a most intriguing specimen of the new and perhaps future type of Israeli spiritual budding. The leader of some youngsters who called themselves Yuvalites, and who were then working as cotton pickers in the tropical valley of Bet Shean, had come to the meeting. I noticed him, a good-looking lad with large, dark eyes and tousled, light hair, leaning his head wearily against the chair in front of him. He saw me watching him, smiled, and shrugged. "*Diburim*—words, words," he whispered, as if to apologize for his lack of attention.

After the meeting we strolled through the streets of Jerusalem, and Joseph Manellah told me about his group. He was careful not to speak overenthusiastically about their immediate possibilities. As a matter of fact, they were at that time going through an organizational crisis. Many of the young people had left for the army. Among those who remained, a few had "gone off the deep end" in their enthusiasm for Yoga and other spiritual novelties. The group lacked permanent leadership, and above all at that time, a permanent home. For several years they had been wandering from place to place, trying to establish themselves. Still, Manellah was hopeful that their experiment would succeed. They had no desire to become a mass movement, but, thought Manellah, there was room for a small group like theirs, which if successful could eventually do more for the larger community by personal example than by preaching.

The ideology, such as it was, of Manellah's group was simple and when expressed could sound banal. They wanted to found a community based on inner bonds of love and friendship in which each member would seek to realize the most essential purpose of life—a purpose which they felt was linked to a consciousness of the "something above man." Above all, the individuals in Manellah's group wanted to close the gap between professed ideals and actual life.

It is an ideal which can be understood in its fuller meaning only against the background of current discussions in Israel of the younger generation's crisis of values. This crisis has resulted, says Yishar, the previously mentioned writer, who is both spokesman for and critic of the new Israeli, in the creation of an "espresso" generation who find their main source of interest in the cinema, the café, and in dreams of personal careers or material self-advancement. They are uninterested or cynical about the ideals which inspired the land's early pioneers. "They are attracted to the easy and the superficial," charges Yishar, who suggests that a reacquaintance with the writings of A. D. Gordon and with life on the kibbutz might be for them a source of regeneration.

But the call to spiritual regeneration by choosing life on a kibbutz has a hollow echo these days, for the kibbutz is going through its own crisis. New immigrants and city youngsters no longer are attracted to it. And in the kibbutz itself, there is a beating of breasts. "We have adopted the ideals of the city, and become bourgeois villages that give little more than lip service to the ideals of human relationships and the spiritual goals which inspired our foundation." This gap between official ideals and actual life in the city and in the kibbutz, in political and personal life, is the essence of what Israelis call their current crisis of values.

It is against the background of this discussion that the efforts of Manellah's group take on intriguing meaning.

The next day at one of the Umana sessions Manellah outlined the thinking of the young people he represented in more detail. Most of them were sabras, graduates of local high schools, and the children of nonreligious parents. The question which had brought them to form their group was simple. "We had asked ourselves as we were about to go out into life, What should a man do in this world? We do not want to just live and be dragged after that which is done. We wanted to reach the root of things, to understand them and to feel them."

260

Manellah explained that city life did not appeal to them, because "man in the city was lonesome. His human relations were usually based on artificial manners which were feigned, or else there was complete indifference." Nor did life in the villages and kibbutzim seem much different. Their goal also seemed to be a higher standard of physical existence, more comfort. Nor did his group feel that a sense of duty to people and state could be the center of a man's life. After much discussion among themselves, and with the guidance of Dr. Joseph Schechter, a high-school principal in Haifa, Manellah's group decided to create a collective settlement which would attempt to achieve a deeper relationship with that which is "higher than man"—with God. They decided that their ideal ought not to "remain in a state of constant discussion, but be realized in deeds." Quickly Manellah sketched some of their admittedly experimental efforts. They had decided to devote themselves to agricultural labor, because this would enable each individual to gain a better sense of being "a part of the cosmic cycle of life." They tried to infuse their work with meaning by various techniques. For example, in the morning before going out to work they set aside moments for solitude, "because it is first necessary to draw oneself together, become aware of oneself, awaken clear. A person draws himself together in order to have a full meeting with the world."

During their work they try to emphasize rhythm, not to begin quickly and to then end tiredly, but to make every moment as meaningful as possible. In the evenings there were also moments set aside for solitude, and occasionally group prayer. Their prayers are very short—"a long prayer is usually a sign of degeneration." They mark the Sabbath, but with a pattern different from both the religious Orthodox, or the so-called freethinking kibbutzim. Thus, they do not take the kind of journeys which the nonreligious kibbutzim like to enjoy on the Sabbath, for "leaving one's place is contrary to the spirit of the Sabbath." On the other hand, they do not have congregational prayers on Sabbath mornings like the Orthodox. Instead, each person goes off by himself to meditate. At one time they ate their Sabbath noon meal in strict silence, but lately they had lightened that rule, though they still avoided the compulsion to talk just for

261

the sake of talking. They also observe the key religious holidays of the year, trying to sense the peculiar significance in each of them. For example, the Day of Atonement is for them an opportunity for renewal, a day of special effort to "drive out the demoniac elements" which have accumulated within individuals and the community during the course of the year. This demoniac took different forms—"inner emptiness, denial of ideals and values, cynicism, anger, weakness, feeble relations between man and his neighbor, and so forth." They also fasted on the Day of Atonement, and when they wash on the morning of that day, "there is a symbolic meaning in this washing."

They wanted to achieve an inner peace by this way of life. "This state of inner peace," said Manellah, "is the place of meeting between the soul and God. The world wants noise and distraction and fears peace. If we attain a fundamental faith, a unity in the community, a life of simplicity and labor, joy will also come. Joy is a feeling that there is a purpose in life."

All of these thoughts were not original, Manellah admitted with a quiet smile. They were common to Indian, Chinese, primitive Christian, and Islamic traditions. But they were also to be found in the Jewish tradition, though sometimes "contact with non-Jewish tradition helps us to understand better the expressions and symbols which in our own tradition have been forgotten because of much use." Therefore the group often discussed existentialist literature, or drew upon Indian writings or even Christian writings in addition to their Jewish sources.

Aware that the kind of life he was portraying might not seem sufficiently Jewish to his listeners, Manellah closed with a quote from A. D. Gordon.

"Jews in the past were first of all human beings, who lived, thought, and felt about God, about man, about their life; and because they were Jews, they afterward called the way of life they had created Judaism. So also, if we will have something to say about great things in the world, and if we shall create a true way of life, it too can be called Judaism."

In conclusion Manellah paid tribute to Dr. Joseph Schechter, the teacher whose inspiration had brought the initial group together, and who is still their spiritual guide, even though he could not live with them.

Dr. Schechter was present at the meeting of Amana. He is stocky, ruddy-faced, husky voiced, and fierce in his opinions—a vigorous personality. In another age he might have been the type that could start a religious sect. This thought has evidently occurred also to Schechter, with whom I spoke after the meeting.

"I do not have enough mana—primal power—though in other ways I am all right. With money, for example, I am O.K. It plays no role in my life. In other ways, too, I'm O.K.—but necessary is this mana." Schechter has a way of opening his eyes wide, and pausing as if to let the full significance of his remarks sink in.

I later obtained some of Schechter's writings and realized how important this concept of mana, primal and direct, was in his thought.

"A community possessing great existential energy," writes Schechter, "is equipped for the struggle with the phenomenon universally characterized in all human communities—the victory of death over life, the disintegration of existence, the phenomena of license, individualism, cynicism, lust, irony, boredom, emptiness, doubt, demonism, fetishism and ossification, 'inner death.'"

It is the quality of *oz,* usually translated as strength, but according to Schechter a term employing the manifest presence of God, a type of mana or life power, which Schechter sees as the main characteristic of the biblical individual and community. This "existential energy," when linked with community needs, becomes "responsibility—the key trait of the religious person's life."

Even a quick reading of Schechter's writings, some of them in books, others in mimeographed sheets got together for pedagogical problems, shows how deeply Manellah and his group, who are sometimes called Schechterists, are influenced by the Haifa educator.

"The kibbutz, the collective settlement," says Schechter, "is the Israeli solution to the problem of man in our time. The kibbutz is not to be appreciated primarily as a solution for economic

263

or security problems, but from the point of view of the spirit. It is a view of life, which comes naturally to young people desirous of returning to a type of communal life which was known of old among the tribes, and in different communities throughout the ages, and its purpose is to renew a positive relationship between the individual and his natural basis of existence."

The essential drive of a person who enters a kibbutz, in Schechter's opinion, ought to be his eagerness to live in the present.

"He whose hopes are always in the future is a coward. He wants something, but does not have the strength to realize it now, in his life, in the present." Similarly, one who is always thinking about the past is simply a "tombstone." He also does not live his own life. He is not present at all. A person who is truly mature, however, and possessed of inner strength, takes upon himself full responsibility for his life, and therefore lives now, today—not tomorrow and yesterday. One who wishes to live in the present finds supreme meaning precisely in repetition. For such a one, the present is one with eternity and eternity is one with the present. Everything both repeats and renews itself. Every morning is like the first morning, every Sabbath like the first Sabbath, and every season of nature and life as if it were met for the first time.

The pamphlet goes on to point out that the "covenant" is the traditional way of forming the community which wants to achieve this kind of life. Every individual who enters a covenant community should experience a "new birth." That is to say, what had previously existed within him as a possibility now becomes reality. He who was previously a "strong man" becomes now a "responsible man," for strength and weakness are only possibilities which have to be realized, and the realization of an individual's strength in a community is achieved through his taking on of responsibilities for the community and its individuals. In that way what was once only a "view of life" becomes a "way of life."

In such a community "people who are together do not mock each other, do not relate to each other ironically, do not close themselves off from each other, do not make little of each other,

264

and never abandon each other in any situation." For mockery, irony, self-enclosure, etc., all of these remove a person not only from the community, but from his own sources of life contact, and deprive him of *oz*—existential energy. They also deprive him of joy, for the absence of joy is present when an individual does not fully carry out the movement from inner desires and thought to realization in life.

One of the keys to a fully realized life lived in the present is an attempt to harmonize all life expressions, both inner and outer, with the natural biological and geographical environment. This is an idea which Schechter says he has culled from Eastern sources. He once read some chapters written by a Chinese scholar which suggested how a person might relate himself to the twelve months of the year. For example, if certain birds appear at a certain time of the year, then one should pay attention to the kind of songs they sing and weave their style of melody into one's own singing. The color of a season's flowers, the texture of the skies, and other natural phenomena are part of the "law of heaven and earth," to which man should harmonize the details of his life, his manner of work, of dress, his thought.

What the Chinese writer did in terms of his country's seasons, Schechter tries tentatively to outline for the land of Israel. For example, the general mood of an Israeli summer is "tiredness, effort, and a yearning for what is ahead. The dominant sense is touch." The sense of sight continues to function, but it is limited, as is also the sense of smell in the summer. The typical flower of this season in Israel is the thorn bush, whose flowers are practically lacking in odor. The main animal of the season is the bird, and its voice is sharp and high (therefore, suggests Schechter, the songs sung in that season ought to be of a similar tone). The dominant color of the season is brown and white, and this might be reflected in the clothes. The major foods to be eaten are fruits and juicy vegetables rather than meat and porridge, and "not too many sweet things." These are the kind of suggestions, admittedly experimental, which Schechter thinks are appropriate to the Israeli seasons.

The Jewish calendar, as Schechter understands it, does reflect a rhythm and mood in keeping with the natural law. It realizes that the day, for example, and particularly the morning, is the time when man goes out to meet the world. "But the essential mood of the evening is withdrawal for the sake of protection. The night is the time of darkness, the time of "the awakening of the harsh judgments" in Cabalistic terminology. Therefore, the night is the time for group meetings, because the group is stronger than the individual. It is also the time for group song and prayer. The morning, on the other hand, including Sabbath morning, might be set aside for individual meditation, because the individual has less need of the group at that time.

Schechter breaks each of the days, holidays, and seasons into this type of pattern, but enough has been quoted to indicate the general tenor of his thought. To the extent that the Yuvalites have an ideology, it is this attempt to bring their rhythm and style of life into direct contact with the laws of "heaven and earth."

Shortly before they moved to their permanent home in Yodephet I visited Manellah and his colleagues in Segev, a newly built village for Moroccan immigrants, located in the western Galilee not far from Yodephet. They had rented some cottages from the villagers and were working in the area, some on road building, others in educational tasks among the Moroccan Jews.

I came there shortly before the Sabbath noon meal and found Manellah helping to prepare the meal in a small wooden shack which served the group as their dining room. Two girls were warming the food and setting the table. Food arrangements among the Yuvalites, Manellah explained, were more informal than among other kibbutzim. The kitchen and the icebox were always open. The idea was to have everybody "feel as if he were living in his mother's house."

Shortly after noon the young people began walking into the room, most of them rubbing their eyes and half-yawning as if not quite emerged from deep Sabbath rest. All of them were in their early twenties or younger, and obviously very individualistic personality types. Manellah lifted a piece of bread and offered

266

a brief blessing—not the traditional Orthodox form, but a simple "Thank Thee, God, for this bread." The rest of the meal was eaten in semisilence, broken by an occasional light comment. Though friendly, it was evident that the Yuvalites were not going to let the appearance of a stranger interfere with their Sabbath rest by letting themselves be drawn into a full discussion of their ideals or problems. After the meal they went to their rooms, some to nap, others to hear a concert on the radio. Manellah took me to his room, where I met his pretty wife. Another point of distinction between their group and other kibbutzim, said Manellah, was that they wanted to keep the family unit, including the children, intact, and living in the same quarters.

Through the windows of the cottage we could see Yodephet, the future home of the group. Manellah was still cautious about the future of his group. He would be happy, he said, if they received some publicity in America. Perhaps some youngsters there might be attracted. When I asked if there was anything I could do to help, he suggested that some books dealing with religious problems in a liberal way might be useful. Otherwise, all they needed were a few more young people. Life in Yodephet would undoubtedly be hard. There would be little opportunity for entertainment. But, said Manellah, there were surely some young people who felt that the kind of entertainment available in the city was taking them away rather than toward the essence of life and even joy. The pursuit of "new" things and "diversions" often came from a sense of inner emptiness and boredom. But in boredom—he quoted his teacher, Schechter—"man senses the eternal, but cannot endure it." Therefore he runs from it, but his running only further scatters his being and leads to more boredom and lack of joy. Manellah had the feeling that there were some young people—not many—who felt this way, and who would fit into his group. Despite his caution about the immediate future, the young sabra did feel that a group like his, soon to be called the settlers of Yodephet, had a contribution to make to Israel's crisis of values—a contribution which was indigenous to that land in both an historical and geographical sense.

In 1961 the Yuvalites moved into their new home on top of

267

a stony hill. In one of their rooms they placed two loaves of bread and a bowl of water on a table under a constantly burning electric light to symbolize the daily, earthly life constantly lighted by a light from above. Here they come, sometimes alone for a moment of meditation, or as a group, to sit quietly on mats and sing songs. Occasionally they read and discuss an unusual mixture of literature—perhaps an essay by Kierkegaard or Sartre, along with some saying of Lao-tse, a selection from Hasidic sources, a chapter from the Bible. On Sabbaths they eat their meal in semisilence, sitting around a table so as to face each other in a style reminiscent of the ancient Essene sects as they were described by the first-century Jewish Roman historian, Josephus.

The attempt to associate these husky Israeli youngsters with an ascetic religious group like the Essenes and Josephus is not as far-fetched as it might seem. They are what in more religious days might have been called a "covenant community"; that is, a group that has adopted a specific spiritual as well as organizational pattern of life. They are also connected with Josephus—by accident of geography. Near their new home are some stone walls, the remains of a fortress called Yodephet, which was defended by Josephus before he deserted the Jewish cause and went over to the Romans. The young people call their collective settlement, or kibbutz, by the name of the ancient fortress.

Kibbutz Yodephet is an intriguing phenomenon on the spiritual landscape of modern Israel, and a meeting with these youngsters can lead to what may be extravagant thoughts. But there is something about them which recalls the biblical commandment to love God "with all your heart, and all your soul, and all your might." A kind of religious expression which is satisfied with nothing less than "all." Their belief that ideals are to be realized in life and not only taught by speeches or pamphlets may seem naïve and even queer to some—but it is a technique which draws its inspiration, conscious and unconscious, from the deepest roots of the Hebrew tradition. But such talk would, I fear, be dismissed by the sabras of Yodephet as mere *diburim*— "words." They are interested in more.

Dialogue with Buber

On a bookshelf in Manellah's room I had noticed a book by Martin Buber. "How do you feel about Buber's religious ideas?" I asked.

"Well, they're not easy to understand," the young sabra replied, smiling.

This is another religious paradox of Israel—that Martin Buber, the famous master of the "dialogue," has not succeeded in quickening much of a dialogue between himself and his own countrymen, or even with his own students at the Hebrew University. At the latter institution, to which he came from Germany in 1932, he taught courses in Sociology, the only label which the University could find for the mixture of theology, philosophy, and social analysis which other professors, not without malice, used to call Buberism. At the University various stories about the difficulty of understanding this Buberism were current. When Professor Buber's Hebrew-speaking vocabulary was still limited, went one anecdote, it was still possible to follow some of his thoughts, but as he became more facile in Hebrew speech, he became more obscure, until now nobody could understand him. It was a fact that in the classes of Professor Buber there was little understanding, and also there were not many students. To some extent Buber's lack of influence at the University and in Israel could be ascribed to his unpopular political views. He was the leader of the Ichud group, which had supported a bi-national state in Palestine.

Some in Israel claim that Buber's antipathy to Ben Gurion, as expressed recently again during the heat of the Lavon Affair, is rooted in the fact that history seems to have been on the side of the latter. "The men of spirit," as they call themselves, who bitterly attacked Ben Gurion for his "immoral" behavior in ousting Lavon do seem to have been extreme in their castigation of their old-time political antagonist, as if eager to even old scores or prove correct their predictions of moral doom for the Jewish state. How else to account for charges like "degeneration" and "moral corruption" in an affair which was at best little more than a political power struggle?

Apart from politics, however, there have always been those, in and out of the University, who dared to claim that there was, in fact, little to understand. Not that anyone doubted the Professor's creative scholarship in the field of Hasidic literature and biblical interpretations. It was when he started talking about "I and thou" and "I and it" that they began to question his meaning. Certainly, Buber's critics agree, other human beings should be treated as important entities in their own right, as a "thou" rather than as an "it"—an object important to us only to the degree that it serves us. Nor did they question his interpretation of life and history as a dialogue between man and man, or between man and God. What the protest amounted to was a rebellion against the idea of confusing incomprehensibility with profundity. The fact is that there are many intelligent readers of Buber who suggest that once Buber's vague and difficult verbiage is clarified, there is little to understand beyond some obvious if important ideas.

I hoped the last time I visited Buber to find a way to ask him some questions about what I supposed would be the delicate problem of his lack of communication in Israel. Miss Rahel Zabari, a member of the Israeli Knesset, had come with me, and we waited for our appointment in the cool, dark foyer of Buber's home. The furniture about us was covered with cloths as if for storage. There was a stillness, a lifelessness in the house, or was it our consciousness of the fact that the then eighty-two-year-old professor lived alone here. His wife had died two years before, while returning with her husband from a trip abroad. I had been in Israel that summer when the papers reported her death—respectfully, but not neglecting to remember that she had been born a Christian. This had always been a tidbit of gossip in some Jewish circles, especially among those who liked to point out that Buber seemed to be much more appreciated by Christians than by Jews.

Once when I had spoken to Professor Buber, I had hinted at this accusation by telling him about a Jewish convert to Christianity who credited Buber for ideas which later led to his conversion. The elderly scholar had shrugged, and said something about not being able to take responsibility. As far as he was concerned, Buber had said, no religion had absolute truth, "all are in exile and God is in the center. We are all removed from Him. I never talk to Christians about dogma. Here we never convince each other. We must concentrate instead on real human relations."

Now, through the glass door opposite us, we heard Buber's voice speaking French with the same Germanic flavor of tone which came through his English and his Hebrew. Then the door opened and Buber came out to greet us. Though it was April, and the weather balmy, he was wearing a sweater and a brown jacket whose heavy material made his small figure even smaller. The fine features of his light-complexioned face had not changed much. His white beard and hair were neatly trimmed. His eyes had that combination of acuteness and peacefulness which usually impress his visitors. But his voice seemed wearier. He had just arisen, he told us, from four weeks of illness. He introduced us to his guest, an elderly visitor from France. We waited in his study while Buber and his other guest concluded their business.

After accompanying his French guest to the door, he asked us to take the two empty seats in front of his desk. His eyes lighted up with added interest when I introduced Miss Zabari as a member of the Israeli parliament.

What party, and what phases of government work particularly interested Miss Zabari, Buber asked. When she told him she was active in educational matters and in social-welfare legislation, he nodded.

"My father, may his memory be blessed, used to be head of the Committee on Charity in his town. I remember how he used to give them money and food. First he would go to their home, sit down for several hours and talk with them, and only incidentally, as he rose, did he give them the monetary or physical help. This is the real meaning of the word *ezra*—'help.' Not the type of organized social services which are given today."

Miss Zabari agreed, and thanked Professor Buber for seeing us on short notice. "Do you see everybody who wants to come

271

here, even if they have only personal matters they want to speak about?"

"*Dafke*—especially if they have personal matters. These, the personal questions, expressed and unexpressed, are the most important to answer."

"Still," Miss Zabari pointed to some open books and a manuscript on Buber's desk, "I hope we are not disturbing you."

"No—there is too much writing, today. What is needed is less writing and more opportunity for genuine direct dialogue between human beings. These," Buber motioned again toward the manuscript in front of him, "are merely some autobiographical notes a publisher wants me to put down—a recording of some important moments in my life which I would like to finish, *Im yir-tzeh Ha-Shem*—God permitting." Buber slowly spoke the pious phrase by which traditional Jews remind themselves of the fragility of human plans. Was it the small picture of his wife on the desk which made me think I sensed special feeling in his words?

I expressed condolences on the loss of his wife.

"Thank you, thank you." Buber lowered his eyes to the desk for a moment. Mrs. Buber had been a talented writer, and all knew that their relationship had been one of great depth and fondness.

He leaned back in his chair, waiting for our questions. I reminded him of our conversation the previous year and of his negative opinions about religious interests in modern-day Israel.

"I still think so." Buber nodded his head. "The whole religious question here is terribly difficult. There is no liberal Jewish movement here—only some Jews who have liberal religious ideas. I am inclined to think that something will happen only after the next generation. After we have overcome this state of excessive politicization."

Miss Zabari leaned forward. She had not caught the English word which Buber had used.

"Politicization." Buber's voice strengthened. "We are too politicized here, eh? Externally and internally. Most of the youth —apart from the Orthodox—are interested in politics; that means military problems, or political problems, or the two of

272

them, eh?" He looked at Miss Zabari to see if she was following him.

"Another part of our youth is interested in just what you might call 'career,' personal career, without any ideas at all. Just knowing something because they must know something in order to make a career, eh? There is, I mean—a cynicism?"

The Israeli demurred. "But there are many young people here who are as disgusted with politics as you. Many of them feel a vacuum within themselves, especially since the war."

Buber interrupted. "You are right. There is a certain number —not very many, I think—but some who feel a certain want, that they don't at all wish to explain, not even to themselves. If you will tell them that there is at the bottom of this a religious longing, they will deny it. I am very doubtful that this can be changed in this generation at all. Today, the sabra is interested in *mamashut*—the 'concrete,' the concrete achievement in science and agriculture. He has little interest in abstract ideas."

There was no tone of complaint. Buber spoke as if explaining something to himself as well as to his listener. Still, wasn't it strange that in a land so steeped in religious associations there was apparently so little religious fermentation? What, in Buber's opinion, was the effect of the land of Israel upon religion, upon Buber's own personal religious thinking?

"I do not know how influences affect me." Buber opened his hands as they lay on his desk. "I just let them work on me and through me, but," he looked out through the window at the bright sunlight outside and spoke even more slowly, "I couldn't live in any place but Jerusalem. I know this after all my traveling. As for the land and its effect on religion—this is very, very hard to know. Not that it is not present, but it is hidden. A land speaks with a still, small voice, and it takes much time. No religious phenomena appear suddenly. They are long in preparation. Then they only *seem* suddenly to appear."

We had spoken at length, I reminded Buber, in our last conversation, about Jewish religion in Israel. Would he have something to say about the modern land of Israel and the Christian religion?

"The effect upon a Christian of living in the Holy Land is

273

something quite interesting. But you must observe it not through the official Christians but through Christians who live here quietly and simply."

I had met a Catholic priest here, who had some interesting ideas about the influence of the land of Israel on the actual life of Christians who came here. Might I outline his ideas to Professor Buber?

"Yes, of course," Buber's voice rose, almost cracked, in quick encouragement.

I outlined Father Stiassny's "archetype" theory. Would it be possible, I asked Professor Buber, to say that Christianity in modern Israel could not help but confront the historical and therefore the Jewish component of its origin?

Professor Buber nodded. "I agree with Baeck. Marcian tried to make a cut between creation and revelation. That is, he did not want to see any continuation between them, and therefore wanted nothing to do with nature. You know, the Marcian view was proposed again not so long ago by a scholar some twenty years before Hitler, by Harnock. 'What have we to do with the Torah?' Harnock asked. Yes," Buber nodded again, "I would say that living here makes you for Jesus and against Paul."

The professor looked at his watch, and I apologized for the time I had taken with my own speculations.

"No, no," Buber assured us quickly, "I have called off my next appointment, and we have time."

But I had little time, I confessed, for my plane was leaving Israel that afternoon. Therefore, I had prepared one last but large question, the kind of question one asks before parting. Buber waited.

Actually, the question I wanted to ask had been in the process of preparation for some time. I approached it by referring to the fact that many of his books, so popular elsewhere, were not published in Israel because there was no market—people didn't understand him, complained the publishers.

"Perhaps they don't understand because they don't want to understand." Buber paused, as if to let his thought sink in. "People say they don't understand because they are seeking to understand an idea, an intellectual thought. What I ask for is not an

274

understanding of ideas but for a change in life, a life response. This people don't want to give."

Buber seemed willing to let his answer stand at that, but I made a last try.

"The rabbis in the Talmud try to sum up the essence of their life understanding by saying something like, 'The world rests on three things. . . .' Then they proceed to mention two or three principles which make up the essence of their life conclusions. Would you be willing to attempt such a summary?"

Buber thought for a moment, then spoke as if he were rethinking his ideas.

"In general, people asking so, want so-called objective answers. Now, I have no objective answer at all. I think," his sentences came slowly, with long spaces in between each phrase, "I think—that everything depends—in what measure a person gives himself or herself to the truth."

"To the what?" asked Miss Zabari. Buber was speaking English and she had not caught the last word.

"I mean not to the objective truth," Buber continued to explain, turning to her, "but to the truth that one can get just by giving oneself. And I don't know—at least for this moment of history—I don't know a more objective answer. I think that now everything depends upon the human person. On the measure in which human persons are willing and able to give themselves to the living and lived truth, the truth that is living and lived by persons. Do you see what I mean? We cannot get the objective truth to put it in our pockets. We can enter into a relation with the truth in such manner that we can know a personal kind of truth. You cannot put it into writing, into speaking. You cannot explain it to another person that this is this and this is that. This is what Micah meant when he suggested three essentials for man: 'Justice, mercy, and walking humbly with God.' This is what I think he meant by 'walking humbly'—not to think that I can get the truth, but to know that I can get something which is most valuable for me and my personal life, if I enter into a personal, total, unrestricted relationship to it."

"Professor Buber—" the Israeli had been trying to follow the explanation but was evidently not satisfied. "This idea that every

275

man must try for his own truth—how do we know then what the real truth is? What is the true, the right way, for example, to respond to the murder that took place yesterday?"

The night before in Jerusalem an elderly watchman had been killed by Arab infiltrators.

"What is the way of finding truth in this situation?" The Israeli went on to make her question clearer. "That is, can our 'truth' influence the Arabs—will they understand the wrongness of acts like these through any type of persuasion, other than actual retaliation?"

"Retaliation—so," Buber's voice suddenly rose and snapped with anger. "So—retaliation—do you really think so?"

Miss Zabari was taken aback by the sudden sharpness of his voice. "But how else can our conception of the truth have influence with them? How can we persuade them toward peace?" she said. "Haven't we tried?"

"Have we tried? Really tried?" His eyes were still flashing.

The Israeli hesitated. "That is true—we have not tried enough."

Buber spoke more quietly. "In my opinion, the people who live in Transjordan live in inhuman conditions. Now we should want to do something to change that situation. So long as we are only citizens of this country and nothing else—even our imagination cannot conceive of life there as it really is."

"But we have people who know how life is there," the Israeli demurred again.

Buber's voice again rose. "I have not seen them. In this and all matters of life you have to touch the concrete reality, otherwise you will not understand it."

The Israeli shook her head. "Look, I can understand speaking this way and taking the blame upon ourselves if a man comes and kills somebody here because he is trying to come back to his original home. He doesn't like it there and in the process of coming back he kills, perhaps in self-defense. But in this case, when individuals deliberately come over for no other purpose but to kill . . ."

Buber stopped her. "What is your opinion, why does man kill?"

276

"Because—it could be for many reasons—because he lacks something, or because he hates, or because . . ."

Buber did not let her finish. "I will tell you why—because—the inner, inner essence of the matter is—fear. Fear, because of fear there is no peace, here and in the world at large. Fear and one other thing—suspicion."

"Then he killed the night watchman out of fear? But he came over deliberately to kill," I said.

"Yes." Buber shook his head. "Because he is—he is afraid all the time and he knows the primitive reaction of the man who fears death to strike out, to hurt."

"Between you and me, when I was in America, I saw this fear in the hearts of people, even in the highest circles. I haven't been to Russia, but I am sure that there, too, the thing that is at the deepest core of their actions is fear and suspicion."

"Then what do we do—what can be done about it?" The Israeli lifted up her hands.

"To your question there is no direct answer," Buber replied. "But I would ask another question. How would it be possible—I have tried to think about it, but can find no reply—how would it be possible for representatives of the people to come together and speak with each other openly and honestly?"

The Israeli sighed. "If only it were possible."

We all remained silent for a while. Professor Buber walked with us to the door and out to the porch. I told him we would be looking forward to the publication of his new book of autobiographical fragments.

"If God be willing, and give me time to finish it," he said, quietly. We shook hands. The anger which had flashed in his eyes a few moments ago was now gone. Again, there was in them that strange mingling of acute vision and far away, peaceful composure.

"Shalom," we said.

"Shalom u'vracha—peace and blessing."

He remained standing on the porch as we walked out through the gate. The bright Jerusalem sunlight glittered on the white hair of the straight little figure in the brown suit.

CHAPTER XIII

The Wild Goats of Ein Gedi

"A land speaks slowly," Martin Buber had said, and the phrase kept running through my mind as I waited in the bus at Beersheba. Surely, whatever it was that this old-new land of Israel was trying to say could not be heard amid the traffic of Diezengoff Street in Tel Aviv. But perhaps in the desert, that part of the land where it all began—the desert of the Patriarchs and the prophets and the Essenes—something might be sensed.

There were about a dozen other passengers in the bus, most of them young, with deeply bronzed faces. That was good, I thought. It meant that I was going to spend the last Sabbath of my visit in Israel with the native-born pioneer element of the population —the sabra—the "new Jew" that Israel is supposed to have produced. They, after all, were the bearers of any secrets about Israel and its destiny. Two khaki-clad older men sitting in front were armed with heavy revolvers. This, too, I found agreeable. Not that two guns can offer much security against a well-planned desert ambush, but their arms proclaimed that we were going to a "pure security area," where one could feel the real heartbeat of Israel's precarious destiny. Surely, that too could not be felt in the air-conditioned lobby of the Dan Hotel in Tel Aviv. It was a rather childish whim, I knew, this sudden decision to take the long bus ride through the Negev and down to the lowest crevice on the earth's surface, where the collective settlement of Ein Gedi was located near the Jordan border. But there had been that impulse which can well up when we are about to leave something precious—a person or even a place—a last shooting forth of the arms, a last attempt to touch what is under the surface. And where can the essence of that phenomenon which some call the mystery of Israel be touched if not in the desert.

279

The bus driver—the pallor of his face and carefully trimmed small black mustache meant that he probably was not from the Negev—politely informed some people standing in the terminal that we were about to depart. A young man in khaki uniform, with shoulder tags marked "medical officer," entered. He was thin, slightly stooped, and his hair was cut in long European style—definitely not the sabra type. He looked at the passengers with moody eyes, as if searching for something. His glance fell for a moment upon a plump, pretty young girl sitting directly behind the bus driver. Her face was too white, and her flesh too soft, for a native of the desert. The army officer sat behind her. Last on the bus were a half-dozen husky men chatting in animated rapid Arabic intermingled with an occasional Hebrew phrase. "Druse," the tall, mustached young Israeli sitting in front of me whispered to his girl friend as the men took seats about us.

"They work in the potash works in the Dead Sea." He pressed his lips against the girl's ear, whispering.

As we drove down the broad main street of Beersheba, the bus driver turned around to speak with the plump young girl sitting in back of him. The medical officer's face showed his disappointment. He turned his attention to the buildings we were passing. Most of them were chipped and unlovely plaster-cube structures, but in the distance we could see the modern, pastel-colored apartment houses and the industrial plants of the new town.

On the outskirts of the town we passed one of the wells which is supposed to account for the biblical name of Beersheba—the Seven Wells. Actually, only three wells are to be found in the town—a fact that has been turned into one of the aggressive anecdotes that circulate among the various ethnic components of Israel's population—namely, Why does Beersheba have only three wells? Answer—the Rumanians (or whatever group is being attacked) moved here and immediately four of the wells disappeared.

We passed a garbage dump where black-robed figures, Bedouin women and children, were scavenging, and the bus stopped to pick up a young Bedouin lad—he could not have been more than seventeen. He was dressed in full desert regalia, a long frayed brown cloak wrapped around a nondescript inner garment. His heavy leather belt supported a leather wallet on one side and a scabbard and dagger on the other. In the boy's hand was a long, polished stick with a knob on the end.

"What's the wallet for," one of the Druse called out, grinning. I heard the Israeli lad in front of me translating the Arabic for his girl friend.

"Identification papers," the Bedouin answered timidly, and all the Druse burst out in laughter.

"Let's see the knife, how do you hold it?" Another Druse reached for the Bedouin's dagger. Embarrassed, but still trying to smile, the Bedouin offered him the dagger. The Druse passed it around, feeling its sharp edge with mock horror. The young Bedouin fumbled awkwardly with his wallet, while the Druse peppered him with teasing questions. The Bedouin was obviously relieved when he could ring the bell and descend from the bus three or four miles down the road.

Conversation in the bus ceased after this bit of excitement and everyone looked drowsily at the monotonous, gently rolling land-scape. It was spring, and the usually brown, dry Negev hillocks were covered with a soft, fuzzy green like the first hair on a baby's head. It was a sparse covering of vegetation, but it enabled the shepherds to lie leisurely on the ground and watch their sheep and goats graze. These were the few weeks of the year when they did not have to walk miles in search of a bit of moisture. The hypnotic roll of the hills and open sky encour-aged the mind to wander. Somewhere among these low-slung hills the Patriarch Abraham had wandered about with his black tents and flocks. It must have been a spring day like this when the normally industrious sheik found it possible to take a few hours from his busy day and "play," as the Bible euphemistically puts it, with Sarah in her tent. That day evidently he forgot to close the tent flap. The impotent Philistine king had observed the scene and reprimanded the Hebrew for ungallantly saying that Sarah was his sister and making her available to the king. It is unfair, though, to judge Abraham's conduct by Western stand-ards of chivalry. Abraham's specialty was not courage or moral

281

character in the stiff-lipped, Anglo-Saxon sense, but a propensity for overwhelming mystical experiences; witness his readiness to kill his own son—an act, Kierkegaard reminds us, quite impossible to defend in moral terms. The desert and mystical religious experience have an affinity according to biblical accounts. Perhaps that is why the mystical Essenes had gone to live in Ein Gedi. How many, I wondered, of the present settlers in Ein Gedi, had any such thoughts in mind?

Our bus route was probably along the way which Abraham traveled on his way to Sodom. He too must have gazed marveling at the white salt world which suddenly reveals itself to the traveler as he looks into the valley of the Dead Sea, 1286 feet below sea level. Even the young people in the bus who had made this trip before looked out with renewed curiosity as we began the steep, circuitous descent between washed-out gullies and whitish-brown sandstone which desert wind and rushing rain waters had sculptured into an endless variety of geometric forms.

"Lot's wife," I heard the Israeli lad tell his girl friend as we passed a hillock faintly resembling a human figure. Within a few moments we were at the bottom of the valley, driving along the shore of the Dead Sea. A few trees were planted near the white-caked machinery of the potash works, but they only set off the torpid barrenness of the scene. Dead is a good name for this sea and the earth about it. No organic life can exist in the salt-saturated soil and water.

The Druse passengers left us at the potash works, and now we followed a narrow stone path along the water's edge. One of the khaki-clad men—the younger one—took out his binoculars. I thought he might be looking for possible trouble in the hills about —we were close to the border—but he trained his glasses toward the sky, where a few birds were circling about slowly.

The texture of the hills to our left began to change in form and composition. Near the potash works they had been smooth brown-and-white cliffs, with sliced-off sections revealing the long, varicolored layers of earth and chemicals. Visible were both the slices and the cliffs from which they had been cut. Now the hills were brownish in hue, and their composition was stone. It seemed as if a gigantic hammer had been at work here and knocked off

282

huge boulders, pounded them into heaps of rocks, and smashed these in turn into pebbles. The most unanthropomorphic mind, looking at this landscape, would find it hard to avoid the image of a giant hand at work or at play. "The voice of the Lord breaketh the rock . . . turneth over the hills. . . ."

Now that everyone in the bus knew that we were traveling to the same destination, the silence which had prevailed throughout most of the five-hour journey began to thaw. I asked a young girl sitting in back of me whether we had yet passed the fortress of Massada. She shook her head and pointed to a cliff still in the distance. I had a tourist guidebook and turned to the page which described Massada.

"Metzada, another form of Metsuda—stronghold—the name has been Hellenized into Massada—is cut off from the surrounding heights by deep gorges. It is mentioned in ancient literature. 'David and his men got them up into the stronghold (Metsuda). . . .' The Book of Chronicles pictures David's followers joining him . . . 'into the stronghold (metsad) in the wilderness men of might, and men of war fit for battle, that could handle shield and spear, whose faces were like the faces of lions, they were swift as the roes upon the mountains.'

"Metzada was the last stronghold that held out against the Romans during the Jewish revolt. The fortress was so impregnable that the Romans never overcame its fortifications. At the end of three years of siege, the defendants put themselves to death rather than fall into enemy hands. The fall of Metzada in 73 A.D. marked the end of Jewish independence."

The Israeli girl interrupted my reading to point out a square-edged cliff about three miles away from our road. On the flat plain around it were the remnants of the three walls which the Romans had built to prevent the people in Massada from escaping. All eyes in the bus turned toward the steep, almost perpendicular walls of the ancient fortress, and there was silence. If there had been any question earlier in the journey as to whether the silent passengers on the bus were sharing common historic associations, there was none now. The strange confluence of past and present which protrudes into even the most prosaic level of

283

existence in modern Israel has no more vivid symbol than the fortress of Massada.

A few minutes later the bus stopped to pick up six youngsters in shorts and sandals, most of them without shirts. They entered laughing, joking, greeting some of their comrades in the bus with loud shouts and slaps on the shoulder. The tall lad in front of me proudly introduced them to his girl friend, pointing out the luxuriant mustaches which these sabras of Ein Gedi had grown. There was a shifting of gears, the bus mounted a little hill, rounded the corner of a cliff, and there ahead of us in stark relief against a brown stone mountain appeared a perpendicular streak of green, following the path of the spring which issued out of the cliff.

"Ein Gedi," the Israeli lad said to his girl friend. Soon we were driving through green acres of vegetation, vineyards and orchards, all drawing their life from the water that poured out of the stone above. The Israeli pointed to some buildings rising on top of a nearby hill—modern stone cabins and halls which would soon replace the present ramshackle wooden structures that presently housed the kibbutz.

It was almost six o'clock when we drove through the barbed-wire gate of the kibbutz. Sunset and Sabbath were only a few minutes away, and in most kibbutzim everyone would have already been showered and be dressed in clean clothes, walking around or playing with their children. But here the tractor was still clanking in the field. The young man with steel-rimmed glasses who watched us get out of the bus wore a khaki blouse open at the neck and chest, skimpy khaki shorts, and no shoes. Tugging his sandy mustache, he silently counted the guests, for whom he would have to find beds. One of the armed men, the younger one, strode up to the kibbutz member and stretched out his hand with a loud, "*Shalom*—what is your name?"

The member of the kibbutz finished counting before replying briefly, "Uri."

"*Shalom*, Uri. My name is Dov." Again the visitor extended a hand. Uri shook it indifferently.

"You are probably expecting us, Uri. We are here on a *tafkid*

284

[an official mission], sent by the Department of Wildlife Conservation."

Uri nodded and with a wave of his hand indicated that we were to follow him. Dov walked ahead with Uri. The rest of us trailed behind.

"Tell me, Uri," I heard Dov say, "why do you walk about here in bare feet—isn't this the place of the famous Ein Gedi viper?"

Uri shrugged. "If I get a bite, it's coming to me for walking this way." Uri showed us some soggy mattresses and blankets on the ground. We dragged them to a bunkhouse which contained about a dozen rooms. As we reached it, the bus driver hurried up and whispered in Uri's ear. Uri turned around to look at the girl with the bus driver and opened the door of the first cabin for them. The older government official, the medical officer, and I were given a room a few doors away. Dov went to another bunkhouse. Our room contained three rusty bedsprings, a broken chair, and some dirty pots heaped up in a corner. After Uri left, the doctor walked ruefully around trying to close up some of the holes in the hopelessly torn screens.

"This is one of the areas in the country which still breeds malarial mosquitoes." He shook his head worriedly and began sweeping the room with a broom he found in the corner. After shaking his blankets outside, he returned to his cot and lay down with an unhappy sigh.

The government official, who introduced himself as Shimon, immediately stretched out on his bed. With a tired groan he told us about his mission at Ein Gedi. There was a species of wild goats in the rocky hills of Ein Gedi called in Hebrew *ayelim*.

"It's mentioned in the Bible," Shimon said, "something about King David and his comrades hiding in the wilderness of Ein Gedi on the rocks of the wild goats." Shimon was not sure of the exact biblical text, but the wild goats were a species related to the generic group Ibex. According to the statistics of the Ministry of Wildlife there were only fifty of these goats left. The members of Kibbutz Ein Gedi had been complaining that the goats were doing serious damage to their crops. They were threatening to do something about the goats themselves unless the Ministry of

285

Wildlife took action. This was the *tafkid* of the two government officials.

A few minutes later Dov returned with Uri. We sat on the wooden porch outside our room. Uri told us about his kibbutz, which had some eighty official members, most of them in their late teens or early twenties. Dov asked about the snakes which were to be found in this area.

"Out there," Uri pointed to a pipe out of which some water was bubbling, "one of our comrades received a bite a few weeks ago. He was picked up by a Piper plane and taken to the hospital. We have no telephone here, but recently we got a wireless, and we can get in touch with Jerusalem." As Dov continued to ask about the wild animal life, Uri's answers became less laconic. He told us of a baby gazelle that had wandered into the camp. Uri had fed it on a bottle for six months, and now the gazelle continued to follow him around the kibbutz like a pet dog. The kibbutznik had built a wire enclosure in which the gazelle dwelt along with a monkey and one or two other pets which Uri had adopted.

"I wish there were more like you, Uri," said Dov, "interested in the preservation of wild animal life."

"One like me is enough." For the first time I noticed that the young Israeli's left arm was partially paralyzed. His long mustache and brusque, clipped manner of speech did not quite match his thin, somewhat tense face and eyes.

"What's the woman situation here?" asked the doctor. Uri shrugged.

"We always have a shortage—it's boring for most girls."

"Have you got a girl?" Dov asked.

Uri clicked his teeth Arabic style in negative reply, and left to make some arrangements for other guests.

"How do you like our sabras?" Dov asked proudly after Uri had left. "Wonderful, eh? I love them."

I asked Dov where he had been born.

"Anik'mat sabra—practically native born"—an answer often given regretfully by those who missed being born in Israel by a few years. "I was very young when my parents settled here."

I asked what plans the Ministry of Wildlife had for preventing the crop damage caused by the wild goats.

"The damage which they *think* is being caused by the wild goats," Dov corrected. He looked at his companion meaningfully. "Our job here is not only a scientific one, eh, Shimon? We have to be diplomats as well."

It had become quite dark, and we hurried to wash and dress for the Sabbath. The primitive outhouse sanitation facilities were nearby, and the odors mingled unpleasantly with the scented blossoms of the adjacent trees. I decided to walk away from the kibbutz toward the dark cliffs which rose in a long, high line behind it. The Essenes, a whiff of unpleasant odor reminded me, carried paddles at all times, which they used to dig a hole in the ground at some point far outside the communal grounds, when they felt the need for discharging their natural functions. It seems wrong for unpleasant odors to have an effect on religious moods, but they do. So do noises, like the clanking of the tractor which was still working in the field. It was not going to be easy, I could see, to evoke that Sabbath atmosphere I had hoped to find in the wilderness of Ein Gedi. I came to a barbed-wire fence, and somebody shouted a warning about getting lost in the dark. It was dark now and I returned to the patch of green lawn outside the dining room, where my roommates and Uri were sitting. I almost stepped on a white, thin, curved form in the grass and started back. Uri laughed.

"I looked twice too. It's only a stick—you can sit down." The incident stimulated Dov and the doctor into a half-hour of lurid descriptions about the manner in which the snakes around Ein Gedi could cause pain and death. "What would you do," the doctor asked, "if you were bitten by a snake up there near the fountain of Ein Gedi?"

"Run for help," I replied, to the delight of the doctor who assured me that I would then be dead—"after a snakebite one must move as little as possible."

"Say, where is the bus driver and his girl?" Shimon asked. No one had seen them since we arrived. "Doctor," Shimon turned to the medical officer, "maybe you had better have a talk with them—about overexertion and health, I mean." A bell rang and everyone walked into the dining room to sit on the benches ranged in long rows against the tables. Most of the young boys —the average age was about twenty—were dressed in white shirts with Russian-style collars of embroidered Yemenite needle-work. Some girls wore slacks and others had put on dresses for the Sabbath. We sat facing each other across the table. A girl played some full chords on the piano, and everyone sang the opening verses of Bialik's Sabbath hymn:

> "The sun on the treetops no longer is seen
> We have gathered to welcome the Sabbath, the Queen
> Behold she descends, the blessed, the holy
> Come oh Queen, come oh blessed Queen."

The full, organlike chords of the piano and the singing were serious and slow, quite different from the frenetic shouting and clapping of the usual Israeli youth song. After the song there was quiet, while the Sabbath candles were lighted by a girl. Then a husky lad whose shirt was open at the neck rose and lifted a cup of wine and recited the traditional prayer of Sanctification. He read it simply with no hint of formal liturgical recitation in his voice. Another youngster read a few verses from the Bible. Then the waiters—on Sabbath the men, wearing aprons, take over the task—brought in platters with roast chicken and potatoes. After the meal I asked Uri why a nonreligious kibbutz like Ein Gedi arranged a religious ceremonial for its Sabbath meal.

"We just had a meeting and decided that we wanted it this way," was Uri's explanation. It was a reply which would have shocked other kibbutzim in Israel, whose settlers came from the lands where the "problematics" of religion were not so easily resolved.

"Now, Uri," said Dov to our sabra host, "about the matters for which we've come. I suggest that tomorrow morning we take a walk around the kibbutz and look at the damage which you claim the wild goats have caused." Uri raised an eyebrow.

"Not the damage which we claim they caused, but which they have caused."

288

Dov slapped him on the back and laughed. "We'll see to-morrow, Uri. Set up a meeting for the end of the Sabbath."

"*B-seder* [O.K.]." Uri shrugged and walked away.

Dov invited me to the meeting. "You may find it an interesting lesson in psychology and diplomacy, right, Shimon?" Dov winked at his comrade.

Back in our room that night, there was a brief discussion about whether to open or close the doors and windows. In summer the temperature at Ein Gedi reaches 130° and even in April the nights are quite hot, and a breeze most welcome. But the doctor's warnings about the malarial mosquitoes prevailed. We decided to close all the shutters, and stretched out on top of our blankets fully dressed.

It was pitch dark and my watch said four o'clock when the sound of people getting up to work woke us. As soon as the sun rose, Dov came in carrying a book and his binoculars. He suggested a pre-breakfast walk around the settlement to inspect the wildlife in this area. His book was an illustrated English text on birds. The doctor began reading it eagerly. It seemed that he too was a bird watcher. The two of them walked ahead, stopping every few paces to train their binoculars on circling clusters of birds, and excitedly correlating what they saw with the descriptions in their book. Ein Gedi, Dov explained, was a favorite resting place for birds on their way from Africa to Europe and back. It was possible to see many nonindigenous species stopping here to rest and drink, and wait for a favorable wind to carry them on their journey.

While Dov and the doctor were occupied with their bird-watching Shimon rested and I inspected a small stone memorial nearby. On it were written the names of seven Israeli youths who had built a campfire here while hiking to Massada. An accidental discharge of a hand grenade they were carrying had killed all seven. There were empty rifle cartridges lying all about, and I picked some up for souvenirs. The sun was now close to the front quarter of the sky. This was the ancient way of reckoning time, quite appropriate in the desert, where life must adjust itself carefully to the sun's varying degrees of heat. The Essenes had been especially interested in guiding their days by the position of the sun, not only because of the heat but because they believed that every act had its precise place in the rhythm of time. Their mystical belief in numbers, which some scholars related to the Greek Pythagorean schools, made them very concerned about the accuracy of their religious calendar, which differed from the calendar followed by the Temple authorities in Jerusalem—one of the facts that drove them to live alone by the Dead Sea.

Shimon too had been watching the sun as a clue to the time when breakfast could be eaten.

In the dining room Shimon again looked around. "Doctor, I still don't see our driver and his friend. Maybe you ought to speak to them. It's really not healthy." After the vegetables, cheese, and tea which form the standard Israeli breakfast we set out to visit the springs of Ein Gedi. We had gone only a few yards when Dov stopped us suddenly, a finger to his lips.

"You see that bird?" he whispered. "He is not a kibbutz type, he doesn't like to live in company. He takes possession of one tree with his mate." Breathlessly, Dov and the doctor walked toward a small blue bird with a sharp tail, sitting proudly on top of a little tree.

"Hello." The call came from the cornfield to our left. A member of the kibbutz in blue jeans and a blue shirt was waving to us. "If you are looking for the damage of the wild goats, I can show it to you," yelled the youngster. With a reluctant sigh Dov turned from the bird. We stepped across the rows of short corn to where the young man was standing.

"All right, let's see," Dov smiled tolerantly. The young lad pointed out several rows of cornstalks which had been nibbled almost down to the ground.

"Hmm, obviously there's damage." Dov rubbed his head. "But whether the damage is caused by wild goats, that is another question my friend. How do you know what caused this damage?"

The youngster, whose blue eyes matched his shirt, looked at Dov with a broad grin. "I know, because I saw them."

"What do you mean, you saw them?" said Dov.

"I mean that you can see them almost every morning or evening when they come down to feed. And I have often seen

290

about a hundred wild goats standing about here and eating."

"What's your name?" asked Dov.

"Yuval," answered the youngster, still smiling.

"Yuval, what would you say if I were to tell you that there were not more than fifty of these wild goats in the world?"

The young lad grinned again. "I would say that I have seen at least a hundred."

"We will talk later," Dov said.

We continued on our way to the springs which flowed out of some cliffs a half mile from the kibbutz. In a clearing below stood three empty buses. Their passengers were already clambering about the cliff or bathing in a pool of water beneath the thin waterfall that issued from sheer rock. We followed a narrow trail upward toward the first spring, which was called the Well of David. The spring of Ein Gedi was higher up. Along the sides of the path were other bubbling pools surrounded by moist green foliage, bushes, and cane reeds. Shimon pointed to small clumps of bushes and trees along the side of the rock path we were climbing.

"A joongle," he said proudly. "Joongle" was evidently one of the many English words, like "sveter" for sweater and "gip" for jeep which have been transmogrified into modern Hebrew. We climbed through a small tunnel in the "joongle" formed by an overhanging rock and some tree branches. A flat-topped rock was placed like a bench in the shade. I sat on it for a moment, trying to visualize David or the Essenes here—they must have climbed along this path too. But the conversation of the people from the bus who were climbing about us, and the sandwich wrappers scattered around the pools of water, made historic reflections difficult. We swam for a while in the warm water under the waterfall, then rested in a small clearing within Shimon's "joongle." The sun shone through the heavy haze which rose from the salt sea. Its white, depressing light added a measure of bleakness to the jagged, sterile cliffs and to the dull metallic water. In the face of the cliff, directly across a gully separating our hill from another barren ridge, was a hole, below which could be seen the remains of steps carved into the rock. Some of the Essenes might have lived in that cave. Why had they come to this sterile wilderness? It was not only because of the conflicts with "evil priests" or dislike of the authorities in Jerusalem. They had a kind of life here in the desert that evidently attracted them.

Josephus describes the mystical aura that pervaded their daily activities: white-robed communities eating their meals in complete silence; communal meetings where awe-inspiring quiet could be broken only by permission of the head priest; rules regulating articles of clothing, encouraging celibacy, inflicting severe punishment for an unguarded word or gesture—it was a monasticism similar in mood and pattern to the strictest orders of the Christian church. It is the connection between these groups and Christianity that scholars find most interesting. But the nonscholarly mind is intrigued by other questions. What did these people find so attractive in a life of labor and abnegation in the desert? But then, what was it that has always attracted some to the desert? What attracted Uri and his comrades to Ein Gedi? It would be fruitless, I supposed, to ask a question like that of the sabras. The answer, if any, would be a shrug, or a negative Arabic click of the teeth. The young people at Ein Gedi would deny any interest in the spiritual moods of the monastic Jews who had lived here two thousand years ago. Still, they had banded together voluntarily in a community which shared property like the Essenes. And they too had left the lights and comfort of the city.

The quiet of our "joongle" was suddenly broken by a new band of tourists climbing past us to the Fountain of Ein Gedi. We descended the hill to find that a truck had arrived and was peddling sandwiches and soda drinks to the tourists. After a snack we started back toward the cornfields, only to be held up again by Dov's suddenly raised hand.

"You hear that sound?" We listened to a bird call. "That sound is going to kill me yet. I will not leave the settlement till I have found out what that bird is."

"Look," Shimon exclaimed joyously. The bus driver and his girl were walking toward us. "I was getting worried about them."

"Well, how do you like Ein Gedi?" Shimon asked the bus driver when we met, nudging the doctor.

"Fine," the driver replied. "We're going bathing in the Dead Sea later, if you would like to join us."

"I hope they're not going to be disappointed in their Dead Sea bathing," the doctor said after the couple had passed by. "You know the chemicals there are very strong, and make the orifices of the body smart. . . ."

"Doctor!" Shimon exclaimed in mock shock, when he had caught on to the implications of the medical officer's remarks.

The sun was standing full in the heavens now. Even the Essenes must have rested at this hot hour, I thought, and after lunch I went back to my room. Later in the afternoon, as the low hills of Moab on the other side of the Dead Sea appeared in purple-blue outline, I decided that it was time to carry out the project that had really brought me to Ein Gedi. I could not define exactly what the project was, but it certainly meant going someplace where it was quiet. I picked up a small Bible, and started toward the rocky hill in back of the kibbutz. I stepped over a barbed-wire fence, and my feet sank in the soggy soil of the terraces which were being watered by the kibbutz sprinklers. After half an hour of climbing the noise of the tractor and generator faded away. I found a rock flat enough to serve as a seat, and was about to sit down when I heard a rustle from a nearby bush and saw the movement of a pebble. Last night's conversations about snakes, vipers, and scorpions were still in my mind, and I poked nervously around with a stick before sitting down to find an appropriate Psalm. The 104th I thought would be fitting, because it mentioned the wild goats.

"Borchu—bless the Lord, oh my soul." Had the psalmist been troubled that day by the prosaic physical problems which I had encountered on my Sabbath at Ein Gedi. After all, there were snakes and scorpions in his day too, and probably distracting noises from some nearby village, even unpleasant smells from the outhouses. Maybe he too had to command his soul to ignore them and slowly work his way up to higher concerns.

"Oh Lord my God, thou hast clothed Thyself in glory and splendor. Thou hast spread the light like a garment and stretched out the heavens like a tent."

The Essene, like the psalmist, had also begun his prayers

293

with contemplation of the heavens. In the morning he had stood, his body turned toward the East, his hands outstretched to heaven as the sun rose. The manual of discipline, one of the newly found Dead Sea Scrolls, describes the prayer when the pious communicant enters into "the Covenant of God" and recites his ordinances "at the beginning of the Dominion of Light, with its circuit, and at its withdrawal to the habitation of its ordinance." Everything to the Essene was guided by ordinances, by immutable laws. To live in perfect harmony with these laws, and according to the demand of each moment of time, was the object of the Essene teachings. His faith would admit no possibility of chaos. A child stumbling upon a venomous snake, a cell in the body suddenly going wild, the thought of pain or death or history being caused by sheer accident—this possibility that life can be affected, even ended, by sheer, purposeless accident, this profoundest of challenges to all claims for a divinely created and purposely governed universe is violently rejected by the Essene, who saw everyplace only the rule of law, like the writer of the 104th Psalm. "Thou makest fountains and rivers to run among the hills . . . thou givest drink to the creatures of the field and sustenance to the wild plants upon which the birds of the sky can rest and from whose branches they can give voice."

The image of Dov and his binoculars came between the lines of the psalm. "There the birds make their nests, and the stork makes his home among the bushes . . . the high hills are for the wild goats. . . ." Did these goats damage the corn of the Essenes? "The rocks are shelter for the coney." Dov and the doctor had had a long discussion about the coney. In America everybody knew of a place called Coney Island, but few in the Bible who read the word *coney* associated it with any real image. Dov said he had seen coneys in the Galilee—small, brown, long-tailed animals looking something like beavers. This, of course, was one of the things that happened to the reading of the Bible in Israel—vague place names, trees and animals and streams and rivers assumed concrete form. It was a process which often resulted in an ambiguous mixture of emotions, fulfillment coupled with disillusion.

294

"All of them turn to you for food, and Thou givest them their food in their time . . . when Thou hidest Thy face, they are confused." God hiding his face—this was the way biblical man explained those happenings which seemed to deny the reality of a God who cared for justice and mercy or even order. God turned his face away because of man's wrongdoing—this was the usual explanation, but sometimes it didn't work. Man's deeds, even if not perfect, were obviously not deserving of the evil and suffering visited upon the innocent. Then the only possible explanation was that God hid his face for reasons of his own, or perhaps He could not help himself. There was a Manichean touch in such an explanation, the great heresy which suggested that the world was divided between the powers of light and darkness and even admitted the possibility that darkness could overcome light. The Essene was attracted to this dualistic division of the Cosmos into light and darkness. But he rejected the possibility that light might not be the ultimate power with an extremism that betrayed the power of the horrible thought being suppressed. A "both/and" world, admitting the possibility of a realm not fully under God's control and therefore a world which harbored both meaning and meaninglessness, offers man confusion rather than sureness of faith. And utter definiteness is the only pattern of faith that has been able to fully engage men's souls. This is the testimony of all "true believers" from Abraham to the Essenes, from Jesus and Mohammed to today's Chinese Marxists. "And when thou takest their spirit, they die and return to dust. When thou sendest forth thy spirit, they are created and the face of the earth is renewed."

Renewal—the power to be born again—if there is a religious doctrine indigenous to the land, it is this.

"May the glory of God be for ever, and may it be my lot to rejoice in all His works. He who looked upon the earth and made it shake, who touched the mountains and caused them to quiver."

Did this psalmist see the earthquake which sliced and pounded the rocks around the desert of Sodom and Ein Gedi?

"I shall sing unto the Lord while I live, sing out to the Lord while I exist. . . . Bless the Lord, oh my soul, my God, Hallelujah."

The clanking of the tractor suddenly filled the air. Apparently I had not really climbed away from its noise—the driver had simply taken a brief respite. As if stimulated by the noise of the tractor, there came again the suspicious rustlings in the ground about me, and thoughts of the famous Ein Gedi viper.

Had the Essene found his efforts to commune with the spirit disturbed with noises, worries about snakes, and the smells of the latrines? Surely he must have. The disturbing influence of the body upon the spirit—noise, smells, mosquitoes upon the desired mood—this had been my problem at Ein Gedi. It was in a way illustrative of the problem of life. How to maintain inner peace, courage, serenity, whatever aspect of the spirit we desired, in this world of "bodies" which smell, ache, grow sick, and die? How to reach for spirit without a cutting off from the body, without the dualism which some religions found to be the solution —that had always been the problem of a faith like Judaism, which even insisted that in the Messianic era body and soul would be united.

Of course, the sabras of Ein Gedi had other problems, like the wild goats. I remembered that Dov had arranged the meeting about the wild goats in Uri's room for the end of the Sabbath, and hurried back to the kibbutz.

Uri's room was neatly furnished with a radio, chairs, and large photographs on the walls. Dov was already there, looking at some pictures Uri had taken of a wild goat who had wandered into the kibbutz some months before. He was a very old goat whose curved horns were so large that they had begun to penetrate his back. He had evidently been blind for some time, managing to keep his footing on the rocks by memory and instinct. One day a member of the kibbutz had found the goat alone in the cornfield, and Uri had brought him back to the barn. The goat's blindness had made him continually bump his head into the walls of the barn. A few days after he was captured the goat had laid down and begun to die with huge shudders. Uri had brushed the flies away from the dying goat's eyes, and taken pictures of his last moments. Afterward Uri had buried the goat near the kibbutz. He drew one of the long, curved horns of the goat from under his bed to show us. Three members of the kibbutz entered the room while we were looking at the horn, and good-naturedly teased their comrade about his interest in wild goats. One of them was the smiling blue-eyed lad we had met out in the cornfields. He brought with him a box of cookies which he had received from home. All of the lads were dressed in white shirts, their faces shining after a day of rest. Passing the cookies around to each other, they seemed like children playing at camp. They must have impressed Dov that way, for in a fatherly tone he asked each one his name and the work he did. The business discussion began only after Shmulnik, the secretary of the kibbutz, arrived. He was a thin, slightly hunched lad with sleepy dark eyes set in a permanently bored expression. Shmulnik sat down on the bed, leaned his back and head against the wall, and waited with closed eyes for the government official to begin.

"*Chevra* [gang]," Dov began, with the word which he knew was all-important to Israeli youth. The young people themselves make fun of their slavish subjugation to the ideals of their *chevra*, but know that it remains the determining factor in their lives.

"*Chevra*, I haven't come here to preach Zionism—I hate *dibburim* [word mouthings] as much as you do. But I have come here and given up my Sabbath in order to acquaint you with some facts. Now you know, *chevra*, that in our country the situation of the wildlife is very poor, very poor to say the least. . . ." Dov went on to speak at length about the lack of wildlife in Israel. The boys listened quietly, though obviously bored. Shmulnik kept his eyes closed.

"And so," Dov finally approached the main subject, "we come to the problem of the wild goats. Now suppose you tell me your problem, and some of the suggestions you have for a solution?"

"We are here to listen, if you have any suggestions, suggest." Shmulnik's dry voice cracked the silence.

Dov cleared his throat, slightly taken aback. When he spoke again his voice was more firm.

"Now, *chevra*, let us remember what we are dealing with.

You may not realize that there are only about thirty or forty wild goats left in the world." The blue-eyed boy grinned.

"Oh, you may think that you've seen more." Dov told a long story about an animal count which had been taken up in the Galilee. The inspector had counted the same animals over and over again, not realizing that they could move on so swiftly from place to place. "These wild goats are very speedy," said Dov. "They travel fast when they see you."

"They don't travel at all when they see you," said one of the boys. "They are not in the least afraid of human beings. Only if you come very close do they retreat up to the mountains, and then very slowly."

"Still, you may have counted the same ones several times. They can appear quickly in places where you haven't seen them before."

"They travel in regular paths," the boy insisted quietly, "and I myself have seen at least a hundred in a day."

"Maybe the count of the Ministry of Wildlife is still from the time of the British Mandate," someone suggested, and they laughed. Dov tried to laugh, but his face had reddened a bit.

"Well, never mind the numbers, let's talk about some solutions. Have you tried chemicals?"

They had tried chemicals.

"How about scarecrows of some sort?"

"They are not afraid of scarecrows."

"Well, what do you suggest?" said Dov.

"That's what we came here for, to hear you make suggestions," Shmulnik said dryly. "You are the third 'mission' from the Ministry of Wildlife. We have yet to hear a good suggestion."

Dov shook his finger. "Now, you boys, ought to realize that I left my house and village and came here to spend my Sabbath trying to help you."

"Some people come here for a vacation and find it very pleasant," said the lad who worked in the cornfields, with a pleasant smile.

"I have other ways to take my vacation," Dov snapped. "I want to tell you—don't you dare raise a rifle against any of these wild goats. First of all, it wouldn't do you any good."

298

"Why not?" asked one of the boys. "It would solve the problem."

"Don't you dare shoot—there is such a thing as a law and courts." Dov's face was red.

"The law of the land does not reach to Ein Gedi," said Shmulnik in a flat voice. His comrades smiled. "Besides, how'd you know if we did shoot one? Are you going to keep a guard here? It would be less expensive for you to compensate us for the damage."

The government official made an effort to control himself. The blue-eyed boy seemed sorry for him.

"Listen, we all love the wild goats and don't want to hurt them, but we are here trying to make a living and this year the damage they have caused has run into thousands of pounds."

Dov was grateful for the proffered hand of peace. "All right, then, if nothing else works, then we must build a fence."

"You must build a fence," said Shmulnik.

"But don't you have any feeling for the national interests which are involved here?"

"*Sh'ma*—listen, my friend," Shmulnik's dry tone crackled. "If you want to have a national park here—then by all means make one. We are trying to farm and make our bread here. If there is damage we will protect ourselves by getting rid of the source of the damage."

"But I am not speaking of a national park. Don't you realize that the eyes of the world are on these wild goats? You have a responsibility to see that they are not harmed." Dov was shouting.

"Listen——" Shmulnik's voice remained flat. "You know we are a generation far from ideas and very *chomreni*—materialistic. If you want a national park, build it. We don't have the money or the hands." Shmulnik rose and said he had to leave for another meeting.

The ensuing silence was embarrassing. Shimon, who had been sitting near me on the cot, whispered, "I told him he shouldn't make speeches." Dov sat crestfallen in his chair. The boy who brought the cookies began to pass them around again.

"Listen," he tried to comfort Dov, "we don't want to hurt the wild goats, but don't go back and send us another report and another delegation."

We left the room. Uri walked with us, and I tried to assure Dov that nobody was going to harm the wild goats.

"I know," he said disconsolately, and went to his room. Shimon went on ahead and for a moment I was alone with Uri. I asked him why he had come to Ein Gedi. He shrugged, and motioned toward his bare feet.

"Because here I can feel things—real things." He pressed his feet into the dust and stone of Ein Gedi.

We bade each other good night. Shimon and I paused outside of our room and looked toward the mountains in back of the settlement. Their jagged black line was sharply etched across the blue of the night sky. The night heavens appeared light blue in contrast to the deep blackness of the mountain wall which seemed to hang over and press down upon us.

"*Ayom* [terrible]," said Shimon looking up at the sky, and went in to bed. I walked away from the cabin toward the silent salt sea. We would be leaving Ein Gedi at five o'clock the next morning, and this was my last chance to take a walk alone here.

"*Ayom*." Shimon had almost shuddered as he looked up at the black mountains above us. *Ayom* is the modern Hebrew expression for terrible. The Biblical meaning of the word is closer to awesome, something like Rudolph Otto's *mysterium tremendum*.

But what is it about the "awe-fullness" of the desert that attracts people away from the light and comfort of the town? Above, the slim crescent of the moon was sharply outlined. Among the lights of the city the contours of the moon are less sharp, if they are noticed at all. In the desert the constant changing of the moon is clear and its implications unavoidable— the passage, the "terrible" passage of time, and the inevitable destruction of our loves and joys. The gadgets of civilization can at least be a buffer between us and the pain of the natural life processes. The frozen meat package in the refrigerator need no longer be related to the death scream of the animal which provided the meat. Why then do men flee from this civilization to the desert? Is it the truth as seen in Plato's myth of the cave—

300

that pain and life cannot be separated from each other and that he who would live in comfort must live with shadows and turn his eyes away from the bright painful fire of reality? The Hebrew, too, described his God, the source of life, as "a consuming fire," separation from whom means death, but at the same time as one whom man cannot see and live. The Essenes believed that this real God could not be found among the pleasant green hills, shady trees, and bubbling springs, the "verdurous glens" where one could languorously be "half in love with easeful death." Those who came to the desert wanted no half-love. They wanted nothing "in-between," and the desert allows nothing in between. All the veils of concealment are torn away to reveal the primal dichotomies—hot sun and freezing nights, blazing light and fearful darkness, the dead, dead desert and the life-giving spring.

"*Ayom* [aweful]." But perhaps as Uri said, one could "Feel things here—real things."

What Will the Land Say?

Yigael Yadin, former commander-in-chief of the Israeli army and now professor of archaeology at the Hebrew University, picked up a stone and threw it accurately at a row of columns which had once supported the roof of King Ahab's stable.

"Notice that they are all leaning in the same direction. That is the result of an earthquake—another archaeological verification of an incident recorded in the Bible."

The brown-mustached young general speaks swiftly and authoritatively, like a man accustomed to translating thoughts into deeds. He swung an iron-tipped cane in a northern direction, toward the brown-blue plateau which marked the Syrian border.

"Damascus is only fifty miles in that direction, and Lebanon," the stick swung eastward toward the massive brown mountain on whose top a white patch of snow could be seen even now in the heat of the summer, "is over there. Any army caravan coming from those regions toward Egypt—and this is the way the armies of Babylonia and Assyria would have to come—has to pass this spot. That's why it was always fortified, even in Canaanite days."

Yadin was taking us on a tour of Tel Hatzor, the high hill covering the remains of the biblical city which he had been excavating. In our group was an Englishman, a rotund gentleman, who despite the heat was dressed in a heavy green sweater and green cloth cap with long ear flaps. While Yadin was speaking the Englishman kept backing about with his camera. He was trying to frame the handsome archaeologist-general against the background of the Lebanon mountains and the flat, marshy, Hule plain below, which stretched between us and the thin blue ribbon of the Jordan river several miles to the west. Several times Yadin threw an irritated look in the direction of the photographer, who grunted with audible satisfaction after every click of his camera.

"Look, he's already delivering the lecture that will go with these pictures," an Israeli schoolteacher in our group whispered to me. *Sotto voce* she offered her idea of the lecture being formulated in the Englishman's mind:

"Two thousand years ago, Jewish soldiers stood here looking toward the hills, from which enemies threatened the life of their people. Now a Jewish general stood again at Hatzor. . . ." Rachel, the schoolteacher, like many young Israelis was a member of the "club" which wanted to outlaw all speeches in Israel that began with the phrase, "Two thousand years ago. . . ." The quality of amazement, unlike the quality of mercy, can be strained, suggests the club, by interminable speeches about the "miracle" of the Jewish return to their ancestral land and language after two millennia of separation.

When our tour was finished, Yadin offered to drive us in his jeep back to the nearby kibbutz settlement which served as a center for his archaeological expedition. We had just started down the narrow dirt road leading from the top of Hatzor to the main road, when the archaeologist said something under his breath and jammed on his brakes. Coming up the path, which permitted the passage of only one car, was a milk truck. Angrily, Yadin jumped off the jeep and confronted the driver, hands on hips.

"You're not in the habit of reading signs? Didn't you see the placard down below saying, 'Entrance forbidden?'" It was the general, not the archaeologist, talking now. Sheepishly the milkman muttered something and then began backing his truck down the hill. Yadin returned shaking his head, but smiling.

"How do you like that? He heard on the radio that we had discovered something new here, so he came on his lunch hour to look. The search for roots, eh, Rachel?" Yadin turned to the Israeli teacher.

"Well, what is it that attracts you to all this digging?" Rachel smiled back. "What are you looking for?"

304

"You are right, Rachel, absolutely right. We are digging into the *moleded*—the motherland—back to the womb."

Rachel and Yadin had served together in the Israeli war, and he knew her propensity for Freudian explanation. "But we have some questions to put to you—for serious answers," the Israeli teacher insisted.

"Not now—we'll talk alone later."

We drove down the hill to the kibbutz, and Yadin asked us to wait for him near a long table, where under a canopy several dozen people were sorting potsherds.

"They are volunteers." Rachel pointed to some of the older workers. "You see, that's our national religion."

The Israeli was referring to the craze for archaeology which today occupies milkmen and youngsters as well as scholars in Israel. The discussion as to why Israelis are so interested in archaeology is almost as popular a subject in that land today as archaeology itself. The native-born Israeli, the sabra, say some, senses in these clay and stone reminders of past Hebraic civilizations evidence of his own historic roots in the land where he now lives. He feels more kinship with the biblical period of Jewish history than with the immediate past of his father or grandfather in Europe, says Ben Gurion. Hence his interest in biblical archaeology or in biblical figures like Joshua and David.

Another theory suggests that there may be some guilt involved in this archaeological craze. A large section of the people who dwelt for centuries in this land have been dislodged and their place taken by Jews. Whether it be the fault of the Jews or of Arab leadership, Israelis do not live with this fact as comfortably as official government statements would suggest. Nor does the Jewish claim to "belongingness" in this land always convince the immigrants who have brought to it the foods, languages, and cultures which they have lived with for thousands of years in the seventy different countries from which they returned to the land of Israel. They too need to convince themselves, and archaeological evidence helps a bit.

Of course, the monk on Mount Carmel had offered a different explanation of the Israeli interest in archaeology. "We watch a sabra like Yadin," he had said. "We watch his interest not only in archaeology but in the Dead Sea Scrolls, which tell of monastic communities very much like our orders. It's part of a process that's going on here, the sabra's sense of a spiritual vacuum and his search for roots. The process has not yet come to the surface, but for us the interest of a sabra like Yadin in the scrolls is like a moving finger—the moving finger of history. . . ." The priest had moved his finger on the table toward himself.

Later, when Yadin returned and took us to a cabin where we could talk alone, I told him about the priest. The general laughed and tapped his pipe.

"As a matter of fact, the members of the Dead Sea communities, though monastic in their ways of life, were very Orthodox keepers of the Jewish law." However, Yadin was very careful to avoid making public statements now on the theological implications of the Scrolls.

"It's become impossible to get an objective evaluation of the Scrolls, because of the perspectives of the various church groups. Now at least I can work comfortably with every religious opinion, including the Orthodox Jewish, and I wouldn't want to change that. Besides, I haven't formulated my own religious beliefs."

Yadin narrowed his eyes, and his usual fluent flow of language faltered as we came to the subject we had discussed at a previous meeting in London. There our conversation had turned to questions about the religious interests of the sabra.

"I don't know about the over-all strategy," the archaeologist had fallen back upon military terminology, "for bringing the sabra and religion together, but the tactics, I think, must include the Bible. . . ."

Now Yadin was speaking slowly, as if again trying to think through his own attitude.

"I don't think Kurzweil is right in saying that we have confused the "Rock of Israel" with Israeli patriotism or that nationalism is our religion. Someday I am going to answer him."

His tone suggested he was not quite sure as yet of the answer.

"But I don't think that Ben Gurion is right either, in the way he uses a term like Messianism." Ben Gurion's Messianism, implied Yadin, had been separated from its other-worldly dimension, overhumanized and secularized.

"With respect to my own belief or understanding about the Jewish religion," Yadin tapped his pipe slowly on the table, "it seems to me that the association of a people's religion with its land is something rather special for Jews, and if there is going to be a vital religion here in the future, I do believe that it has again to have some special association with this land."

The General shrugged and turned for a minute to look through the window at the brown mass of Mount Lebanon. He turned to the Israeli teacher.

"But if you ask me, Rachel, as you did on the hill, what it is we are looking for in all this archaeology—and I think my attitude is also the attitude of the sabra—what we want in all these matters, religion and all the other subjects, is simply the truth—all the truth about our past, about what happened here, about our tradition. That's our sole concern—not to protect preconceived ideas, but to get the concrete facts."

We all shook hands and left the comparative darkness of the cottage for the bright light outside, the light which Yadin had said "is about as bright a light as you can find anywhere."

Can the light of a land, the shape of its hills, and the memories that cling to its soil affect the soul of a people and influence their perception of truth?" This was the question that we asked at the beginning of our "digs" into the spiritual landscape of modern Israel. Of course, we knew even then that it was the kind of question that could beget not an answer, but at the most a wondering. This wondering began with a fact of history—the fact that this soil did produce at one time a remarkable time of *Homo religiosus,* whose thoughts and moods became the main ingredient of half the world's spiritual diet.

The late poet laureate of modern Israel, Chaim Nachman Bialik, eloquently pointed up the question which this past fact of history poses when it is juxtaposed with the latest "return" of the Jews to their homeland.

"Four thousand years ago there gathered in this land, from Ur of the Chaldees, from Aram, from Egypt and from the Arabian desert, some groups of wandering shepherds divided into a number of tribes. They became in time, in consequence of events of apparently no great importance, a people small and poor in its day—the people Israel. . . . This people produced men—for the most part of humble station, shepherds, plowmen, and dressers of sycamores, like their brethren—who carried the tempest of the spirit of God in their hearts and His earthquakes and thunders in their mouths. Those men, in speaking of nations and individuals and in discoursing upon the history of their times and the apparently trivial affairs of the moment, dared to turn to eternity, to the Heavens and Earth. And it was they who in the end provided the foundation for the religious and moral culture of the world. . . . After the proclamation of Cyrus, some tens of thousands of exiles rallied again to this poor, waste country and again formed a poor small community, even poorer and smaller than the first. After only some three hundred years, there arose again in this land a man of Israel, the son of an Israelite carpenter, who conveyed the gospel of salvation to the pagan world and cleared the way for the days of the Messiah. Since then, two thousand years have elapsed, and we are all witnesses this day that idols have not yet disappeared from the face of the earth; the place of the old has been taken by new ones, no better than the former. And then came the Balfour Declaration. Israel is assembling in Eretz Israel for a third time. . . . Surely not for nothing has the hand of God led this people for four thousand years through the pangs of hell and now brought it back unto this land for the third time."

Whether or not the Jews have been brought back to the land of Israel for nothing is the question which concerns those who are interested in the mystery of Israel. As we have seen in our encounters with Christians, Moslems, and Jews in today's Holy Land, not all of them are convinced with Bialik that the end result of the Balfour Declaration will be a "new Gospel, the gospel of redemption, for the whole of humanity."

It all may be, as one of the priests we met said, "just a mistake."

Those who think it is more than a mistake confront a problem

308

in modern Israel. If the return of the people of Israel to their ancestral land is destined to reveal the "great lights" of spirit that Rabbi Kook talked about, where is the evidence? If two thousand years of survival and martyrdom have resulted in the establishment of but another shade in the twentieth-century patchwork of nationalisms, was it worthwhile? And where in modern Israel is there any sign that this return is connected with the "Divine Matter"?

The fault may have been in our own eyesight. But we have not found evidence of great religious stirrings in the Holy Land, at least on the surface. On the contrary, we have seen that the historic religious institutions and traditions which call this land holy seem to lie about sterile and lifeless on the cradle soil of their faith. If anything, they appear to have less power for spiritual creativity here than in other lands. We have called it a riddle as puzzling in its way as the peculiar capacity which the land obviously has had in the past for producing a gifted type of *Homo religiosus*.

To call something a riddle is to tempt a guess at a solution. Our guess, of course, is little more than a thought—Yehudah Halevi's thought that this soil will receive and give root only to a particular kind of religious seed, and "vomit out" all imitations.

It has been this thought which accompanied us in our meetings with groups as diverse as the Little Brothers and Sisters of Jesus, the Darmstadter Nuns, and the Yuvalites in Yodephet. These "seeds in the desert" have, despite their obvious differences, a peculiar affinity for the desert—every kind of desert, either of soil or of soul. They wither where there is tepidity, and take root only in an atmosphere of "allness"—total commitment —the giving of "all of your heart, and all of your soul, and all of your might." They produce a blossom which prefers the lonely and unseen locale for its growth, though it would offer its flower and fruit to all. There is something about this kind of religiosity, when it appears in the land of Israel, be it within Judaism, Christianity, or Islam, that seems somehow to "fit," to find roots here, while all other types of spiritual expression lay barren or decaying in putrefaction.

We asked another question at the beginning of our survey. How does life in modern Israel affect Moslem, Christian, and Jew religiously? We have not been able to say much about Moslems, either because we do not know, or because there is not much to say. As to Christianity and Judaism, an image used by the anthropologist Ruth Benedict comes to mind as a final thought. She compares the range of human emotional capacity and variety to a piano keyboard. There are cultures that can play on wider or narrower ranges of this keyboard. There are ages when a particular civilization may be tone deaf to notes on a certain part of the keyboard. We have wondered, in the course of these religious dialogues in the Holy Land, whether a certain amount of tone-deafness has not characterized the historic Jewish-Christian dialogue. Have there not been centuries when the ears were closed to certain notes on the spiritual keyboard simply because they were being played by the "other side." After Judaism and Christianity became two separate religions, it was enough for something to be "Jewish" in order to have Christian ears flee from its sound. On the other side, the knowledge that a certain kind of spiritual experience was at the center of Christian life was enough for Jewish groups to push it to the periphery of their own religious consciousness. I am thinking of religious phenomena like monasticism, or "seizure by the Holy Spirit," or "second birth"—terms which have acquired loaded meanings on both sides of the Christian-Jewish dialogue. Look how differently, for example, the biblical words describing a figure like Elijah have been heard by Jewish and Christian ears through the centuries. For the monk on Mount Carmel, Elijah is the prototype of a Carmelite priest—celibate, lonely, almost contemptuous of family life, and interested mainly in lonely mystical exercises. To the Jew, Elijah is a family prophet, visiting Jewish homes at all gay occasions, a sort of benign and gentle miracle worker. What has intrigued us about the "leap backward through time" which Judaism and Christianity both take in modern Israel, is that in a sense it brings them back to a period in history before they were divided. Will the ears through which the "new Israeli" hears his Bible—and he does hear tones different from those heard by Diaspora Jews or Diaspora Christians—reveal to him a new kind of biblical figure? Going back to the piano keyboard metaphor, may it be that such a leap backward through time can affect the range of the spiritual keyboard within each group and perhaps sensitize the ears to notes which have not been heard for centuries? Of course, this too is the kind of question which can result at the most in only a kind of "wondering."

In the last analysis, all guessing about future religious phenomena in the new Israel should bear in mind the main characteristic of the land's peculiar type of religious seed—its insistence on the utter openness of the future. If there is a way of thought and faith indigenous to the Holy Land, it is the affirmation that an utterly new and different level of life is possible. The prophetic dream of a "new heaven and earth," the early Christian expectation of a "new order," A. D. Gordon's vision of man and nature transformed and lifted to a never before experienced dimension of life—all share the absolute refusal to accept a future which merely repeats the past.

"There will come a time" and "in that day" are the key words of the dreams and visions which come from this land. Any expression of religiosity which does not share this Messianic hope, lies rootless and lifeless on its soil.

We are left, then, at the end of our journal, with the choice that will always be left to those who examine the pages of life. We can find in them enough evidence to break our every hope, or proof that dreams are not entirely in vain. All that has happened and is happening today in the land of Israel offers us the same choice—only, as is the way in this land, in a focus particularly sharp. We can look at what has transpired there, at what goes on there now, and feel the absurdity of man's dreams, including religious visions. Or we can look at words written on a card of greeting sent by the Darmstadt nuns to the new state on one of its anniversary occasions, and read:

> Who hath heard such a thing?
> Who hath seen such things?
> Is a land born in one day?

Is a nation brought forth at once?
For as soon as Zion travailed
She brought forth her children.

—*Isaiah 66:8*